CW01024261

# *In* PURSUIT *of* Angelic POWER

## A Path Towards Divine Healing Energy

SHAYKH NURJAN MIRAHMADI

PUBLISHED BY THE

NAQSHBANDI CENTER OF VANCOUVER

In Pursuit of Angelic Power

Copyright © 2018

by Shaykh Nurjan Mirahmadi

ISBN: 978-0-9958709-5-6

Published and Distributed by:

Naqshbandi Center of Vancouver
3660 East Hastings
Vancouver, BC  V5K 4Z7  Canada
Tel: (604) 558-4455

nurmuhammad.com


*Special thanks to the Publishing Team for making these books possible*

Mrs. Amina K.  &  Mrs. Saira K.  &  Mrs. Hafsa M.  &  Ms. Wida M.


First Edition: May 2018

# TABLE OF CONTENTS

# ABOUT THE AUTHOR

## PROFILE

For the past two decades, Shaykh Nurjan Mirahmadi has worked hard to spread the true Islamic teachings of love, acceptance, respect and peace throughout the world and opposes extremism in all its forms. An expert on Islamic spirituality, he has studied with some of the world's leading Islamic scholars of our time.

Shaykh Mirahmadi has also founded numerous educational and charitable organizations. He has travelled extensively throughout the world learning and teaching Islamic meditation and healing, understanding the channeling of Divine energy, discipline of the self, and the process of self-realization. He teaches these spiritual arts to groups around the world, regardless of religious denomination.

## BACKGROUND

Shaykh Nurjan Mirahmadi studied Business Management at the University of Southern California. He then established and managed a successful healthcare company and imaging centers throughout Southern California. Having achieved business success at a remarkably young age, Shaykh Nurjan Mirahmadi shifted his focus from the private sector to the world of spirituality. In 1994 he pursued his religious studies and devoted himself to be of service to those in need. He combined his personal drive and financial talents to work for the less fortunate and founded an international relief organization, a spiritual healing center, and a religious social group for at risk youth.

In 1995, he became a protégé of Mawlana Shaykh Hisham Kabbani for in-depth studies in Islamic spirituality known as Sufism. He studied and accompanied Shaykh Kabbani on many tours and learned about Sufi practices around the world. Together with Shaykh Kabbani, he has established a number of other Islamic educational organizations and relief programs throughout the world.

Shaykh Nurjan Mirahmadi has received written *ijazas* (authorization) to be a Spiritual guide, from two of the World Leaders of the Naqshbandi Nazimiya Sufi Order; Sultan al-Awliya Shaykh Muhammad Nazim al-Haqqani ق and Mawlana Shaykh Muhammad Hisham Kabbani. He is authorized to teach, guide, and counsel religious students around the world to Islamic Spirituality.

Shaykh Nurjan Mirahmadi has taught and travelled extensively throughout the world from Uzbekistan to Singapore, Thailand, Indonesia, Cyprus, Argentina, Peru, and North America. He teaches the spiritual sciences of Classical Islam, including meditation (*tafakkur*), subtle energy points (*lataif*), Islamic healing, the secrets of letters and numbers (*ilm huroof*), disciplining the self (*tarbiyya*), and the process of self-realization (*ma'rifah*). He teaches the Muslim communities the prophetic ways of being kind, respectful and live in harmony with people. He emphasizes on good manners and respect, and often reminds his students that the spiritual journey begins from within and "You can't give what you don't have."

## ACCOMPLISHMENTS

One of Shaykh Nurjan's greatest accomplishments has been the worldwide dissemination of the spiritual teachings of Classical Islam through his books and online presence. The Prophet Muhammad ﷺ has told us, "Speak to people according to their levels." In an era of social media, Shaykh Nurjan's ability to reach a new generation of spiritual seekers through the Internet has been remarkable. His *NurMuhammad.com* website alone has over 1,500 unique visitors each day, and since its inception has seen more than 200,000 downloads of the book *"Dailal Khairat"*, 1.5 Million free downloads of *Naqshbandi Muraqabah*, and another 700,000 downloads of the *Naqshbandi Book of Devotions (Awrad)*, as well as many more articles. His Facebook pages "Shaykh Nurjan Mirahmadi" and "Nur Muhammad" combined have over 1 million likes and followers. Furthermore, his YouTube Channel "The Muhammadan Way" has over 2 million views, and his Google page, "Shaykh Sayed Nurjan Mirahmadi" has over 2.7 million views.

Shaykh Nurjan Mirahmadi focuses on the worldwide social media presence working on ways to bring knowledge to all seekers around the world. In 2015 he launched an Online University, called "SimplyIman.org", to spread these traditional Spiritual Islamic teachings even further and make it accessible to all seekers around the world.

For over 20 years Shaykh Nurjan has dedicated his life to spreading the true Islamic teachings of love, acceptance, respect and peace. He has established several non-profit organizations since the early 1990s and, over the past decade, he has founded numerous educational and charitable organizations. In the Greater Vancouver region alone, he has established the following:

**Divine Love: Hub-E-Rasul TV Series** – launched in May 2017, this weekly half-hour Islamic television show covers a wide range of topics, focusing on spreading Prophet Muhammad's ﷺ message that Islam is a religion based on peace, love, and acceptance.

The show airs every Saturday at 1:30 pm (PST) on Joytv, reaching 7 million viewers Canada-wide. It reaches the online community through social media and through its website **huberasul.net.** For a full channel listing please visit **www.huberasul.net/schedule.**

**Muhummadan Way App** – a comprehensive resource of Islamic information for all mobile devices. Created for both Muslims and non-Muslims, it provides users with a wealth of knowledge including access to books, supplications, prayer times, month-specific practices, a media library of audio and video files, an events calendar, and much more.

**Ahle Sunnah wal Jama of BC** – this organization is a resource for authentic content, books, and articles from the Qur'an & Sunnah from around the world. It works in collaboration with the well-known international organizations, Al Azhar University of Cairo, Dar al Ifta of Egypt and Islamic Supreme Council of North America.

**Hub-E-Rasul ﷺ Conference** – monthly Milad & Mehfil-e-Dhikr events are organized and held throughout the Lower Mainland. The aim is to revive the teachings of the Qur'an and *Sunnah* by celebrating holy events in true Islamic spirit (*Isra wal Mi'raj, Laylatul Bara'h, Laylatul Qadr, Milad un-Nabi* etc.)

**Naqshbandi Nazimiya Islamic Centre of Vancouver** – this Centre is a place for people of all faiths and beliefs to attend weekly *zikr* programs (circles of remembrance) three times a week (Thursdays, Fridays, and Saturdays). Shaykh Nurjan teaches above and beyond the principles of Islam including the deep realities of *maqam al-iman* (belief) and *maqam al-ihsan* (excellence of character).

**SMC** – an outreach organization that spreads teachings to the Western audience including concepts such as meditation and charity. It reaches out to other faiths to increase peace, love, and acceptance in the interfaith environment.

**Simply Iman Cloud University** – an international online platform allowing people from around the world to pursue studies in various aspects of faith and spirituality from a classical Islamic perspective. Students have the opportunity to learn at their own pace and engage in an open dialogue with a teacher in real-time.

**Fatima Zahra Helping Hand** – this charity organization runs a food program every two weeks which feeds more than 500 less fortunate people in the downtown eastside of Vancouver. It also collects clothing and non-perishable food items for the BC Muslim Food Bank and the Burnaby Homeless Shelter.

**Shaykh Nurjan's Published Books** – these titles are available at all major retailers and online.

- **Levels of the Heart – Lataif al Qalb**
- **Secret Realities of Hajj**
- **The Healing Power of Sufi Meditation**

Shaykh Nurjan has also established an international presence through many social media outlets including:

- **FaceBook (Shaykh Nurjan Mirahmadi)** with over 1 million likes
- **YouTube Channel (NurMir)** with over 600 videos
- **NurMuhammad.com,** a comprehensive website containing many resources covering the deep realities of classical Islam.

Shaykh Nurjan's sincere mission is to spread the love of Sayyidina Muhammad ﷺ throughout the city for our families and children. If you would like to be a shareholder in all these blessings we invite you to support our Center by any means possible. We hope to strengthen our efforts by joining our hands in raising the Honourable Flag of Sayyidina Muhammad ﷺ.

# UNIVERSALLY RECOGNIZED SYMBOLS

The following Arabic and English symbols connote sacredness and are universally recognized by Muslims:

The symbol ﷻ represents *Azza wa Jal,* a high form of praise reserved for God alone, which is customarily recited after reading or pronouncing the common name Allah, and any of the ninety-nine Islamic Holy Names of God.

The symbol ﷺ represents *sall Allahu 'alayhi wa salaam* (God's blessings and greetings of peace be upon the Prophet), which is customarily recited after reading or pronouncing the holy name of the Prophet Muhammad ﷺ.

The symbol ﷵ represents *'alayhi 's-salam* (peace be upon him/her), which is customarily recited after reading or pronouncing the sanctified names of prophets, Prophet Muhammad's ﷺ family members, and the angels.

The symbol ؓ represents *radi-allahu 'anh/ 'anha* (may God be pleased with him/her), which is customarily recited after reading or pronouncing the holy names of Prophet Muhammad's ﷺ Companions.

The symbol ق represents *qaddas-allahu sirrah* (may God sanctify his or her secret), which is customarily recited after reading or pronouncing the name of a saint.

# Chapter One

## Take a Path of Acquiring Angelic Power and Energy

إِنَّا أَنزَلْنَاهُ فِي لَيْلَةِ الْقَدْرِ (١) تَنَزَّلُ الْمَلَائِكَةُ وَالرُّوحُ فِيهَا بِإِذْنِ رَبِّهِم مِّن كُلِّ أَمْرٍ (٤) سَلَامٌ هِيَ حَتَّىٰ مَطْلَعِ الْفَجْرِ (٥)

*97:1, 4-5 – "Innaa anzalnaahu fee lailatil qadr. (1) Tanazzalul malaa-ikatu war roohu feeha bi izni-rab bihim min kulli amr. (4) Salaamun hiya hattaa mat la'il fajr. (5)" (Surat Al-Qadr)*

*"We have brought it down on the night of power. (1) The angels and the Spirit descend therein by permission of their Lord for every Command/affair. (4) Peace it is until the emergence of dawn. (5)" (The Power, 97:1, 4-5)*

1

# We Are Energy Beings: Build It or Lose It

## At the Core of Everything is Energy

*I*nshaAllah, in a very simplified and very basic language, it doesn't have to be complicated, but it has to be understood, that we are people who are understanding energy. A good and solid understanding of energy should lead to a happy life, *InshaAllah*, and a guarded and protected life, *InshaAllah*. It becomes so simple in our day and in our time when you reduce everything to the understanding of energy. Everyone has an energy and there are so many energies surrounding us and that we are an energy being. We are a spiritual being.

## Every Communication is Through Energy

Every communication now is through energy; that every radio wave, microwave, every type of television signal and transmission – all of these are energies. When you reduce them and reduce them to the core, it's energy. The most powerful energy is the human, *insaan*, "*Wa laqad karamna Bani Adam*," that Allah ﷻ says, "I have honoured your creation."

وَلَقَدْ كَرَّمْنَا بَنِي آدَمَ وَحَمَلْنَاهُمْ فِي الْبَرِّ وَالْبَحْرِ وَرَزَقْنَاهُم مِّنَ الطَّيِّبَاتِ وَفَضَّلْنَاهُمْ عَلَىٰ كَثِيرٍ مِّمَّنْ خَلَقْنَا تَفْضِيلًا (٧٠)

*17:70 – "Wa laqad karramna banee adama, wa hamalna hum filbarri wal bahri wa razaqnahum minat tayyibati wa faddalnahum 'ala katheerin mimman khalaqna tafdeela." (Surat Al-Isra)*

3

*"And We have certainly honoured the children of Adam and carried them on the land and sea and provided good and pure sustenance and bestow upon them favours, and preferred them over much of what We have created, with [definite] preference." (The Night Journey, 17:70)*

One of the true honours of creation is the amount of energy that flows from the soul, from the being, from the *nafs* (ego), and from everything around *insaan* (human being).

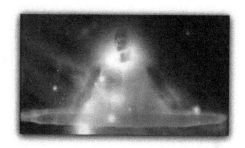

A very simple understanding of the *tariqas* (spiritual paths) is to perfect the energy. Everything that they give us, every practice that is given to us, every teaching of Holy Qur'an, of Hadith an-Nabi ﷺ, of all the *amal* and the actions – all reduced to energy, building our energy, perfecting our energy, and building a shield of perfection and protection around us.

## Take An Account of Your Actions and the Energy They Produce

When we begin to think at the level of energy, then we begin to understand cause and effect. If all my thinking is based on energy, then am I producing enough positive charge? Are my actions producing a positive charge? Are my prayers, my meditation, my *zakat* (charity), my pilgrimage, all my *amal,* all my actions – are they producing enough positive charge? Then I keep a mental understanding within my mind and my heart about roughly what my positive charge is.

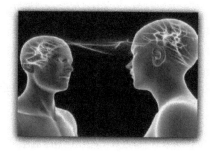

Then begin to take an account and *hisaab* (account) of our lives and our everyday actions. That, everywhere I go and everyone I meet and everything I come in contact with, also has an energy charge. The people that I work with, the people that I communicate with, the people I go to school with, the people that I socialize with – all of them are producing an energy. Now if their energy charge is positive, you feel an abundance of good feelings and good energy.

## You Either Take or Lose Positive Energy

By coming to the *masjid* (mosque), coming to the *ahlul zikr* (people of remembrance), coming to the holy places, people feel a positive

 energy and they don't really rush to go home. They stay within that energy. They are being charged within that energy. Then we know, because again the energy people and the people of *tafakkur* and contemplation,

the people of *zikrullah*, *"Zikrullah tatmainnal quloob"* (In the remembrance of Allah do hearts find satisfaction, Holy Qur'an,13:28)

الَّذِينَ آمَنُوا وَتَطْمَئِنُّ قُلُوبُهُم بِذِكْرِ اللَّـهِ ۗ أَلَا بِذِكْرِ اللَّـهِ تَطْمَئِنُّ الْقُلُوبُ (٢٨)

*13:28 – "Alladheena amano wa tatma'innu Qulobu hum bidhikrillahi, ala bi dhikrillahi tatma'innul Qulob." (Surat Ar-Ra'd)*

*"Those who believe, and whose hearts find satisfaction in the remembrance of Allah. For without doubt in the remembrance of Allah do hearts find satisfaction." (The Thunder, 13:28)*

It means that the tranquility within the heart is that the heart becomes very subtle. It begins to understand with the little bit of *zikr* (remembrance), it feels the energy. It knows that when it goes

5

somewhere it's feeling a heaviness, that this place I went, it's very heavy. The heart is not going to lie. It is telling you the charge that is being emitted from the people, from the place, from that location is a very heavy energy.

If it's not positive and giving to you, it's very simple; it must be negative and taking from you. It means that if we go to enough places that take energy, your battery becomes empty. The more this negative charge goes, the more this negative charge goes, then as the battery becomes empty; your field of protection has now dropped.

## Importance of Iron in Creating a Field of Protection

Again you will see the sign within *dunya* (material world) and within yourselves.

$$\text{سَنُرِيهِمْ آيَاتِنَا فِي الْآفَاقِ وَفِي أَنفُسِهِمْ حَتَّىٰ يَتَبَيَّنَ لَهُمْ أَنَّهُ الْحَقُّ... (٥٣)}$$

*41:53 – "Sanureehim ayatina fil afaqi wa fee anfusihim hatta yatabayyana lahum annahu alhaqqu…" (Surat Al-Isra)*

*"We will show them Our signs in the horizons and within themselves until it becomes clear to them that he is the truth…"*
*(The Night Journey, 41:53)*

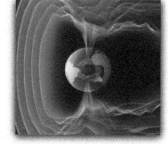

The *dunya*, the earth, has a field of protection they call the Van Allen belt. They say that belt of protection is actually from the core of the earth, the magnetic core of the earth. The earth is spinning with its magnetic core. The iron within the magnetic core is

6

producing an energy. This energy is emitting and providing a protection for the earth.

## Purification of Iron Leads to Perfection of Energy

Allah ﷻ is teaching, 'You are the same'. Your skin is like the *ard* (earth), you are from clay.

$$وَلَقَدْ خَلَقْنَا الْإِنسَانَ مِن سُلَالَةٍ مِّن طِينٍ (١٢)$$

*23:12 – "Wal laqad khalaqna al Insaana min sulalatin min Teen."*
*(Surat Al-Mumineen)*

*"And certainly did We create man from an extract of clay (water and dirt)."*
*(The Believers, 23:12)*

And you have a very holy ingredient within your being which is iron. That iron is what makes your blood to be red. Pumping through your blood, it moves into your heart and the heart's *zikr*, the heart's energy, is stamped upon the iron. It's not stamped upon the water; water just allows energy to flow. But what really captures and holds the energy of the body is the blood and the iron within that blood.

The perfection of *insaan* and the perfection and purification of the iron within the body is the perfection of its energy; its energy field. The energy that it begins to produce provides a protection against an attack.

## Be Vigilant With Your Energy – We Are Constantly Under Attack From Negativity

When the energy is depleted and the energy goes down, or there has been a major sin or transgression against the body, immediately the veil of

protection is dropped and *Shaytan* (Satan) is piercing because he is waiting. A very basic understanding that Prophet ﷺ is teaching is that your life is a state of vigilance. At one point or some point in your life you wake up and realize that this fight with *Shaytan* is very real, that this fight with *Shaytan* is constantly against me. He is waiting for me to make a mistake and full attack.

You watch movies where there is a hole blown into the castle and every type of *shayateen* (devils) are running through that hole. And as soon as the *Shaytanic* attack comes, it begins to drop the energy of the person. It begins to make the person to come down because he's now reducing the energy force of that servant.

## The Negative Energy Changes the Character

When the energy force is reduced and reduced and reduced, the abundance of negative charge begins to then change the character of that person. They become very negative and they become very angry. A sign of that negative energy is now that *zikr* moving through their heart is *zikr* (chanting) of a horrible language and horrible tongue. It's no longer the *zikr* of Allah ﷻ and the praising of Sayyidina Muhammad ﷺ, because the negative energy has overtaken that body.

The guides teach us that when you go out and about you see. You turn on TV, you turn on movies, and you see how they talk like that, nonstop?! Their *zikr* is the f-word and every word that they speak is a cursed word. It means *Shaytan* is in their heart and all their *zikr* is the *zikr* of *Shaytan*. And that is the only energy that they are producing.

## Clean Your Energy By Asking Divine's Forgiveness

So then it is very real for us, that if my heart is filled with the love of Allah جل جلاله, love of Sayyidina Muhammad ﷺ, then it should be busy asking Allah's جل جلاله forgiveness and praising upon Sayyidina Muhammad ﷺ and making *salawat* (praisings) on Prophet ﷺ, making *salawat* on Prophet ﷺ, and asking Allah's جل جلاله Divinely Forgiveness.

وَلَوْ أَنَّهُمْ إِذ ظَّلَمُوا أَنفُسَهُمْ جَاءُوكَ فَاسْتَغْفَرُوا اللَّـهَ وَاسْتَغْفَرَ لَهُمُ الرَّسُولُ لَوَجَدُوا اللَّـهَ تَوَّابًا رَّحِيمًا (٦٤)

*4:64 – "...Wa law annahum idh zhalamoo anfusahum jaooka fastaghfaro Allaha wastaghfara lahumur Rasolu lawajado Allaha tawwaban raheema."* (Surat An-Nisa)

*"...And if, when they had wronged themselves, they had but come to you and asked forgiveness of Allah, and asked forgiveness of the messenger, they would have found Allah Forgiving, Merciful." (The Women, 4:64)*

I know that I'm making mistakes left and right. I'm not claiming to know anything. I'm not claiming to be perfected. *Ya Rabbi, astaghfirullah al-Azim* (I ask for forgiveness O' Magnificent). *Sifat al-Azim* (Attribute of the Magnificent) is that from Your Might and Magnificence and Munificence, grant me Your *Istighfar, ya Rabbi.*

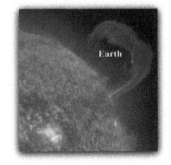

I'm nothing, I am an epsilon, I'm not even visible throughout your universes. Just in the *had* (limit) of creation, from the highest point of this universe, our galaxy, and if you look to this earth, we are not even visible. It means that, '*Ya Rabbi*, I am nothing in Your Presence, grant me Your Forgiveness, grant me Your Forgiveness.' It means that our *zikrs* have a power. By making *istighfar* we are asking Allah's Forgiveness. 'Where I'm coming short, where I know I'm coming short, where I don't know I'm coming short, grant me Your *Maghfirat* (forgiveness).

And what is Allah's reply? Most definitely, as you know the back of your hand, you know that Allah says, 'If you ask Me, you should receive.'

وَإِذَا سَأَلَكَ عِبَادِي عَنِّي فَإِنِّي قَرِيبٌ ۖ أُجِيبُ دَعْوَةَ الدَّاعِ إِذَا دَعَانِ ۖ فَلْيَسْتَجِيبُوا لِي وَلْيُؤْمِنُوا بِي لَعَلَّهُمْ يَرْشُدُونَ (١٨٦)

*2:186 – "Wa idha sa alaka 'ibadi 'anni fa inni qareebun, ojeebu da'watad daa'i idha da'aani, fal yastajeebo lee wa liyumino bee la'allahum yarshudon." (Surat Al-Baqara)*

*"And when My servants ask you, [O Muhammad], concerning Me - indeed I am near/close (to them). I respond to their prayer/invocation of the supplicant, when he calls upon Me. So let them respond/listen to Me [by obedience] and believe in Me that they may be [rightly] guided." (The Cow, 2:186)*

As soon as we say, "*Istaghfirullah al-Azim wa atubu ilayh, ya Rabb*" (I ask your forgiveness O' Allah, the Most Magnificent, and I repent), Allah's reply is, "*Bismillahir Rahmanir Raheem*" (In the Name of My Mercy and My Compassion), 'I'm forgiving you; I'm forgiving you; I'm forgiving you'.

## Once Cleansed, Be of Service to Allah's ﷻ Creation

So all day long busy with *istighfar; astaghfirullah, astaghfirullah, astaghfirullah.* After we are cleaning and cleaning our self, cleaning our loved ones, and cleaning everyone that we know from our community. Everyone that we are coming in contact with, their energy is affecting us.

Again, a very simple energy understanding is that when you put out a positive charge, the positive charge by its nature picks negative charge because two positives repel. So the positive charge goes out and the negative charge is attracted. That is what Allah ﷻ describes as a *khidmat* (service). 'If I'm going to give you a positive charge, you are your brother's keeper.' If you are an abundance of positive charge, you are responsible. You go out amongst mankind and their negative energy is going to be dressing you.

So then now, our *zikr* is not only by choice. It's a responsibility. It's in Allah's ﷻ Divinely Service, unless you want to be loaded by negative energy. So then just the understanding of energy, '*Ya Rabbi* dress me from these positive lights, dress me from these positive lights.'

## Praising and Spiritual Practices Are For Our Protection

Then the guides begin to teach that your *zikr*, your *awrad* (daily practices), your *salawats*, they are a protection for you, they are a dressing and a blessing upon your soul and you begin to purify and perfect that light. Then they begin to teach that wherever you are going, there is a light, there's an energy.

Then begin to take a *hisaab*, and an account, that this energy going out, is it positive? Then, *alhamdulillah*, that that association and that time was a positive charge. But if everywhere I'm going are negative charges, I have to increase my *zikr*, I have to increase my *istighfar*, and I have to increase my *salawat*. I have to constantly make my *wudu* (ablution), I have to go home and make my washing, or my shower. If the abundance of energy was too much, too heavy, too many sick

11

people, too many *hasad* (jealous) people, then you have to wash, you have to shower. You have to take away all these negative charges.

## Everything Produces Energy – Positive or Negative

Then the guides begin to teach us that when you have a real strong grasp of energy, they begin to teach everything produces an energy. So

if you watch a television show, Hub-e-Rasul, Muhammadan Way, or Sufilive on YouTube and Mawlana Shaykh is making *zikr*, you feel the positive charge. You feel the energy, you feel the excitement, because there are *malaika* (angels) coming through; the *mumin* (believer) souls are coming through. All that energy is flowing and you feel the charge. So then you know in that half an hour that you were watching, you are filled with a positive charge.

Now, again, the other side is if we watch negative and horrible TV shows. You keep watching them; you keep watching them and keep watching them; where is that energy going? And then put on top of that horrible sounds, horrible sounds, horrible sounds; where is that energy going?

That is very simple energy because before you talk about it in too much of a religious term, they say, 'Oh Shaykh, you know it's like hocus pocus stuff.' No! It's very basic energy. When you are listening to somebody cursing all day long, where is that cursing energy going? It's entering into your heart; it's entering into your being. How are you going to rid yourself of that difficulty? How are you going to cleanse yourself and purge yourself of those difficulties?

## Taking an Account of Yourself is a Sign of Maturity – *Rijalullah*

It means to take an accounting of ourselves and the energy charge that is coming in. That is the concept of growing up. It's the concept of coming out of heedlessness and moving towards *Rijalullah* (Men of God). What make the men of God, be it men or women; it means that they are entering a state of maturity. When you enter a state of maturity you begin to realize everything has a consequence.

Whatever I'm doing, either I'm making the energy or losing the energy. If I'm listening to these sounds, I am most definitely losing the energy, because Satan is next to me making his chanting, chanting, chanting. I'm listening to it, absorbing that negative energy and my positive energy is going down.

## We Either Gain or Lose Energy Through Our Actions

*"Qul ja al haqq wa zahaq al-batil."* (The truth has come, and falsehood has perished, Holy Qur'an, 17:81). Either the *haqq* (truth) is coming and falsehood is going, or you are inviting falsehood and the *haqq* is going; the two don't stay in the same place.

وَ قُلْ جَآءَالْحَقُّ وَزَهَقَ الْبَطِلُ، إِنَّ الْبَطِلَ كَانَ زَهُوقًا (٨١)

*17:81 – "Wa qul jaa alhaqqu wa zahaqal baatil, innal batila kana zahooqa." (Surat Al-Isra)*

*"And say, "Truth has come, and falsehood has perished. Indeed falsehood, [by its nature], is ever perishing/ bound to perish." (The Night Journey, 17:81)*

So when Prophet ﷺ was sitting and somebody became angry, Prophet ﷺ would get up and walk away, because he said, 'I cannot be in the proximity of Satan.' As soon as you lose the character and the satanic influence comes, the reality of Prophet ﷺ begins to move.

## If You Watch Many Crazy Shows, You Begin to Copy Them

Then the guides begin to teach us that everything has a consequence,

that what you're doing and what you're hearing and what you're watching, it's dressing you. And you watch enough of these crazy shows and you begin to emulate and copy them. You see people change.

They watch a crazy biker movie and they begin to wear the rings that they wear. They begin to talk like they talk, and they begin to walk around and dress like they dress. They don't realize they are being influenced by that satanic reality and it begins to dress them because that is all that *Shaytan* wants.

## Go to *Zikr* Associations – They Are Circles of Cleansing

Then the guides begin to teach that make your *istighfar* (seek

forgiveness); go make your *zikr* and most definitely attend the circles of *zikr*. The circles of *zikr* are a *ni'mat* (blessing) from Allah ﷻ, from Prophet ﷺ as a cleansing and a washing. They are the circles of washing. Everybody

is coming with their burdens, bringing those burdens into the Centre.

*Alhamdulillah*, with the *barakah* (blessings) of Sultan al-Awliya Mawlana Shaykh Muhammad Nazim Haqqani ق, and his representative Mawlana Shaykh Hisham Kabbani, they are responsible and their *du'a* (supplication) is moving. Prophet's ﷺ *nazar* (gaze) is

looking and Allah's ﷻ Support is moving and descending. As soon as Allah's ﷻ Support comes, the negativity is lifted. So there is tremendous cleansing in the associations.

## Be *Rijal* (Mature) – You Are Responsible For Protecting Your Family

The guides begin to teach us that everything we are doing is about energy. Once I take a personal account that, '*Ya Rabbi*, am I building my energy that day? Am I reducing the loss of my negative charge? Am I watching crazy, nasty, horrible things, and listening to horrible things? I lost my charge for that day.' If you have no charge for the day, you have no protection for your home, your wife, and your children.

## You Are Responsible for Your Family's Energy and Protection

Then what are you considered in Prophet's ﷺ eyes? It's not a man. A man is somebody who has energy and has a protection to protect himself, his wife, and his children with his energy. It's not about everybody for themselves. It's about building your energy, building your protection. When you have enough charge for yourself, enough for your reality, enough for everything; then what was Prophet ﷺ saying, "*Ummati, ummati, ummati*" (my nation, my nation). Prophet ﷺ wasn't teaching everybody to just you take care of yourself and the rest go to *jahannam* (hellfire)!

It means the *Rijal* (men) and what they are teaching for what is coming. What is coming into this *dunya* and what's opening into this

*dunya* is unimaginable difficulty. If my circle of protection is enough, enough for myself, then who's protecting my wife and children? Or wives, who is protecting their children, if they don't have a husband? It means then everyone's *amal* (deeds)

should be strong enough for themselves and they take a daily *hisaab* (an account). That, 'Ya *Rabbi*, am I doing enough good? Is my *amal* good; is my love for Prophet ﷺ strong? Am I doing my *wazifah*, am I doing my *awrad*, am I reading my *juz* (part) of Qur'an? Am I reading my *Dalail al-Khayrat* (book of praising on Prophet ﷺ)? Am I doing everything I possibly can? If not, give me *himmah* (zeal) to do more.'

## Build Your Energy By Increasing the Spiritual Practices

You begin to understand the energy charge, energy charge, energy charge; and then the selflessness begins to open within the heart. 'Ya *Rabbi*, now I'm not feeling a sense of protection for my loved ones. Who's going to watch over them? What type of energy is going to protect them? What's going to happen to all of them?' Then my *ibadah* (worship) should be increased again, increased again, because we are spiritual people more than physical people.

Now, if you turn on the TV you watch physical people buying guns. They are not buying 1 gun, they buy 10 guns, they buy 50 guns, 10,000 rounds, 20,000 rounds – this is from lack of faith. What they fear is coming they think that they can solve it with force because they have no *iman* (faith). Allah ﷻ is saying, 'What is coming, all the guns in the world won't help you if My Love is not within your heart and I haven't signed your heart'. If Prophet ﷺ hasn't signed the heart, if *awliyallah* (saints) haven't signed the heart, and you carry a bazooka with you, it won't help you.

It is very simple; build my energy, perfect my energy. Then begin to have a sense of responsibility that kids are not on their own; I'm responsible for them. My wife's not on her own; I'm responsible for her. I have to increase my *ibadah* and increase my worshipness if I want to know Allah ﷻ is satisfied with me.

## Disasters Are Everywhere – Are You Good With the Divine?

These difficulties are coming. Watch TV, watch every country in the world and what's happening to every place on earth – there are 10,000 people in one flood gone and they say even more, 100,000, they don't want to show the numbers. In every war, in every continent and every country there is a war, there is a flood, there is a disaster.

'*Ya Rabbi*, am I good with you? Am I good with Prophet ﷺ? Am I good with the *Ulul amr* – the *Ulul amr*, the unseen or seen *Rijalullah* – are they happy with me?' It's very simple; if they are happy with you, you should be seeing them. Because when Allah's ﷻ *Rida*, Allah's ﷻ Happiness dresses you, you should be seeing; you will be *ahlul basirah*, the people whose hearts are opened.

$$\text{أَطِيعُوا اللهَ وَأَطِيعُوا الرَّسُولَ وَأُولِي الْأَمْرِ مِنْكُمْ... (٥٩)}$$

*4:59 – "...Atiullaha wa atiur Rasola wa Ulil amre minkum..."*
*(Surat An-Nisa)*

*"... Obey Allah, Obey the Messenger, and those in authority among you..."*
*(The Women, 4:59)*

## Be With the 4 Categories –
### *Saliheen* (Righteous), *Shuhada* (Witnesses), *Siddiqeen* (Truthful), and *Nabiyeen* (Prophets)

Allah ﷻ has four categories: *Nabiyeen, Siddiqeen, Shuhadahi wa Saliheen* (Prophets, Truthful, Martyrs/Witnesses, and Righteous). They are with Allah ﷻ.

وَمَن يُطِعِ اللّهَ وَالرَّسُولَ فَأُوْلَـٰئِكَ مَعَ الَّذِينَ أَنْعَمَ اللّهُ عَلَيْهِم مِّنَ النَّبِيِّينَ وَالصِّدِّيقِينَ وَالشُّهَدَاء وَالصَّالِحِينَ وَحَسُنَ أُولَـٰئِكَ رَفِيقًا (٦٩)

*4:69 – "Wa man yuti' Allaha war Rasola fa olayeka ma'al ladheena an'ama Allahu 'alayhim minan Nabiyeena, was Siddiqeena, wash Shuhadai, was Saliheena wa hasuna olayeka rafeeqan." (Surat An Nisa)*

*"And whoever obeys Allah and the Messenger ﷺ are in the company of those on whom Allah has bestowed His Favors/Blessings – of the prophets, the sincere Truthful, the witnesses (who testify), and the Righteous, and excellent are those as companions." (The Women, 4:69)*

They are with Allah ﷻ. Anybody who says, 'No, I'm with Allah ﷻ', Allah ﷻ says, 'Okay then are you from *Nabiyeen* (Prophets)?' 'No.' 'Are you from *Siddiqeen* (Truthful)?' 'No.'

We have two choices, to be either *Shuhada* (Those who Witness), or *Saliheen* (Righteous). It means that every association, if they think that they are from the *Saliheen*, they must have *Ahlul Basirah* amongst them. They must have somebody who is *Shuhud* (Witnesses) and whose heart is open. What that *Shuhud* is

witnessing is the next one, is the *Siddiq* (Truthful). He must be witnessing the Shaykhs and the masters of the *tariqa* (spiritual path), either Sayyidina Ali ؓ or Sayyidina Abu Bakr as-Siddiq ؓ. From that *Siddiq*, they must be directly connected to Prophet ﷺ.

If their *amal* is correct, their actions are correct, their *ibadah* (worship) is correct, Allah ﷻ signed their sincerity. When they practice their practices, their heart must be witnessing their teacher. And when the teacher's happy with them, Mawlana Shaykh is happy with them, and their heart must be witnessing Sayyidina Muhammad ﷺ.

At least at that level, their Islam now is entering to be real because as soon as you say in every *salah* (prayer), *"Ash hadu an la ilaha illallah wa ash-hadu anna Muhammadan RasulAllah* ﷺ" (I bear witness that there is no God but Allah, Muhammad ﷺ is the Messenger of Allah), it means you are saying, 'I bear witness, I see Sayyidina Muhammad ﷺ'. So it's an imitation until it becomes real.

So anyone who thinks that their group is *Saliheen*, that their actions are *saliheen*, well they must have from the *Shuhada* (Witnesses). They must have somebody whose heart is open. As a result that their heart is open, those *Saliheen* (Righteous), their hearts will be opened. Because the practices and the *amal* of the one whose heart is open is what he is teaching the *Saliheen*, so that they can be from the *Shuhada* and connect to the energy of the *Siddiqs*. And the *Siddiqs* take you to the hand of Sayyidina Muhammad ﷺ. So at that time, your *salah*, your Islam is real, that you are witnessing Prophet ﷺ. You say *"Assalamu alaika ayyuhan Nabi"* (Peace be upon you O Prophet ﷺ) and you are witnessing Prophet ﷺ through your heart. And then Prophet ﷺ is in the Divinely Presence.

## Understand *A'udhu Billah* – 'Seeking Refuge in the Divine'

This is just the understanding of *"A'udhu Billah"* when we say, *"A'udhu Billahi Minash Shaytanir Rajeem"* (I seek refuge in Allah from Cursed Satan). We are asking *A'udhu Billah*, asking, 'Ya Rabbi, I'm seeking refuge in You from every *Shaytan*' – basic energy. If you are not seeking refuge then you must be inviting *Shaytan*. If whatever you're doing is not seeking refuge from *Shaytan*, then know that you are inviting *Shaytan*. So then that is not *A'udhu Billah*, that is sitting with *Shaytan*. Basic energy – am I inviting or am I repelling?

Then when I'm really repelling, I'm asking Allah ﷻ, 'Ya Rabbi, keep me with whom You are pleased with. I'm asking for Your Protection, I'm asking to be under Your Shade of Mercy.' And Allah ﷻ begins to inspire, 'My Shade, My Protection with Sayyidina Muhammad ﷺ'. *"Qul in kuntum tuhibbon Allaha fattabi'oni, yuhbibkumUllah."*

قُلْ إِنْ كُنْتُمْ تُحِبُّونَ اللَّـهَ فَاتَّبِعُونِيْ يُحْبِبْكُمُ اللَّـهُ وَيَغْفِرْ لَكُمْ ذُنُوبَكُمْ ۗ وَاللَّـهُ غَفُورٌ رَّحِيمٌ (٣١)

*3:31 – "Qul in kuntum tuhibbon Allaha fattabi'oni, yuhbibkumUllahu wa yaghfir lakum dhunobakum wallahu Ghaforur Raheem." (Surat Al-Imran)*

*"Say, [O Muhammad], "If you should love Allah, then follow me, [so] Allah will love you and forgive you your sins. And Allah is Forgiving and Merciful."*
*(Family of Imran, 3:31)*

Allah ﷻ says, 'If you want that protection, then you must be with Sayyidina Muhammad ﷺ.' So then the reality of Muharram (start of Islamic calendar) is the reality of the opening up of these energies, that at every moment asking to seek refuge. And the only refuge we are interested in is to be with Sayyidina

Muhammad ﷺ, to be with the lovers of Sayyidina Muhammad ﷺ, to be with *Ashab al-Kahf* of Sayyidina Muhammad ﷺ, and to be with *ashiqeen* of Sayyidina Muhammad ﷺ. And who are they? They are, *"Ateeullah, wa atee ar Rasul wa Ulul amrin minkum."*

يَاأَيُّهَا الَّذِينَ آمَنُوا أَطِيعُواللهَ وَأَطِيعُواالرَّسُولَ وَأُولِي الْأَمْرِ مِنْكُمْ...(٥٩)

4:59 – *"Ya ayyu hal latheena amanoo Atiullaha, wa atiur Rasola, wa Ulil amre minkum..." (Surat An-Nisa)*

*"O You who have believed, Obey Allah, Obey the Messenger, and those in authority among you..." (The Women, 4:59)*

They are the *Ulul amr* (saints). *Alhamdulillah*, we are under the banner of Sultan al-Awliya Mawlana Shaykh Muhammad Nazim Haqqani ق. He is the master of the *Ulul amr* for all this earth – our belief. And one of his highest ranking representatives is Mawlana Shaykh Hisham Kabbani. So, *alhamdulillah*, we have love of them, example of them, the way of them, and that we are asking to hold tight to that rope. Asking that, *'Ya Rabbi*, let me to understand my energy, to build my energy, to bring the perfection of my energy.'

وَاعْتَصِمُوا بِحَبْلِ اللَّهِ جَمِيعًا وَلَا تَفَرَّقُوا (١٠٣)

3:103 – *"Wa'tasimo bihab lillahi jamee'an wa la tafarraqo..." (Surat Al-Imran)*

*"And hold firmly to the rope of Allah all together and do not separate..." (Family of Imran, 3:103)*

## Understand the Power of Jealousy and Negative Energy

Then we begin to understand negative energy. How much negative energy people are able to produce. How important it is to understand *hasad* (jealousy). When we understand how powerful we are as energy people, we have to understand how powerful *hasad* is and what type of energy emits from *hasad*. Then we begin to guard our lives appropriately. Watch where you go, watch who you speak to, watch what type of actions you are doing because all that negativity is around.

Our way is a humble way, a low profile way, a way in which not to attract and not to engage in difficulties. It is to build ourselves and build our practices and to be aware that we are not inviting negativity within our lives.

We pray in the beginning and the opening of the holy month of Muharram. Muharram means no *haram*, 'Ya Rabbi', at every Muharram is a new opening, a new chance. *Ya Rabbi*, let me to move away from *haram* (forbidden) at every moment and moving towards Your Oceans of *Rida* and Satisfaction.'

*Subhana rabbika rabbal 'izzati 'amma yasifoon, wa salaamun 'alal mursaleen, walhamdulillahi rabbil 'aalameen. Bi hurmati Muhammad al-Mustafa wa bi siri Surat al-Fatiha.*

# Acquire Angelic Power:
## The Force = Energy

### We Seek the Truth and the Angelic Presence

What we seek is a Divine Grace and Divine Mercy. This Divine Energy, what we know, is the angelic presence. *"Bismillahir Rahmanir Raheem. Qul ja al Haqq wa zahaq al-batil."*

وَ قُلْ جَاءَالْحَقُّ وَزَهَقَ الْبَطِلُ، إِنَّ الْبَطِلَ كَانَ زَهُوقًا (٨١)

*17:81 – "Wa qul jaa alhaqqu wa zahaqal baatil, innal batila kana zahooqa."* (Surat Al-Isra)

*"And say, "Truth has come, and falsehood has perished. Indeed falsehood, [by its nature], is ever perishing/ bound to perish." (The Night Journey, 17:81)*

This, what they call the truth, has many levels of understanding but the most basic for us that Mawlana Shaykh is teaching is that this Divine Mercy is an angelic force. Everything that we are trying to do on a spiritual path is to bring the excessive angelic force within our being.

### The Angelic Energy Pushes Away Falsehood

From the verse of Holy Qur'an (17:81), *Awliyaullah* (saints) take from the heart of Prophet *"Qul ja al-Haqq"*, verily when truth comes and when truth faces falsehood, it obliterates the falsehood. And falsehood, by its nature, is ever-perishing. It means that the falsehood in the face of Divine Realities; the two are polar opposites. Falsehood is the lack of Divine Light, the Divine Reality, and the angelic force.

The Divine reality, for us to understand in very simplified terms, is the  abundance of angelic energy. When the angelic energy comes, it is a Divine Light and the Divine Grace. When that energy comes, it pushes away, by its nature, the falsehood, all that is from the ego and bad desires, the negative energy. Our quest in life as spiritual seekers is to fill ourselves with that angelic force. That angelic force comes with such a tremendous light, such a tremendous amount of blessings that as it begins to approach, it begins to push out the negativity from within our being.

## Like a Bus, We Pick Up Many Negative Energies

We are like a bus; our physical being picks up many passengers along the day. Many negative energies come on board and occupy us, most of which we invite, some of which we don't. These negative energies come and they begin to fill us. Then we are in need of positive energy.

The way to get this angelic force is by keeping the company of those that are producing and bringing excessive amounts of that positive energy.

يَا أَيُّهَا الَّذِينَ آمَنُوا اتَّقُوا اللَّـهَ وَكُونُوا مَعَ الصَّادِقِينَ (١١٩)

*9:119 – "Ya ayyuhal ladheena amanoo ittaqollaha wa kono ma'as sadiqeen." (Surat At-Tawba)*

*"O you who have believed, have consciousness of Allah and be with those who are truthful/pious/sincere (in words and deed)." (The Repentance, 9:119)*

24

It means that by coming into the associations of remembrance, by coming into the associations of *zikr* and chanting and what the guides have been taught of these chants, they bring an angelic force and bring an angelic energy. When that energy begins to emanate, it begins to move into the heart.

## Who Occupies the Heart Controls the Entire Being

The chakra that Sufis are most concerned is the heart chakra, *Lataif al Qalb*. It means who occupies the heart controls the entire being. Somebody got your feet, they still don't have you. But if they got your heart, they have your entire being under control. So then the Divine is teaching that, 'I am sitting upon the heart of the one who loves Me.'

مَا وَسِعَنِيْ لَا سَمَائِيْ ولا اَرْضِيْ وَلَكِنْ وَسِعَنِيْ قَلْبِ عَبْدِيْ اَلْمُؤْمِنْ

*"Maa wasi`anee laa Samayee, wa laa ardee, laakin wasi`anee qalbi 'Abdee al Mu'min."*

*"Neither My Heavens nor My Earth can contain Me, but the heart of my Believing Servant." (Hadith Qudsi conveyed by Prophet Muhammad ﷺ)*

It means for us it's then the symbol of the focus; that we are asking for the Divine Kingdom, the Divine Light, the purified light, the angelic force to enter within our heart. So then the focus of the energy, focus of the *lataifs*, focus of all the practices is that, '*Ya Rabbi*, my Lord, send that light into my heart.'

## Fortify the Heart in Order to Handle Divinely Energy

So then everything the spiritual guides begin to teach is that the chanting, the reciting, the meditation; all of these practices are to bring that energy and begin to flow. As that flow of energy begins to hit, it begins to push away negativity. Then all of their practices are supporting. Again for us to understand, they teach always by analogy. This angelic force is like liquid gold, so hot and so valuable. Again, for us to understand, that we are asking to pour that liquid gold into something plastic! It means if we are not fortified and certified; that if we don't build our self and build the heart, build the practices, build the being, then that's a path of annihilation. That energy, if it comes and hits, it is going to completely obliterate.

So much so that in Holy Qur'an, Nabi Musa ﷺ, Prophet Moses

(peace and blessings be upon him) asked, 'Oh my Lord, let me to see You.' He is given the gift of speaking with the Divine Presence. He wanted a higher *darajat* (level) of energy. 'Let me see You.' The Divine is saying that, 'Just like that, it's not possible. If I release that energy, you will be *khashiya;* you will be dust! I'm going to show you now; look at the mountain. I'm going to just release a drop of that energy.' And the teaching is that the mountain was completely obliterated. And the Prophet Moses ﷺ went unconscious.

وَلَمَّا جَاءَ مُوسَىٰ لِمِيقَاتِنَا وَكَلَّمَهُ رَبُّهُ قَالَ رَبِّ أَرِنِي أَنظُرْ إِلَيْكَ ۚ قَالَ
لَن تَرَانِي وَلَٰكِنِ انظُرْ إِلَى الْجَبَلِ فَإِنِ اسْتَقَرَّ مَكَانَهُ فَسَوْفَ تَرَانِي ۚ
فَلَمَّا تَجَلَّىٰ رَبُّهُ لِلْجَبَلِ جَعَلَهُ دَكًّا وَخَرَّ مُوسَىٰ صَعِقًا ۚ ... (١٤٣)

*7:143 – "Wa lamma jaa Musa limeeqatina wa kallamahu Rabbuhu, qala rabbi
arinee anzhur ilayka, Qala lan taranee wa lakini onzhur ilal jabali fa inistaqarra
makanahu, fasawfa taranee, falamma tajalla Rabbuhu lil jabali ja`alahu,
dakkan wa kharra Musa sa'iqan, ..." (Surat Al-A'raf)*

*"And when Moses arrived at Our appointed time and his Lord spoke to him, he
said, "My Lord, show me [Yourself] that I may look at You."
[Allah] said, "You will not see Me, but look at the mountain; if it should remain
in its place, then you will see Me." But when his Lord manifested His glory on the
mountain, He made it as dust, and Moses fell unconscious..."
(The Heights, 7:143)*

From that and from the prophetic teaching, and from the teaching of
pious people, that what we are asking for, the Divine wants to send.
He wants to fill us beyond our imagination of that light. But they are
teaching that that light comes in a clean environment. That light has to
come in a fortified environment. You cannot pour that abundantly
pure, unimaginably pure, merciful light in something that is not yet
purified.

## Purify the Body – It is the Temple That Holds the Heart

The guides teach us that our entire spiritual path is then begin to
purify. Purify the body
because the body is the
temple that is holding the
heart. How can you have a
dirty form and say, 'My heart
is good'? The two have to be
correct. If the heart is good,
the form is good. If the form
is good and the heart is defect,

it is corruption. The guides come into our lives and begin to teach us to fortify the body. The body is the temple. It is going to be the presence of the Divine. It is your *Ka'bah*; it is your place of worship. Perfect it.

$$ ... وَطَهِّرْ بَيْتِيَ لِلطَّائِفِينَ وَالْقَائِمِينَ وَالرُّكَّعِ السُّجُودِ (٢٦) $$

*22:26 – "...Wa tahhir baytee liTayifeena, wal qaayimeena, wa ruka`us sujood."*
*(Surat Al-Hajj)*

*"...Sanctify and purify My House for those who perform Tawaf*
*(circumambulation), or stand up, or bow, or prostrate [in prayer].*
*(The Pilgrimage, 22:26)*

## You Can Live Without the Brain, But Not Without the Heart

Then focus within that body. The most important organ of the body is going to be the heart, not the head. You can live without a head. There are people in comas all the time and they have no brain activity, or very little. But there is nobody who lives without a heart. The Divine is teaching, fortify the body, sanctify the body, and now prepare the organ of your heart for that Divine Grace to begin to enter.

That angelic light comes with such a force and such an energy that, 'I'm not going to send it if it's going to melt everything.' Hence, all the recitations, all of the practices, all the backup practices that are required for that energy.

## A Sign of Abundant Angelic Light is the Heavenly Knowledge

The abundance and the sign of that energy are the heavenly knowledges and many different blessings that emanate from pious people. It means their hearts are like fountains of angelic light. One of the results

of angelic light is heavenly knowledge. When the being is overwhelmed with angelic lights and angelic energies, all that comes out is going to be from heavenly realities. So then the guides are teaching us that if you want the heavenly reality, then what you are really asking for, to clarify, is the angelic light.

## People Who Talk From Books Teach From the Mind

There are people who talk from something they have read. And you know that when you hear them speak about it, it makes no sense and it's confusing. It's not coming from their heart. It's coming from their mind. They read two or three wisdoms and they begin to convey. Usually their speech is scripted, written, with many books, and looking at all the books and having to remember. Those are a learned people and learned people always have a fear that they are forgetting what they have learned. Hence, they carry their books with them everywhere they go. They take them all out, put 500 books all over the place, and keep trying to make references. And all they fear is that what they learned will evaporate because as the age goes up, the mind begins to forget.

## Real Masters Teach From the Heart, the Divinely Knowledge and Wisdom

But the wise have no books. Those are instilled with wisdom, *ilm al laduni wa hikmati bi Saliheen* (Heavenly knowledge and wisdom of the Righteous). Wisdom is from the heart. Wisdom is from the abundance of angelic energy, that as soon as they open their mouth, these knowledges, these lights, these emanations begin to pour out.

Then if you want what they have, and we are all seeking that reality and going towards many different masters. Then the masters begin to teach, the body has to be prepared. You

29

have to prepare your physicality, perfect it, clean and purify it. You are asking for Divine Presence, angelic presence. That angelic presence is always accompanying you and watching you. And they cannot stay in the presence of falsehood because the angels are under the same rule that, verily when the truth comes, falsehood is perishing. It's obliterated; the two are opposites.

وَ قُلْ جَاءَالْحَقُّ وَزَهَقَ الْبَطِلُ، إِنَّ الْبَطِلَ كَانَ زَهُوقًا (٨١)

*17:81 – "Wa qul jaa alhaqqu wa zahaqal baatil, innal batila kana zahooqa."*
*(Surat Al-Isra)*

*"And say, Truth has come, and falsehood has perished. Indeed falsehood, [by its nature], is ever perishing/ bound to perish." (The Night Journey, 17:81)*

## Sufi Masters Are the Real Alchemists – Changing the Iron Within the Body

Then, begin to perfect the heart with the chanting, with the recitation, with the practices, with the disciplines, and with the meditations. So that the heart now becomes purified, and this is the truth in alchemy. People come and ask that, 'Do the Sufis have the understanding of alchemy and changing matter into gold?' Of course they have that reality; but they are not using that knowledge to turn this metal into gold for material purposes.

They take the metal within our entire being. They take all the iron that 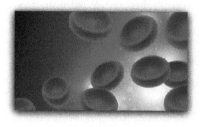 is on every cell of the blood, making it to be red and they begin to turn that iron like gold, perfect and purified. The perfect conductors of energy and light so that every cell of the body, every piece of iron within the body, is almost like gold, perfected. It is perfected and connecting perfectly with Divine energies. And every hair on the body is like a satellite receiver. How many trillions of cells are in the body? And each has a drop of that light and that energy. Then the entire being becomes a satellite dish, receiving these Divine emanations, the *ruhaniyat*, Divine lights, Divine energies, angelic forces.

## Focus on Your Heart, the Real House of Allah

Then they are teaching us, and Mawlana Shaykh is reminding us, to sanctify your body, purify your body. And within the body, look to the heart, at the *Ka'bah*, center of focus, the center of worshipness, the temple within the temple; the mosque within the mosque is the heart.

قَلْبَ الْمُؤْمِنْ بَيْتُ الرَّبْ

*"Qalb al mu'min baytur rabb." (Hadith Qudsi)*

*"The heart of the believer is the House of the Lord." (Holy Hadith)*

## Don't Be Lost in the Form of Prayer and Place of Worship

Many people are lost on the outer form of praying and going to the places of prayer. They are being lost in the form of prayer, but yet the inner mosque is dirty, the inner temple is dirty, the inner heart is dirty. And there is no benefit in what they do. You can go all you want, everywhere you want to go, but if the inside temple and the inner reality of the heart is not sanctified, not purified, then there is no angelic presence.

So the guides come to remind us in our lives that all those forms are very good, very nice, very entertaining, but for Sufis and Sufism it means focus on the heart. Perfect the physicality; perfect the presence within the heart. Pray that, 'Ya Rabbi (O my Lord), bring Your angelic force into my heart. Let my heart to be filled with that emanation.'

And then everywhere you go is a *masjid* (mosque) because the *masjid* is within your heart, and the Divine Presence is within your heart. Your heart becomes the *Ka'bah* and you become a *qibla* (direction of prayer). A *qibla* means people look at you and they regain their faith. They look at you and they are reassured with hope of the Divine Presence.

*Subhana rabbika rabbal 'izzati 'amma yasifoon, wa salaamun 'alal mursaleen, walhamdulillahi rabbil 'aalameen. Bi hurmati Muhammad al-Mustafa wa bi siri Surat al-Fatiha.*

# Chapter Two

## Reality of Light and the Power of Sound and Praise

## Form → Atom → Light → Sound

اللَّـهُ نُورُ السَّمَاوَاتِ وَالْأَرْضِ ۚ مَثَلُ نُورِهِ كَمِشْكَاةٍ فِيهَا مِصْبَاحٌ ۖ الْمِصْبَاحُ فِي زُجَاجَةٍ ۖ ... ۞ نُورٌ عَلَىٰ نُورٍ ۗ يَهْدِي اللَّـهُ لِنُورِهِ مَن يَشَاءُ ۚ وَيَضْرِبُ اللَّـهُ الْأَمْثَالَ لِلنَّاسِ ۗ وَاللَّـهُ بِكُلِّ شَيْءٍ عَلِيمٌ (٣٥)

*24:35 – "Allahu noorus samawati wal ardi. mathalu noorehi kamishkatin feeha misbahun, almisbahu fee zujajatin, ... noorun 'ala noorin. yahdellahu linoorihi man yashao. Wa yadribullah ul amthala linnasi, wallahu bikulli shayin 'Aleem."*
*(Surat An-Noor)*

*"Allah is the Light of the heavens and the earth. The Parable of His Light is as if there were a Niche and within it a Lamp: ... Light upon Light! Allah guides whom He will to His Light: Allah present examples for the people: and Allah knows all things." (The Light, 24:35)*

يُسَبِّحُ لِلَّـهِ مَا فِي السَّمَاوَاتِ وَمَا فِي الْأَرْضِ ۖ لَهُ الْمُلْكُ وَلَهُ الْحَمْدُ ۖ وَهُوَ عَلَىٰ كُلِّ شَيْءٍ قَدِيرٌ (١)

64:1 – *"Yusabbihu lillahi ma fis Samawati wa ma fil ardi, lahul Mulku wa lahul Hamdu, wa huwa 'ala kulli shay in Qadeer."* *(Surat Al-Taghabun)*

*"Whatever is in the heavens and whatever is on the earth is exalting Allah. To Him belongs dominion, and to Him belongs [all] praise, and He is over all things competent."*
*(The Manifestation of Losses, 64:1)*

# Reality of Light and
# Intercession of The Flag of Praise

### 1. Remember Me and I Will Remember You

From Mawlana Shaykh's teaching and from our understandings, they are reminding us that Prophet ﷺ is teaching that Allah ﷻ, the Divinely Presence says, 'Remember Me and I will remember you in a higher association.'

فَاذْكُرُونِي أَذْكُرْكُمْ وَاشْكُرُوا لِي وَلَا تَكْفُرُونِ (١٥٢)

*2:152 – "Fadhkuronee adhkurkum washkuroli wa la takfuroon."*
*(Surat Al- Baqarah)*

*"So remember Me; I will remember you. And be grateful/ Thankful to Me and do not reject faith." (The Cow, 2:152)*

From this one saying and holy understanding, the Divine is asking that, 'Remember Me and I'm going to remember you in a much holier and higher understanding.'

### Open the Heart Because the Mind Blocks the Heart

We can have physical understandings and then the guides begin to remind us that transcend the physical; begin to open up the heart. When they say, 'Open the mind', for us it is actually close your mind and open your heart. It's your mind that is causing the problems; it's the mind that's blocking the understanding and says, 'No, no, I understand this,' and puts a lock and a block.

So they teach us first the *zikr*. *La ilaha illallah* (there is nothing but Allah); there is nothing but God, there is nothing but the Divine. It means *La ilaha illallah*, the *la* means No head. Shut the faculty of the head and open the reality of the heart. The heart is the house of the soul and the timeless, eternal reality where the heart has infinite capacity for understanding. The mind is very limited based on conditions and based on experiences.

## 2. Reality of Light and Intercession

From that contemplation they begin to teach us of these holy teachings and holy understandings and intercession. There are two understandings; first, 'Remember Me, I remember you at higher.' And second, the intercession and the concept of the intercession: intercession of the prophets, intercession of saints, intercession of holy people. At the reality level of understanding, they begin to teach that break your physicality understandings. Take it outside of the understanding of form and now understand from the reality of the soul, the reality of light.

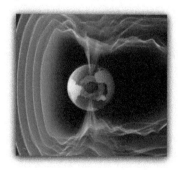

Allah's ﷻ releasing onto this earth is quantum and sciences that are the science of light. And every light is energy; energy is merely manifesting in the form of light. Our souls are lights – energy. Light is an infinite spectrum and the lowest level of light is the electromagnetic field, like a drop. We consider that dirty light

36

because it's mixed with everything from the dirtiness of this earth.

## Can You Purify Your Light and Produce More Energy?

If I have the ability to take my light and increase its frequency, to lift myself from difficulties. They are trying to teach that the spiritual path is not hocus pocus and just a bunch of crazy things you tell people that they don't understand. But Prophet ﷺ was teaching that teach them to know themselves; they will know their Lord.

مَنْ عَرَفَ نَفْسَه فَقَدْ عَرَفَ رَبَّه

*"Man 'arafa nafsahu faqad 'arafa Rabbahu"*

*"Who knows himself, knows his Lord."* Prophet Muhammad (ﷺ)

The science of the self is what *tariqa* (spiritual path) and Sufism comes to lay out its realities, ancient realities. If I'm trying to elevate my soul, then they begin to seek to contemplate at the level of light and energy and to leave the understanding of the form. It means open the horizon of the understanding.

So I want my light to be purified. Can I lift my light to a frequency higher by itself? How can you produce more energy than the energy you are producing? Again, if anyone has that ability, they should go into engineering and make engines for governments. Something that you can produce, put five dollars in and it gives you fifty dollars worth of energy back! We don't have the ability to lift our own energy because of the circumstances of this material world; we are surrounded by negative energy.

## *Haqq* (Truth) and Falsehood Have Different Frequencies of Light

So then the guides are reminding this frequency of your light, that if you really want to develop it and you want to make its *mi'raj* (ascension) or elevate the frequency of that light, it's a power. The frequency of that light, as it begins to move, it becomes more powerful energies. That's why, *"Qul jaa al-Haqq wa zahaqal batil"* (The Truth comes and the falsehood perish).

وَ قُلْ جَاءَالْحَقُّ وَزَهَقَ الْبَطِلُ، إِنَّ الْبَطِلَ كَانَ زَهُوقًا (٨١)

*17:81 – "Wa qul jaa alhaqqu wa zahaqal baatil, innal batila kana zahooqa." (Surat Al-Isra)*

*"And say, "Truth has come, and falsehood has perished. Indeed falsehood, [by its nature], is ever perishing/ bound to perish." (The Night Journey, 17:81)*

Devils and angels, they don't meet each other; they don't come into proximity. Not because of physicality but because of the frequency of their light. That level of frequency of light, if it becomes present, anything of negative Allah ﷻ says, *"Qul ja al Haqq"*. It means when the truth – the truth being eternal divinely dress lights of the soul – we are all God's creation.

When those lights come, there can't be a falsehood in their presence. The nature of the falsehood is that it's perishable. It means that light comes, the frequency of that light hits and it obliterates that which is false, that which is negative, that which is untrue.

## The Power of Light, Sound, and Frequency is Abused

 This is the reality that we are trying to understand. Now the material world is understanding that. They weaponized light. They use it for encryption and computing. All the telephones and communications are through fiber optic. Then they begin to take that light and use it as a weapon. Why? Because of its power. It means when we want to understand spiritual realities, it is difficult to meet angels; they are not readily available to us. But we can find it in the negative world. The negative world is taking light and weaponizing it, and using it for harm. Then they understood from that light that they are able to condense it.

Now they know that that light has a frequency and has a sound. That sound can be weaponized. They have equipment and the understanding that they can begin to release a frequency and begin to shake structures. Because everything emits a frequency; everything emits a sound. At its atomic, molecular level, it's emitting a sound. If you have that sound and begin to emit the opposite of it and begin to hit it with that, they say they are able to shake and move structures.

This is important for the last days, to understand the self. It begins to open the understanding of intercession. When you are talking about intercession, when you're talking about, 'Why should I seek out holy people; why should I seek out holy gatherings? I can sit here myself and do whatever I want to do'.

The guides are teaching to look, look at everything around you. These are the proofs in this world that sound can hit and cause harm; it has an effect. It's not that it doesn't happen. It has an effect. Light has an effect if directed upon someone.

## We Are Heavenly Beings, Sent Here for a Worldly Experience

Now imagine from the Divinely realities. When Allah ﷻ says, 'Remember Me and I will Remember you.' (Holy Qur'an, 2:152). And, that the *'fee kum'* (within you, Holy Qur'an, 2:151), that reality, the Prophetic reality is in everyone's soul. It's sent from heavens to this earth.

كَمَا أَرْسَلْنَا فِيكُمْ رَسُولًا مِّنكُمْ يَتْلُو عَلَيْكُمْ آيَاتِنَا وَيُزَكِّيكُمْ وَيُعَلِّمُكُمُ الْكِتَابَ وَالْحِكْمَةَ وَيُعَلِّمُكُم مَّا لَمْ تَكُونُوا تَعْلَمُونَ (١٥١)

*2:151 – "Kama arsalna feekum Rasulam minkum yatlo 'Alaykum ayatina wa yuzakkeekum wa yu'Allimukumul kitaaba walhikmata wa yu'Allimukum ma lam takono ta'Alamon." (Surah Al-Baqarah)*

*"Just as We have sent among (within) you a messenger from your own, reciting to you Our Signs, and purifying you, and teaching you the Scripture/Book and Wisdom and teaching you New Knowledge, that which you did not know." (The Cow, 2:151)*

We are not made and invented here. We are heavenly creatures sent for an earthly experience. It was in our package; we already packed it in our suitcase. The Prophetic reality is inside the soul; the love of the Divine, the angels and the prophets and all holy books are inside the soul.

### *Zikrullah* (Divinely Remembrance) Obliterates Negativity

So then Allah ﷻ begins to expand the understanding that you want to elevate your frequency to begin to obliterate all negativity around you. 'Remember Me!' because 'I am a Divinely frequency'. So the remembrance of our Lord, means the chanting, the remembrance. Just remembering by mind, remembering by tongue, remembering by heart begins to open the remembrance by soul. Because as you are bringing

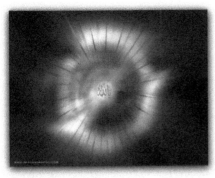

His Divinely Frequency and mentioning His Holy Names, chanting His Holy Praise; when you say *"La ilaha illallah"*, it means 'there is nothing but Allah'. When you say, *"Ya Rahman, ya Raheem"* (The Most Compassionate, The Merciful), all of these are frequencies that are moving towards the soul.

And as they begin to come to the light of the soul, they are like those weaponised understandings. These are Divinely weapons that are meant to improve the condition of mankind. It's a weapon against evilness and the evilness that we surround ourselves with, internal and external. By the remembrance of the Divine, this light and this energy begins to come and begins to smash our frequency. It begins to obliterate the negativity and then begins to dress from that Divinely Light.

## Divinely Energy Cleanses and Uplifts the Frequency of Light

As soon as that light comes and the reality of light and the wave of light, is that it merely begins to move; it obliterates everything of a lesser frequency and brings it up to its higher frequency. The lesser gets obliterated in light. It can't tolerate that energy of light that is coming. That energy begins to obliterate and lift, because it doesn't go anywhere. The reality of energy is that it cannot be destroyed.

So Divinely energy upon the soul comes and begins to obliterate everything negative. It obliterates the low level frequency of that light of the soul, which is based on conditionings and what we are doing in this material world. That Divinely energy begins to elevate it and begins to lift the frequency of that light. The more chanting, the more elevation, the more remembrance, the more elevation.

## Remember Holy People and Be Cleansed By Their Powerful Lights

Then, 'Remember Me and I will remember you'. Then the guides come and teach us then all your life, remember the holy people. Mention them in your lives, mention them over your  food, mention them over what you drink. Sit and mention their names, remember their lives. Why? Because the frequency in which they are emitting from their soul obliterates difficulties, obliterates negativities and lifts the frequency of all the souls because God is Great! They send infinite capacity and lights and emanations, and those merely begin to hit your frequency and elevate your frequency.

Then imagine the intercession by remembering the lives of the prophets. Now you are remembering holy people and attend their associations of holy people. The holy people who are trying to improve themselves, clean themselves, struggle against themselves, there are tremendous lights and energies; the souls are now uplifting, the frequencies are improving.

As a result of the frequencies, there are many cleansings. It's not an easy way; you are taking yourself from one frequency rising to a Divinely frequency. There is going to be a lot of cleansing because the light is changing, the energy is changing, the power of that soul is magnifying.

Then begin to remember the prophetic realities in our lives. Praise upon the prophetic reality; remember the stories of the prophets through the real love and the real actions. Then imagine now the prophets are coming. And the prophets are coming with Divinely Grace and they begin to remember. Again, also they are not cheap. They are saying, 'If you are remembering us in your material world, we are remembering you from our heavenly paradise stations'.

## The Remembrance Dresses the Soul With Medallions of Light

That remembrance begins to change the soul. And each change and each dress, each attribute has its own colour and has its

own frequency. Each of those frequencies and colours are the dress upon the soul and the medallions upon the soul. You see people in the army, they have these jackets with badges up to here; each medallion, all police or fire, usually the services have it.

The Divine is teaching that every attribute and every remembrance,  every association, every praising upon the prophetic reality, every recitation of Divinely holy books are lights and frequencies and colours. They dress the soul and they are medallions for the soul. What Allah ﷻ says then, bring the best of your dress to your *masjid* (mosque).

يَا بَنِي آدَمَ خُذُوا زِينَتَكُمْ عِندَ كُلِّ مَسْجِدٍ وَكُلُوا وَاشْرَبُوا وَلَا تُسْرِفُوا إِنَّهُ لَا يُحِبُّ الْمُسْرِفِينَ (٣١)

*7:31 – "Ya bani Adama khudho zeenatakum 'inda kulli Masjidin wa kuloo washraboo wa la tusrifo, innahu la yuhibbul musrifeen." (Surah Al-A'raf)*

43

*"O Children of Adam! Take (Wear) your beautiful apparel/ adornment at every Masjid/places of worship: eat and drink: But waste not by being excessive. Indeed He, does not love those who wastes/commit excess." (The Heights, 7:31)*

It means it is not only the best of our dresses, that everybody go buy a Versace shirt and come to the *zikr* (association of remembrance). But bring the best of your dress means dress your soul from these realities and these lights. And when you begin to attend the holy association, the soul is emanating all of these Divinely dresses.

## Lights of Powerful Souls Obliterates Lower Frequency

Then we begin to understand how powerful these souls can be. The

frequency and the light and the energy in which they are emitting are so powerful that it obliterates everything in its presence. Merely just a gaze from their eyes, if their light and their soul is of that reality, it obliterates everything of a lower frequency. Many people can't be in their presence. Many people can't attend their associations because the light at which they are emanating, they don't have that desire to progress.

It means the light is so powerful, such unimaginable reality; but if it comes from Toshiba or Mitsubishi or Sanyo, we believe it. When we say the light is coming from the heavens, they say, 'I don't know about that.' But that is from the One who made us. And the things we are making from our hands, we have more confidence in.

## Reality of Intercession in the World of Light

The Divine says, *"Wa laqad karamna Bani Adam."* (I have honoured your creation and I have given you the reality of your soul).

وَلَقَدْ كَرَّمْنَا بَنِي آدَمَ...(٧٠)

*17:70 – "Wa laqad karramna bani adama..." (Surat Al-Isra)*

*"We have certainly honoured the children of Adam..." (The Night Journey 17:70)*

If you elevate that soul, empower that soul, what type of power that has. So when we talk about *shafa'at* and intercession, it means every light and powerful soul emits frequencies that begin to obliterate all of the lower frequencies and elevates everyone who comes into their presence.

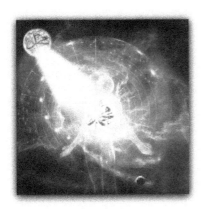

Light and light's nature is that it moves and it blends in. It's beginning and ending is not known. Their lights merely begin to emanate out, obliterates difficulties and bad characteristics, and then begin to dress the souls. The more and more and more dress upon their soul, the higher and more powerful the frequency of their souls is becoming.

This is an understanding from just the reality of the soul and the world of light. Many times people talk at the physical level of intercession and chanting and they say, 'What is this?' But just the understanding of light and energy begins to open an understanding within the heart. As much as we can recite, as much as we can attend, as much as all of these realities and praising upon the Divine Light, it begins to elevate the soul.

## The Power of the Pious People's *Du'a* (Supplication)

Then you begin to find people who are entrapped within negativity and they are surrounded by negativity. Until they have the willingness or inspiration to begin to emanate on that light. Allah ﷻ says, 'I know everything.' It is not the matter of the knowing that we are talking about, because yet your understanding is very *dunya* (material world).

The *dunya* understanding is that you are saying, 'Okay, can you please pray for me to take away the sickness?' Okay, me, you, and God already heard that; the angels heard that and many different spiritual beings in the room may have heard that. That wasn't the necessity. But the prayer of that pious person begins to emit an energy. The energy of their soul, the energy of their heart begins to move onto that and begins to obliterate the difficulties in front of them.

It means many of these understandings and realities, when you begin to think at the level of light, the level of the soul. Think of the level of sound and the level of colour. All of these are in the material world that they use them for negativity. We pray that we expand our heart and our understanding.

*Subhana rabbika rabbal 'izzati 'amma yasifoon, wa salaamun 'alal mursaleen, walhamdulillahi rabbil 'aalameen. Bi hurmati Muhammad al-Mustafa wa bi siri Surat al-Fatiha.*

# Light and Energy Originates From Sound
## Sound → Energy → Light

### Everything is in Praise of Allah ﷻ

We know through science that energy cannot be destroyed. As much as we put our focus upon energy, that energy will always be; it's eternal. That energy is what we will take with us on our departure from this earth. So everything for us is in the focus of energy and building that energy.

Now, in science, they know that every energy has a frequency, in which it's vibrating. Everything around us, at the energy level, has different frequencies. So now they understand that if they can find the frequency of this glass and begin to resonate with their devices a frequency back; resonate the same frequency of the glass, why? Because Allah ﷻ says in Holy Qur'an, 'Everything is praising Me.' Everything has a chant, everything has a frequency; that it is existing by sound.

تُسَبِّحُ لَهُ السَّمَاوَاتُ السَّبْعُ وَالْأَرْضُ وَمَن فِيهِنَّ ۚ وَإِن مِّن شَيْءٍ إِلَّا يُسَبِّحُ بِحَمْدِهِ وَلَٰكِن لَّا تَفْقَهُونَ تَسْبِيحَهُمْ ۗ إِنَّهُ كَانَ حَلِيمًا غَفُورًا (٤٤)

*17:44 – "Tusabbihu lahus samawatus sab'u wal ardu wa man fee hinna wa in min shayin illa yusabbi hu bi hamdi hi wa lakin la tafqahoona tasbeehahum innahu kana haleeman ghafoora." (Surat Al-Isra)*

*"The seven heavens and the earth and whatever is in them exalt [praises] Him. And there is not a thing except that it exalts [Allah] by His praise, but you do*

*not understand their [way of] exalting. Indeed, He is ever Forbearing and Forgiving." (The Night Journey, 17:44)*

## Everything Has a Frequency and It Could Be Crushed By Sound

It means that sound is the source of energy; energy is the source of light; light is the source of all manifestation. They know it to be true scientifically. Everything that is manifesting is a light; it is quantum reality. That light can be reduced or deduced into an energy. That energy is actually a vibration and a sound.

Now they can manipulate that sound. So if they find the frequency of this glass, they begin to just play the frequency of that glass and it shatters. They have more sophisticated devices that they can apply upon a wall and upon steel. You know Hutchinson's theory; that they put a frequency back, for everything has its sound; everything has its frequency. They apply that frequency and it begins to shatter and begins to crush.

## 'It Was Not But One Shout, We Destroyed and Raised You' (Holy Qur'an, 36:29)

Allah ﷻ said in Holy Qur'an, *"Sayhatan wahidatan."* 'It was but one shout, We froze you in your place; you won't be able to move' (36:49). 'It was but one shout and We destroyed you' (36:29). 'It was but one shout that We raised you' (36:53). It is Divine teaching that everything is based on sound. The sound is the origin of our being and the secret of our reality.

إِن كَانَتْ إِلَّا صَيْحَةً وَاحِدَةً فَإِذَا هُمْ خَامِدُونَ (٢٩)

36:29 – *"In kanat illa sayhatan wahidatan fa idha hum khamidoon."*
(Surat Yaseen)

*"It was not but one shout, and immediately they were extinguished/destroyed."*
(Yaseen, 36:29)

مَا يَنظُرُونَ إِلَّا صَيْحَةً وَاحِدَةً تَأْخُذُهُمْ وَهُمْ يَخِصِّمُونَ (٤٩)

36:49 – *"Ma yanZhuroona illa sayhatan
wahidatan ta akhudhuhum wa hum
yakhissimoon." (Surah Yaseen)*

*"They do not await except a single Blast/Shout: it will seize them while they are
disputing among themselves!"* (Yaseen, 36:49)

إِن كَانَتْ إِلَّا صَيْحَةً وَاحِدَةً فَإِذَا هُمْ جَمِيعٌ لَّدَيْنَا مُحْضَرُونَ (٥٣)

36:53 – *"In kanat illa sayhatan wahidatan fa idha hum jamee'un ladayna
muhdaroon." (Surat Yaseen)*

*"It will be no more than a single Blast/Shout, when at once, they will all be
brought up before Us!"* (Yaseen, 36:53)

## Your Frequency Emits Energy – Energy Manifests Light
## Sound → Energy → Light

Based on the sound and the vibration we make it is going to be this same formula: sound, energy, light – it's three. You can't say, 'I have light,' but you have no frequency. Then your frequency is a very low level sound. Where your actions are very low and then you claim to have a very luminous soul; it's impossible. The frequency of your light will be emitting your energy; your energy will be manifesting its light.

So then our whole pursuit is in timeless realities; not the time reality. The time reality is to eat, drink, and sleep and do the physical things like walk and talk. But what the guides want is that your timeless reality

49

of your soul, it needs an energy. It needs more energy; your light is not emitting the spectrum that it needs to. It has an infinite capacity on a spectrum of light.

### Elevate Your Light Spectrum by *Hamd* (Praise) and *Zikr* (Remembrance)

When they show you light they realize light has an infinite capacity. What we use of the spectrum of light is the lowest level of the electromagnetic. The frequency and the degrees of light, consider them to be infinite in their *darajat* and in their ranks.

It means we are here at this low level of light and God wants for us to move and elevate our light, make your soul more powerful. How are you going to make your soul more powerful? You need more energy. How are you going to get more energy for the soul? It is by the sound that you make. The sound that you make, the *zikr* and the chanting that you make, has a direct effect upon 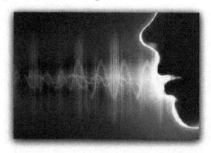 your energy and upon the light and the frequency and the level of the light and the soul.

It means everything for us and they're beginning to explain that reality. As much as we're making changes, as much as we are making recitations, as much as we are breathing in that energy, the spectrum of that light is going higher, higher, higher, and higher.

## Reality of Sound and Intercession of Holy Souls

Then the guides begin to teach, just like now, they can introduce a frequency from another device. This glass has its own frequency and it's making its own chanting. They can introduce an outside frequency to it and shatter it.

The concept of intercession is that same reality and from very holy souls, the devices that, you remember Me (Allah ﷻ and remember these holy souls). Again because they want us to think through reality; we think it through and contemplate. When you call upon holy souls and in association and praising upon God that, 'Bring Your prophets, bring Your saints, bring the angels, bring them to be in this association'. These lights, and the reality of light, are that it doesn't stay separate. When a light comes into this room, it immediately begins to dress everything from that light.

Now we are here at a low level and their lights are unimaginable in their power and are up high. When that energy begins to enter into the room, immediately the frequency of that light, the energy of that light, is elevating our frequency. It is shattering all of the wrong and bad characteristics that block our frequency from going higher. They shatter it, they shatter it, they shatter it, and they begin to dress

it from their frequency. They dress it from their level of lights and from their level of power.

Now those souls become elevated in a timeless reality because there's no time. They don't come for the five minutes that we sat here. It's a very difficult thing to even put into words, what they are teaching of this reality. It's like a window that opens, like a sci-fi movie.

## The Guides Dress Our Light From a Timeless Realm

As soon as the chanting begins and these associations begin, it's like a window opens that this spiritual light comes through and begins to dress our lights. That dress is now in a timeless dimension. It's a pocket of energy that now is eternal, because that from the heavens dressed something from the earth, from our being on this earth. It immediately opened a dimension, opened a reality that is timeless.

It is like a page. Every chant, every association, every heavenly action that we do, opens an eternal page of reality, that eternally, that energy is taking place. Those angels eternally dressing the souls; the prophetic

realities eternally dressing the soul; saints eternally dressing the soul. It means the association with them is eternal, it is entering now an eternal realm; that which is higher, that which is eternal, that which is timeless.

## Build a Relationship With the World of Light and Eternity

So they teach us then the greatest gift and the greatest reality that we can achieve is to contemplate. Prophet ﷺ described that, 'If you contemplate for one hour, *tafakkur sa'ati*, and make a good *tafakkur* for one hour, it's as if 70 years of worship to somebody else.'

تَفَكُّرْ سَاعَةٍ خَيْرٌ مِنْ عِبَادَةِ سَبْعِينْ سَنَةً

*"Tafakkur sa'atin khairun min 'Ibadati sab'een sanatan."*

*"One hour of contemplation is more valuable than seventy years of worship."*
*Prophet Muhammad (ﷺ)*

It means he gave Einstein's theory because Einstein said that if you travel at the speed of light, you leave and come back, 70 years will have passed on this earth.

The guides are teaching that as soon as you enter the world of contemplation, that you use all of Islam, you use all of your practices to discipline the physicality. But then begin to open the reality of the soul and the reality of light and meditating on that light. As soon as the world of light begins to open and you call upon these souls, call upon these masters, call upon these angels, call upon the Divinely Presence, that pocket of energy that opens,

it begins a relationship with eternity. From our temporal world, from a very temporary existence, we can actually have a relationship with that which is eternal – the world of light.

## Keep the Company of People of Light

That's why you find all the traditions call upon the people of light, call upon the realities of light because their relationship that when you make your meditation and contemplation, when you call upon them, where Allah ﷻ says in Holy Qur'an, "*Ittaqullahi wa kunu ma'as Sadiqeen.*"

يَا أَيُّهَا الَّذِينَ آمَنُوا اتَّقُوا اللّٰه وَكُونُوا مَعَ الصَّادِقِينَ ١١٩

*9:119 – "Ya ayyuhal ladheena amanoo ittaqollaha wa kono ma'as sadiqeen."*
*(Surat at Tawba)*

*"O you who have believed, have consciousness of Allah and be with those who are truthful/ Pious / sincere (in words and deed)." (The Repentance, 9:119)*

It means keep the company of the *Siddiqeen* (Truthful), why – because it's that reality. They keep the company of the people of light because if their company comes and you begin to train yourself on how to keep their companionship, you are now opening pockets of eternity. Every time you meet with

them and connect with them, that's an eternal dress. There is no way that if you are able to connect with Mawlana Shaykh, connect with Prophet ﷺ, that that association would ever end. It's an eternal association; there is no time in their realm.

So imagine that you are able to unlock the reality of your heart, and as soon as you contemplate, you are with them. That pocket of eternity is eternally teaching you, eternally dressing you, eternally blessing you. And every association you have in the world of light becomes an eternal page in our reality.

That is something that is not in comparison to anything from the material world. What can we do in the material world that would even compare with that? That's why Prophet ﷺ was directing us to *tafakkur*, contemplate. Once you contemplate you begin to open your heart and call upon the angels, call upon saints, call upon Divinely Presence, call upon the prophets because you are asking God, 'Let me to be with those whom you are pleased with.'

If that pocket of energy opens, it is not something you could even talk about as the tongue has a hard time to describe it. And that's what they want for us, a timeless reality. It is to enter the realm that is timeless and is eternal and that eternal dress, *InshaAllah*, eternally to dress us. Above that is timelessness, where it becomes the Will of the Divine that manifests within the prophetic heart.

*Subhana rabbika rabbal 'izzati 'amma yasifoon, wa salaamun 'alal mursaleen, walhamdulillahi rabbil 'aalameen. Bi hurmati Muhammad al-Mustafa wa bi siri Surat al-Fatiha.*

# Reality of Sound and Praise –
# Why *Hamd* and *Zikr* are Powerful

Science and its understandings begin to open for humanity, to give us an understanding of our reality, especially if the science is correct. Because this is *akhir zaman* (end of time), Allah ﷻ is opening of these realities the importance of sound. We said many times before, but you never know if the third, fourth, or fifth time it may click into somebody's heart. They may say, 'Huh, I didn't hear that before.' It takes a little bit of digesting spiritually to truly understand.

## Everything is in Existence Because of its *Hamd* (Praise)

In the world of form; for form to be manifesting there must be "*Yusabbi hu bihamdihi*" (Holy Qur'an, 17:44); there must be a *hamd*, and a praise.

تُسَبِّحُ لَهُ السَّمَاوَاتُ السَّبْعُ وَالْأَرْضُ وَمَن فِيهِنَّ ۚ وَإِن مِّن شَيْءٍ إِلَّا يُسَبِّحُ بِحَمْدِهِ وَلَٰكِن لَّا تَفْقَهُونَ تَسْبِيحَهُمْ ۗ إِنَّهُ كَانَ حَلِيمًا غَفُورًا (٤٤)

*17:44 – "Tusabbihu lahus samawatus sab'u wal ardu wa man fee hinna wa in min shayin illa yusabbihu bihamdihi wa lakin la tafqahoona tasbeehahum innahu kana haleeman ghafoora." (Surat Al-Isra)*

*"The seven heavens and the earth and whatever is in them exalt [praises] Him. And there is not a thing except that it exalts [Allah] by His praise, but you do not understand their [way of] exalting. Indeed, He is ever Forbearing and Forgiving." (The Night Journey, 17:44)*

The world of form has an atomic reality; the atoms are moving at such

a high speed that you see the form as if it is something solid. These are all atoms moving. These atoms have a *zikr* (remembrance). It means the form, the atomic reality of it, and then when they found the atoms and went into the atomic level, it is light. So form, the atomic reality, becomes a light.

Everything is a *noor* (light) manifesting with a *zikr* that Allah ﷻ gives to it and allows it to manifest. The science of light, the existence of light is from an energy. There is an energy making that light to manifest and that energy is a *hamd* (praise). It means that *zikr*, the *hamd* is bringing the energy, so the source is what? *Hamd*.

## Muhammad محمد (ﷺ) Has the Secret of *Hamd* حمد (Praise)

Our Prophet's name is *Hamd* حمد (*Ha* ح, *Meem* م, *Daal* د); it is not a coincidence. 'Most Hamd' '*Mu-hamd* محمد' ﷺ means 'Most Praised One'. Also within the name is the secret of praise. Because *akhir zaman* (end of time) is that Prophet ﷺ is coming to bring that reality, because we said the world of form and *dunya* is collapsing.

## Holy Qur'an is Coming Through the Divinely Tongue

The earlier Messages were based on form. For Nabi Musa (Moses) عليه السلام the Torah was revealed as written text on Stone Tablets. The last two holy books are based on sound. From Ruhullah Sayyidina Isa (Jesus) عليه السلام it came as *Injeel* (Gospel), 'the Spoken Word' which was based on sound, based on what is coming from the tongue. Then came the Holy Qur'an, which means it is a *kitab* (book) that is recited. It rhymes and it is melodious and it is through a sound, through whom? A *hamd*! Coming to you a Messenger who is the Most Praised (MuHamd), *Liwa al Hamd* (Flag of Praise).

Prophet's ﷺ tongue is the tongue of the Divinely Presence. Through that Divinely Tongue that Allah عز وجل is giving to the soul of Prophet ﷺ, is coming Allah's عز وجل *Kitab* (book) that is not created. *Azhamatul Qur'an* (Greatness of Holy Qur'an) is that it is not created; it is from Allah's عز وجل Ancient Words coming through the holy tongue of Prophet ﷺ.

## 'String Theory' – Everything Has a Praising and Vibration

When we understand the world of form, then it becomes atoms and molecules. These atoms and molecules are light. This light, for it to be in existence, there is a *hamd*, it is a praise. They call that in science 'String Theory'. Everything has a praising and a vibration. Allah عز وجل says, 'For Verily everything is praising Me.' Allah عز وجل gave everything a *zikr*.

تُسَبِّحُ لَهُ السَّمَاوَاتُ السَّبْعُ وَالْأَرْضُ وَمَن فِيهِنَّ ۚ وَإِن مِّن شَيْءٍ إِلَّا يُسَبِّحُ بِحَمْدِهِ وَلَٰكِن لَّا تَفْقَهُونَ تَسْبِيحَهُمْ ۗ إِنَّهُ كَانَ حَلِيمًا غَفُورًا (٤٤)

*17:44 – "Tusabbihu lahus samawatus sab'u wal ardu wa man fee hinna wa in min shayin illa yusabbihu bihamdihi wa lakin la tafqahoona tasbeehahum innahu kana haleeman ghafoora." (Surat Al-Isra)*

*"The seven heavens and the earth and whatever is in them exalt [praises] Him. And there is not a thing except that it exalts [Allah] by His praise, but you do not understand their [way of] exalting. Indeed, He is ever Forbearing and Forgiving." (The Night Journey, 17:44)*

## Control the Body and Free the Light of the Soul

You contemplate on that world of form and we want to break down the world of form. Because we are not here for the form. You are not here to perfect the body, because the body is going into the *qabr* (grave). All the actions we do in Islam is to contain and control the donkey and we call the body 'the donkey'! The body is not going to Allah ﷻ. So don't be preoccupied with the body. You have to tame and bring Islam to tame the body, control the body, control the bad characteristics, and control the bad desires so that the *noor* and light of the soul can become free. The light of the soul is entrapped within that body.

## *Malakoot* (Heavenly Realm) and the Quantum Theory: Study of Light

Everything that is important for us is *malakoot* (heavenly realm). We exist within *mulk* (earthly realm) to return back to the heavenly realm. And the *malakoot* is *"kulli shay"*, in *Surat Yaseen*; Allah ﷻ describes, 'It is all encompassing'.

فَسُبْحَانَ الَّذِي بِيَدِهِ مَلَكُوتُ كُلِّ شَيْءٍ وَإِلَيْهِ تُرْجَعُونَ (٨٣)

36:83 – *"Fasubhanal ladhee biyadihi Malakutu kulli shay in wa ilayhi turja'oon." (Surat Yaseen)*

*"Therefore glory be to Him in Whose hand is the kingdom of all things, and to Him you shall be brought back."(Yaseen, 36:83)*

Allah ﷻ says, 'It is all encompassing' because He is giving us the science of it that the world of light encompasses the world of form. You see it as a form but these objects are atoms, these are molecules. When they look at these atoms and molecules under their 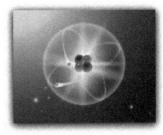 electron microscopes and devices, they see lights, which became known as 'Quantum Theory'. Quantum is the theory of light.

## Reality of 'Quantum' from Holy Qur'an, 'In Kuntum' tuhibbonAllah (3:31)

قُلْ إِنْ كُنْتُمْ تُحِبُّوْنَ اللَّـهَ فَاتَّبِعُوْنِيْ يُحْبِبْكُمُ اللَّـهُ وَيَغْفِرْ لَكُمْ ذُنُوَبَكُمْ ۚ وَاللَّـهُ غَفُورٌ رَّحِيمٌ (٣١)

3:31 – *"Qul in kuntum tuhibbon Allaha fattabi'oni, yuhbibkumUllahu wa yaghfir lakum dhunobakum wallahu Ghaforur Raheem." (Surat Al-Imran)*

*"Say, [O Muhammad], "If you should love Allah, then follow me, [so] Allah will love you and forgive you your sins. And Allah is Forgiving and Merciful." (Family of Imran, 3:31)*

***In Kuntum:*** "In Kuntum tuhibbonAllah" (If you love Allah..., Holy Qur'an, 3:31). This is the study that Allah ﷻ is releasing to them; the Quantum theory is the study of light. Because they wanted to study this form, these atoms and these molecules, they saw all those lights. So they merely made this word 'Quantum' from the *"Kuntum"*.

Then they find that all of this is towards the *"liwal al Hamd"* (Flag of Praise) ﷺ. So in that Holy Qur'an, in that *ayah* (verse) 3:31 is this whole reality. So *"Kuntum"*, Allah ﷻ revealed to them that this creation of yours, all its atoms and molecules are all lights.

***Fattabi'oni*** **(Follow):** The electrons spin around the nucleus because they have fallen in love with the nucleus and want to get closer. So when they saw all these sparkling lights in the atoms, then they realized that this *"fattabi'oni"* is the energy. They are now following Allah's ﷻ order and they are looking to the energy. So when they 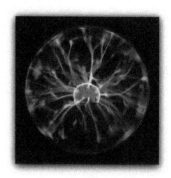 are looking into all these lights, they see that these lights are all moving in an amazing speed. They don't know where they are going and why they are moving so fast. So these are massive energies. This little thing has so much energy, spinning so fast, and making all these different colours.

When the scientists saw these lights in the atom, and that they spin so fast, and make all these different colours, they realized there are massive energies in an atom. Then they said what is this energy? What they found was that these are vibrations.

## The Power of *Liwal al Hamd* (Flag of Praise) in Each Atom

This is then the *"fattabi'oni"* (Follow, Holy Qur'an, 3:31), because this is now the secret of *"liwal al Hamd"* (Flag of Praise), the praise of Prophet ﷺ. All the praises are upon Prophet ﷺ. That is why Allah ﷻ calls Prophet Muhammad ﷺ *"liwal al Hamd"* (the flag of Praise). Because, *"in Allahi wa malaykatahu yusalona alan Nabi..."* (For verily Allah and His angels are praising upon the Prophet ﷺ..., Holy Qur'an, 33:56).

When they reached to the string, *Awliya* (saints) come now and teach them, that string means the *zikr* (Divine's Remembrance). *"Yusabihu bi hamdeh"* (Everything praises Him, Holy Qur'an, 17:44). Allah عز وجل says, 'Verily everything is praising me, you don't have the ears to understand', except my *mutafakkiron* (those who contemplate).

تُسَبِّحُ لَهُ السَّمَاوَاتُ السَّبْعُ وَالْأَرْضُ وَمَن فِيهِنَّ ۚ وَإِن مِّن شَيْءٍ إِلَّا يُسَبِّحُ بِحَمْدِهِ وَلَٰكِن لَّا تَفْقَهُونَ تَسْبِيحَهُمْ ۗ إِنَّهُ كَانَ حَلِيمًا غَفُورًا (٤٤)

*17:44 – "Tusabbihu lahus samawatus sab'u wal ardu wa man fee hinna wa in min shayin illa yusabbihu bihamdihi wa lakin la tafqahoona tasbeehahum innahu kana haleeman ghafoora." (Surat Al-Isra)*

*"The seven heavens and the earth and whatever is in them exalt [praises] Him. And there is not a thing except that it exalts [Allah] by His praise, but you do not understand their [way of] exalting. Indeed, He is ever Forbearing and Forgiving." (The Night Journey, 17:44)*

**Yuhibkumullah (Allah Will Love You):** The *mutafakkiron* understand the praise. As a result *"Yuhibkumullah"* (Allah will love, Holy Qur'an, 3:31), because they went after the Prophet صلى الله عليه وسلم as *"liwal al Hamd"* and they gained Allah's عز وجل love and Allah عز وجل loves them. All that science is to bring that reality out.

## It Is But One Shout – *"Saihatan Wahidatan"*

They found that light is having a praise and a *zikr*. It means for everything, when you go back to its source, it is based on a praise, based on a sound. Why is the last and final Messenger to bring the end of the world based on praise? Prophet Muhammad صلى الله عليه وسلم is the Flag of Praise, to bring the Message of Allah عز وجل, to bring the realities of Allah عز وجل. And on the resurrection he will make another praise that will bring everything down and then bring everything back. When Allah عز وجل resurrects all Creation and the intercession of Sayyidina Muhammad صلى الله عليه وسلم.

مَا يَنْظُرُونَ إِلَّا صَيْحَةً وَاحِدَةً تَأْخُذُهُمْ وَهُمْ يَخِصِّمُونَ (٤٩)

*36:49 – "Ma yanZhuroona illa sayhatan wahidatan ta akhudhuhum wa hum yakhissimoon." (Surat Yaseen)*

*"They do not wait for aught but a single Shout/Blast: it will seize them while they are yet disputing among themselves!" (Yaseen, 36:49)*

إِن كَانَتْ إِلَّا صَيْحَةً وَاحِدَةً فَإِذَا هُمْ جَمِيعٌ لَدَيْنَا مُحْضَرُونَ (٥٣)

*36:53 – "In kanat illa sayhatan wahidatan fa idha hum jamee'un ladayna muhdaroon." (Surat Yaseen)*

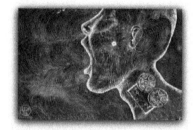

*"It will be no more than a single Shout, when at once, they will all be brought up before Us!" (Yaseen, 36:53)*

It means then the importance of sound is everything. Then our whole life's pursuit is based on the sound.

People who are overly thinking about the form they have got it wrong. The emphasis on the form is very temporary. You wash, you clean, you discipline the body and that is it. You are not taking the body into the Divinely Presence; that body is actually going into the *qabr* (grave). When you begin to understand that, *ya Rabbi*, I cleaned the body but let me energize my soul and my light.

## Light is Manifested Based on Sound – It is Raised by Praising

Then the guides teach, if you want to energize the light, fix your praise. Your light is manifesting based on a sound. Then why is *zikrullah* so important? Why is praising on Sayyidina Muhammad ﷺ so important?

يُسَبِّحُ لِلَّهِ مَا فِي السَّمَاوَاتِ وَمَا فِي الْأَرْضِ ۖ لَهُ الْمُلْكُ وَلَهُ الْحَمْدُ ۖ وَهُوَ عَلَىٰ كُلِّ شَيْءٍ قَدِيرٌ (١)

*64:1 – "Yusabbihu lillahi ma fis Samawati wa ma fil ardi, lahul Mulku wa lahul Hamdu, wa huwa 'ala kulli shay in Qadeer." (Surat Al-Taghabun)*

*"Whatever is in the heavens and whatever is on the earth is exalting [praising] Allah . To Him belongs dominion, and to Him belongs [all] praise, and He is over all things competent." (The Manifestation of Losses, 64:1)*

It means it is the best of *amal* (deed) because it is an *amal* that will raise the *darajat* (level) of your light. So now your light is at a certain praise.

## Negative Energies Lowers Your Frequency

You will see it now in the world of negativity and darkness. Every sound that they emanate, 'uuuu rrrr hh', like a rock concert; all their bad noises that they are emanating is what? To take the frequency to the lowest level. The *shaytanic* and satanic frequency emanates a sound which is very low on the spectrum of sound, and to bring what? Because *Shaytan* knows the reality. That if I want to collapse this human, if he is emanating from this higher frequency and the light which Allah ﷻ gave, because everybody is born on purity and Allah ﷻ gave a pure light and they are emanating at a certain frequency; *Shaytan's* role is to bring that emanation down.

## Listening to Negativity Lowers Your Spectrum of Light

By listening to rap and listening to these horrible sounds, horrible words, *Shaytan* is bringing that person's soul down. Because what you hear is affecting the soul; what you hear affects the heart. What you praise and what you say affects the heart, affects the soul; they are both linked. So *Shaytan's* duty is to take your frequency down and as soon as he brings it down he brings the spectrum of your light down. If he brings the spectrum of your light down, you can become possessed, you can be under satanic attack. That is the whole desire of *Shaytan*.

Now turn and look to the *dunya* (material world); what do they have? An iPod. From the time the walkman came out, the whole world is covered with the bitten apple. Why the bitten apple? Because Allah ﷻ is merciful and great, Allah ﷻ says this *dunya* is a program, I already wrote it; if you are a little bit clever you can pick up

all these different signs. *Shaytan* is using the apple that took us from Paradise; their logo is the bitten apple. So you don't have to think so hard. He uses that device to do what? To lower the frequency of the believers. By lowering the frequency of the believers, he affects their light, lowers their light; they have lowered their defense system. By lowering the defense system, the satanic attack can begin, and difficulty and harm, everything comes to the body.

## 'The Flag of Praise' Brings the Frequency Back Up

So now, *Liwa wal Hamd* (the Flag of Praise) and *Rahmatan lil 'Aalameen* (Mercy to the Worlds). Prophet Muhammad ﷺ comes onto *dunya* and brings the frequency back up.

$$\text{وَمَا أَرْسَلْنَاكَ إِلَّا رَحْمَةً لِّلْعَالَمِينَ (١٠٧)}$$

*21:107 – "Wa maa arsalnaka illa Rahmatan lil'alameen." (Surat Al-Anbiya)*

*"And We have not sent you, [O Muhammad], except as a mercy to the worlds." (The Prophets, 21:107)*

As much as you are reading Holy Qur'an, as much as you are reciting, as much as you are in *durood shareef* and in praising, your frequency is moving, moving towards *haqq* (truth). What does Allah ﷻ describe as *haqq*? That *haqq* and *batil* (truth and falsehood) don't mix. When the frequency goes up, the light emanating from the soul is becoming more powerful. When the light of the soul is becoming powerful, then *haqq* and falsehood don't get along.

وَقُلْ جَاءَ الْحَقُّ وَزَهَقَ الْبَاطِلُ ۚ إِنَّ الْبَاطِلَ كَانَ
زَهُوقًا (٨١)

*17:81 – "Wa qul jaa al Haqqu wa zahaqal Baatil, innal batila kana zahooqa."
(Surat Al-Isra)*

*"And say: Truth has (now) arrived, and Falsehood perished: for Falsehood is (by
its nature) bound to perish." (The Night Journey, 17:81)*

It means if falsehood and evilness begins to come towards you, with that frequency of light, with that frequency that the *zikr* and *salawat* and *durood shareef* is making upon the soul, and raising the power of the soul, that negativity moves away. It doesn't want anything to do with that soul. It is going to be *zahooqa* (perished). Allah ﷻ says, 'Haqq will destroy it.'

## Build the *Haqq* (Truth) in You through *Zikr* and Praising

The *haqq*, as much as we can build the *haqq* (truth) through recitation

and praising, that is the way to raise the frequency. So *awliya* and pious people come into our lives and say, 'That is the best of your *amal* (deeds) because it is not mandatory, it is *Sunnah* (way of

Prophet ﷺ) and that *amal* will raise you to the Heavens. By attending the *majlis* of *zikr* (association of Divinely remembrance), by making your *durood shareef*, by making your *zikr*, by doing recitations and reading of Holy Qur'an, first of all.' All of those recitations, those *amals* (actions) are powerful *amals* for the frequency of the soul. It changes the frequency; it begins to shatter the frequency and raises it. Anything towards the Divine when it shatters, it raises and rebuilds, raises and rebuilds.

Now in *dunya*, as we have said it before, that *Shaytan* will introduce sound weapons. He understands that reality; he understands that he can take a structure, and with sound, begin to manipulate the structure; play the frequency and then shatter it! So if you Google the physics of sound, you see many items they put up and manipulate the physicality of that item based on its sound. This is that reality. *Shaytan* knows that reality and is going to weaponize that reality, to make a weapon out of sound.

## *Zikrullah* is Our Best Defense Against Negativity

Allah ﷻ gave us the best defense which is *zikrullah*! It means every time we are in praising, every time we are in *durood shareef*, every time we attend the *majlis* of *zikr*, the energy that is coming from

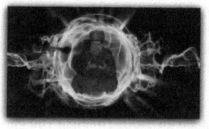

that is not something that can be imagined. You raise the frequency of the soul, the light; the illumination of the soul is changing and that is the defense of the body that pushes away difficulty, pushes away bad characteristics and brings us closer to the reality that Prophet ﷺ wanted for us.

## Every *Majlis* Should Have *Zikrullah* and *Durood Shareef*

Twenty people talking has no benefit to anybody's soul. If you have an event and twenty people come to talk and keep the audience listening

to talk after talk has absolutely no benefit for your soul. If they are not a real guide and they are not from *Ibaad ur Rahman* (Servants of the Most Compassionate). When *Ibaad ur Rahman* speak, they speak from their heart and the energy coming from their heart will affect your heart and will affect your soul. If not of that caliber, all the talk of the world goes to your head and your head takes it, shuts down, and falls asleep.

But *zikrullah* and *majlis* of *zikr*, means that anytime there is a gathering, there has to be *zikr* and there has to be a *mehfil* of *durood shareef* on Prophet ﷺ which becomes a Paradise *halaqa* (circle).

*Ahadith (sayings of Prophet Muhammad (pbuh):*

*"Hazrat Anas (RA) narrates that RasulAllah (pbuh) said: When you pass the gardens of paradise then graze well. They asked: What are the gardens of paradise? He replied: The gatherings of Zikr."*

Why? Because now the lights of Paradise are coming.

*"In Allaha wa malaikatahu yusaloon alan Nabi ﷺ"*

*'Allah and His angels send blessings on the Prophet ﷺ'* (Holy Qur'an, 33:56)

إِنَّ اللَّـهَ وَمَلَائِكَتَهُ يُصَلُّونَ عَلَى النَّبِيِّ ۚ يَا أَيُّهَا الَّذِينَ آمَنُوا صَلُّوا عَلَيْهِ وَسَلِّمُوا تَسْلِيمًا (٥٦)

*33:56 – "InnAllaha wa malaaikatahu yusalluna 'alan Nabiyi yaa ayyuhal ladhina aamanu sallu 'alayhi wa sallimu taslimaa." (Surat Al-Ahzab)*

*"Allah and His angels send blessings on the Prophet: O you that believe! Send your blessings on him, and salute him with all respect."*
*(The Combined Forces, 33:56)*

It means then Allah's ﷻ praising begins to descend, the angels praising begins to descend and people begin to heat up. Their energies and frequencies are changing, the illumination of their light begins to change and their whole being begins to change.

*Ahadith (sayings of Prophet Muhammad ﷺ):*

*"Hazrat Abu Hurairah (RA) narrates from RasulAllah (Prophet Muhammad pbuh) that `there is a group of angels who patrol the earth and wherever they find any gathering of Zikr they call out to each other and form a circle around this gathering that reaches to the sky. When this gathering disperses, they return to the sky…"*

We pray that Allah ﷻ grants more and more understandings and keep us surrounded with the *majlis* of *zikr* and *majlis* of *sallu alan-Nabi* ﷺ.

*Subhana rabbika rabbal 'izzati 'amma yasifoon, wa salaamun 'alal mursaleen, walhamdulillahi rabbil 'aalameen. Bi hurmati Muhammad al-Mustafa wa bi siri Surat al-Fatiha.*

# Chapter Three

## The Guides Are Responsible For Training You On Energy

...وَقَالُوا الْحَمْدُ لِلَّهِ الَّذِي هَدَانَا لِهَذَا وَمَا كُنَّا لِنَهْتَدِيَ لَوْلَا أَنْ هَدَانَا اللَّهُ ۖ لَقَدْ جَاءَتْ رُسُلُ رَبِّنَا بِالْحَقِّ ...(٤٣)

7:43 – "...*Wa qalo Alhamdulillahi al ladhee hadana lihadha wa ma kunna linahtadiya lawla an hadana Allahu, laqad jaa at Rusulu Rabbina bil Haqqi,...*"
*(Surah Al-Araf)*

"... *And they will say, 'Praise be to Allah, who has guided us to this [joy and happiness]; and we would never have been guided if Allah had not guided us. Certainly the messengers of our Lord had come with the truth...*"
*(The Heights, 7:43)*

كَمَا أَرْسَلْنَا فِيكُمْ رَسُولًا مِّنكُمْ يَتْلُو عَلَيْكُمْ آيَاتِنَا وَيُزَكِّيكُمْ وَيُعَلِّمُكُمُ
الْكِتَابَ وَالْحِكْمَةَ وَيُعَلِّمُكُم مَّا لَمْ تَكُونُوا تَعْلَمُونَ (١٥١)

2:151 – "Kama arsalna feekum Rasulam minkum yatlo
'Alaykum ayatina wa yuzakkeekum wa yu'Allimukumul
kitaba walhikmata wa yu'Allimukum ma lam takono
ta'Alamon." (Surat Al-Baqarah)

"Just as We have sent among (within) you a Messenger of your
own, reciting to you Our Signs, and purifying you, and teaching
you the Scripture/Book and Wisdom and teaching you New
Knowledge that which you did not know."
(The Cow, 2:151)

# Internal Energy and External Protection

Keeping the negative energy away is our whole path; our path is based on that. To give a little sort of summary of what we are trying to accomplish is an internal protection and external protection. External and internal protection are related. It means that the strength of the internal protection and the practices begins to create a field of energy that protects us externally. So the internal practices would involve washing, the understanding of how to wash, and the understanding of what to eat and what not to eat.

## Clean Your Food's Energy With a Prayer

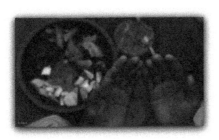

What we are going to bring into the body through our mouth and through our eating and drinking has tremendous amounts of negative energy. There is a power of praying over our food; mentioning the names of pious people over the food. Prophet's ﷺ teaching is that any time you mention pious people, *"tanzil ar-rahmah"*, it brings a *rahmah* and a mercy.

عِنْدَ ذِكْرِ الصَّالِحِينَ تَنْزِلُ الرَّحْمَةُ

*"Inda dhikres Saliheena Tanzilur Rahma."*

73

*"In mentioning the names of the pious people, Allah's Mercy descends."*

*Prophet Muhammad (ﷺ)*

So then pay attention to the power of praying over that food, watching what type of food you eat, the energy from that food, and who is preparing that food. Then how to eat and drink; the *adab* (manners) of the eating and drinking. Preferably eat with the right hand because we use the left hand for cleaning ourselves. All of those mannerisms are then going to determine the quality of energy that is entering within ourselves.

Then our practices; our *zikr* (remembrance), our *wudu* (ablution), our *namaz* (daily prayer), the different prayers – all of those again begin to build the inner energy. Then the most important in that development is when we are trying our best to perfect our self.

## Negative Energy Moves Through the Blood

Prophet Muhammad's ﷺ teaching is that the evilness is moving through our blood.

قَالَ رَسُولُ اللهِ صَلَّى اللهُ عَلَيْهِ وَسَلَّمَ :إِنَّ الشَّيْطَانَ يَجْرِي مِنْ الإِنْسَانِ مَجْرَى الدَّمِ (صحيح مسلم)

*Qala RasulAllah (ﷺ): "Innash Shaytana yajri minal Insaani majrad dami."*

*The Prophet (pbuh) said, "Satan circulates in the human being as blood circulates in the body." (Sahih Muslim, 2174)*

Evilness gains access into the being, to a black spot onto the heart. So it operates in the heart at the level of the *qalb*, enters into the heart, moves throughout the body through the blood. That's why in the purification

74

of meat, we eat meat where the blood has been taken out of the animal, because the dirtiness and the bad energy is within that blood. So that is the concept of the *halal* (permissible), the *zabiha* (slaughter).

All of those are tremendous energy practices. As we begin to open up and understand the energy I have within me, now how am I going to control that negativity? So then what I'm eating and what I'm drinking, I'm praying over it. Then understand the energy internally; the different chantings, the different *zikr*, the different practices; all of that is going to build the energy purification internally. Then that energy begins to provide an energy and a force field outside and begins to push away negativity.

## Like the Earth, Our Core Determines the Quality of Our External Protection

The analogy that Mawlana Shaykh is giving to us is that we are very similar to the earth. The earth is

in a fast motion and the core of the earth has a magnetic core, the iron within the earth. It moves and because of the speed and the movement, it creates a force field around the earth. That force field is protecting the earth from all sorts of penetration. As things are penetrating, and asteroids and all sorts of rays and things that are trying to hit the earth, by the force field inside the earth, it produces an energy that is called the Van Allen belt.

So then the core is going to determine the quality of the external. If the core is not strong then the external has no protection. So if the earth's core stops there is no more shield. The sun will completely burn us, annihilate us. So then in ourselves, the strength of the core practices within ourselves, the part that people don't see, is going to determine the field of energy that we have as a protection. And the strength of that protection will repel and push away negativity.

## Attune Yourself to the Master's Energy Through *Muraqabah* (Spiritual Connection)

So the fastest way towards that perfection is in the *madad* (support) of the master. That is, bringing the presence of the master and the perfection of his light or their light into my life. As he begins to dress me from his perfection, then it's no longer only me trying to build myself to push things back. Because God wants us to know that our life is about a companionship and fellowship – a fellowship of the ring.

يَا أَيُّهَا الَّذِينَ آمَنُوا اتَّقُوا اللّهَ وَكُونُوا مَعَ الصَّادِقِينَ (١١٩)

*9:119 – "Ya ayyuhal ladheena amano ittaqollaha wa kono ma'as sadiqeen."* (*Surat At-Tawba*)

*"O you who have believed, have consciousness of Allah and be with those who are truthful/pious (in words and deed)." (The Repentance, 9:119)*

It means the company we keep is going to be very important. So when we seek out that pious company, then we are trying to attune our self to their energies. The whole concept of the meditation and Sufi *muraqabah* (spiritual connection) is that we are calling upon these masters to dress us from their spiritual presence; visualizing their presence, keeping them always around

us, looking at their picture, remembering them, remembering them, remembering them.

## When Practices Are Strong, Master's Energy Dresses the Core

Then doing all of my practices, my eating and my drinking. This becomes a very deep subject so we are trying to keep it as basic as possible. It is that when my practices are solid, it means now my energy field is good. When my practices are solid, the *madad* (support) of the Shaykh can come.

So it's a connected reality; if my practices are not good, the master's *madad* can't come because I'm doing things wrong, I'm doing things bad. He cannot accompany me spiritually if I'm not keeping myself good, otherwise how can he accompany my badness? He accompanies at a distance but not in the sense of moving within me. So I'm asking that when that badness is going, I'm trying, taking my steps towards purifying myself, doing my chantings. I'm not going to be perfect otherwise that would be a defeated concept, but I'm taking steps towards sincerity. They know what is sincere versus what we say is sincere.

So again, there goes all of the examples of Sufism. Everything we do in this *tariqa* (spiritual path), every action and reaction, is a step towards that sincerity. When they see that sincerity in the action and words and daily life of the student, they begin to come. As they begin to come, and that eating, drinking, practicing, *zikr*, all of that is strong, their energy begins to dress the core.

## The Master's Energy Pushes Away All Negativity and Difficulties

When their energy dresses the core and everything is in their light, their energy begins to push away all negativity. The guides push away so powerfully. The relationship is so strong that they see when a danger is coming before I see it. It means that even in that submission, if we are to go somewhere and there is a danger and the connection is

so strong, they begin to dress before even arriving there. When that person arrives there and that dress is dressing, they begin to open all their energy and everything moves away out of fear of what that energy is bringing, because we are talking in the worlds that we don't see. They see the negative energy, it sees from its light. When it sees that light, it runs, that it's not a light that it even wants to attempt to make a problem with. But me, on myself, ooh he comes and slaps me around with no problem!

## Our Path is Based on Companionship – Physically and Spiritually

So our entire way of protection and building is based on that *madad* (support). So that we bring them into our lives, asking to be purified, to be perfected. *Tariqatuna as Suhba wal khairu fil jamiy'ah* (Our *tariqa* is based on the discourse and companionship, Shah Bahauddin Naqshband). Our *tariqa* is based on companionship.

That companionship is physical, but more important is the spiritual. So then I'm spiritually always in the company of my master. If I'm not in their company, then I will be crushed immediately from the difficulties that I'm facing. So they cannot send you out without that support, otherwise you would be dead in an instant. All the demons from yourself and the demons from other people would be ripping the whole of our lives apart.

So then they bring their support, they bring their *madad*; then they are responsible for you at that time. So everything is based on that *madad*; building our energies, what we eat, what we drink. Do all of our

practices, all of our chantings, all the recitations that they begin to give us. We are reciting, reciting, reciting, reciting, reciting – it's cleaning, cleaning, cleaning, cleaning. As it's cleaning, then we are asking to come, to come, to come, to come, and it's a whole training process. We are asking them to come into our life and spiritually always be with your master.

## True Spiritual Guide Has An Unbroken Connection to His Masters

The ancients would call upon their ancestors. So when you talk to all of these spiritual people, they have the same thing. The Indians, they call upon their ancestors; the Chinese call upon their ancestors. Sufism is the same concept. Our ancestors that were pious, we are calling upon these Shaykhs, these saints, and they are calling upon their ancestor, and they are calling upon their master, all the way back, connected to a prophet.

So the Naqshbandiya, and the power of the Naqshbandi Sufi way, is that it has an unbroken chain of masters. So if I find a master that read a book that says, 'I can be a master for you. Let's go.' The physical is not the problem; the unseen is the problem. When you are going to come and support me, how exactly do you do that? If he is not connected, how is he going to connect to masters? Where is that lineage of living masters connecting all the way? It has to be connected with the unbroken *shajarat*, a tree, that says you are directly linked to Prophet ﷺ.

### True Guide Needs a Signed Permission From Their Master

Our way is based on each one had something signed, all the way back to Prophet Muhammad ﷺ, is signed, that that master signed, that that master signed, that that master signed, all the way to the ones that are in front of you. They have a signed agreement by their masters that they are fully supported. It means that we have your back, we are holding you, you move forward. Don't

worry. Your support comes; it comes to the extent that they deem it's needed. I may go somewhere and say, 'Bring lots of *madad* and make everybody collapse.' So it's not based on us. It's based on them. They already know what's coming and what's happening.

So the concept of *madad* (support) is our whole way. Our way is to be in that annihilation, to be in that light, to be under their discipline.

### Reality of Star –
### Upward Triangle is Hierarchy of Spiritual Government

That's why we have said before many times that our way is based on the triangles, upward and downward. The star has many different realities. But the upward star is the power of the soul that is coming up [gestures from head to left and right side of chest to form a triangle]. The downward star [gestures from right of chest, to left, downwards to belly] is the power of the body.

The upward star, the pyramid that Mawlana Shaykh is always talking about, is this pyramid. This pyramid, it denotes the hierarchy of the spiritual government. That it's not a free for all; it's not like a bazaar, everybody just running towards the Divine. There has to be a pyramid; there has to be a whole corporate structure. There has to be a boss who has to be the one chain, another chain below that, and another chain below that. There is a whole chain of command in which operates and governs God's universe. So then that pyramid, the upward triangle, is what we are trying to connect with.

## Downward Triangle is Like a Shovel –
## Spiritual Path Collects Many People But Only a Few Stay

Then for *dunya* (material world), it looks like a downward triangle. So you are going to see the *dunya* like a shovel. Then Sufism shovels many people; they go around collecting people from many, many places. You go places, there are hundreds of people; and go somewhere with Mawlana Shaykh Hisham, there are thousands of people. It doesn't mean thousands of people are reaching that reality in this world. It means that they shovel them up like that, then they shake them, shake them, and many start to fall out, fall out, fall out, fall out. That's okay because they catch them for intercession in the grave.

But to work through that system, you are going to be shaken; the shake and bake! Shake, shake, shake; shake, shake, shake; they cook you the whole time. They cook you the whole time until from that whole crowd, you are lucky if one comes out. Because the end of the shovel is small; at the top there was a lot, a lot of people come. But at

81

the end, one gold nugget comes out. That gold nugget is now headed for the upward triangle because the space at the top is limited. The downward triangle is unlimited; you can bring everybody in. Shake them and you see that what comes out is

going to be very pure, when they go through that whole testing. That's *tariqa* (Islamic spiritual path).

So a lot of people are coming, but a lot of people are not staying because the testing intensifies, the teaching intensifies. Their life's trials and tribulations intensify and the guides keep asking, hold on, hold on, hold on, hold on. And then we move through the pattern and then the guides are taking us towards perfection. That's the symbol of *tariqa*.

## Other People Don't Understand the Struggle of Seekers

So this has to be understood, because a lot of times people come and say, 'Oh!' They talk amongst each other and they talk to people who have been here before or come and go, and say, 'They are all crazy.' And that's going to be a given because the people outside the cave, they think their life is very normal. That their life is the life to have, and to do those things and to enjoy those things. When they come and see this upward down shaking, they say, 'Those people are all crazy. They are *wahshi*, they are wild, they are not nice. They are like this, they are like that.' Say, 'Most definitely, you are correct. That's true, because we are being cleaned, we are being purified.'

## The Process of Purification is Not Pleasant

The process of purification is not pleasant; it's not something that's always so easy. If you have seen anybody go through cancer and chemotherapy, it's not a pleasant experience. They start to throw up,

82

start to vomit, start to become very sick looking, whereas just weeks before they looked so nice – what happened? So people come and say, 'Why you are living your life like this?' 'Because we are going through chemotherapy and that chemotherapy is much better to go through in this life than in the grave.'

In the grave you can't imagine the difficulties. And the only time that you can say that is from people who have been through difficulties in life. Why did they go through difficulties, if it's not going to be difficult in the grave? So by the Grace of the Divine Presence, is that rather you be cleaned outside of the grave. You take your difficulties now. At least you can stop, have some coffee, watch a little bit of TV, try to regain yourself, and you go back into your testing. Our lives are all about that. It's important to know, so that when somebody else complains, then we have an answer.

## The Real Path Applies Heat to Cook and Purify You

The proof of that craziness is the reality of the path. We have taken a vow to purify ourselves so all of the badness has to come out. If you sit amongst the group and there is no badness, then there is no cooking. There is nobody there that has enough energy to cook the group. So then they stayed the same. It's like a whole bunch of chickens that  nobody turned the oven on; hey, what happened? They all look the same; nothing is happening! Nothing is happening.

These masters, their way is so real. You walk in, it's like a microwave. Everything is popping, smacking; everything is cooking very fast. That is the power to know that we are on a real path, that the Divine has taken notice of us, out of billions of people in creation, billions of universes, billions of galaxies, the Divine is noticing me. And I'm seeing His Miracle in everything I do. As soon as I stop and contemplate, that's the most amazing. *'Ya Rabbi*, how You are noticing me?'

And Divine is saying, 'You are taking a step towards purifying yourself. I'm accepting your step. Move towards Me.' Then you begin all the processes of difficulty.

But with the help of Mawlana Shaykh, and asking for their *madad* (support); we live and breathe in that *madad*. Their *madad* is the only way to defend ourselves against this evilness.

*Subhana rabbika rabbal 'izzati 'amma yasifoon, wa salaamun 'alal mursaleen, walhamdulillahi rabbil 'aalameen. Bi hurmati Muhammad al-Mustafa wa bi siri Surat al-Fatiha.*

# Fighting Desires *(Nafs Ammara)* to Build Internal Energy

We are asking to enter the oceans of Divine *Rahmah* and Mercy. There are many different realities and what we are in search of, and most of all what we are in need of, is protection. Protection from bad desires. Protection from many different difficulties that are constantly moving towards us and attaching themselves towards us, making us to fall, and to make wrong choices, and make bad actions. And eventually trying to cause difficulty upon the eternal soul.

## If You Only Focus on Physicality, There is No Protection

Those whom are inspired by the Divine to be seekers in life, they find themselves in such spiritual associations. They are seeking and their soul is seeking its reality and pushing the physicality and the body, and says, 'Come, let's go find our reality and our secret.'

*Tariqa* (spiritual path) and Sufis come to begin to explain the physiology of the self and the understanding of the self. From Mawlana Shaykh's teachings that if you focus on your external and you build all the external and you focus all on the physicality, there is no protection. There is no light, there is no feeling and there is no taste; all of it becomes only a facade.

We described before that you can cook a turkey very fast, put it on high heat and make the whole outside look brown. But if it's not well

85

done, and you bite into that, it's all raw in the inside. It means that those that focus only on the external, on the form, on the body, they find themselves to have no protection. They have no ability to defend against bad desires, and are always afflicted by confusion. Because again it is like everything else in the material world. If you make a beautiful structure that only on the outside is beautiful and inside is of no substance, is of no power, of no benefit, just the facade of the outside, then anyone who comes can blow that house down. I huff and I puff and I blow that house down.

If *Shaytan* comes to any form and anyone just working on their external form, they do all their practices and that's all and they only do the form, they have no taste and they have no feeling. They are not feeling what they are saying; they are not tasting what they are reading. And many different energies attack them and make them to lose to their desires and fall in the oceans of difficulty.

## Focus on the Core of Your Being – The Heart

Mawlana Shaykh comes into our lives and begins to teach that you focus on the inside. That is the secret of *qudra*, that is the secret of power. That is the secret that the Divine wants for us, that build the inside, strengthen your inside, build your heart. The only chakra that you focus, we call it *lataif*; the only *lataif*, the only subtle energy point

that you focus on is the heart. It is the core of the entire being.

Build the energy within the heart, build the power of the soul; it means then the core becomes powered. When that core becomes powered, the soul is energized. The heart has been cleansed and purified with the chanting and with the practices, with the breathing, with everything that has to do with the spirit and not only the physicality.

## When the Inner Core is Strengthened, It Protects the Physicality

You can't leave the physicality. You put a discipline upon the physicality. But Sufism comes and says that you first focus on the inside. You begin the cooking process. Don't worry about the browning of the turkey right now. Cook yourself inside. Make your *zikr*, your practices; look into your heart. Meditate and contemplate and sit by yourself with yourself in the presence of your Divine Creator. Have a daily accounting, a daily *hisaab*, breathing and meditating.

As that energy begins to build, as that core begins to strengthen, it begins to send the energy that will protect the physicality. If there is nothing happening inside, the outside is like paper, what we call a paper lion; immediately you blow and it falls. One test comes, one difficulty comes, one hardship comes and that falls to pieces.

We have had examples before that if the inside is strong, if they come and try to break the door down, never are they going to enter because the inside is built, the inside has power. It means if a burglar comes from the outside and there is

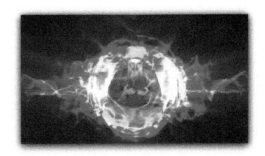

87

nothing on the inside of any value to the Divine Presence, it breaks it, smashes and goes straight through. Because there is nothing inside to protect and the outside was very flimsy. It could be a very subtle glass door, so easy to get through. But if there is a power on the inside and there is a protection on the inside, the protection on the inside will begin to send a shield to the outside and there is no way to penetrate that. That becomes the reality of our self.

## Heart of the Believer is the House of the Divine

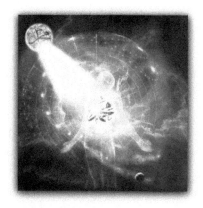

As much as we focus on our heart, focus on our practices, build the reality of the heart, build the reality of the soul, all of the meditations and contemplation and the breathing, all of the accounting, all of the chantings, the *awrad* (daily practices) and the *zikr*, it brings the Divine Gaze within the heart. Allah ﷻ says, 'I'm not in heavens and I'm not on earth but I'm in the heart of my believer' and *Qalb al mu'min baytullah* (Heart of the believer is the house of Allah). So if *baytullah*, if the Divine Light begins to shine within the heart, it means an energy begins to emanate; that energy begins to protect the body.

مَا وَسِعَنِيْ لَا سَمَائِيْ ولا اَرْضِيْ وَلَكِنْ وَسِعَنِيْ قَلْبِ عَبْدِيْ اَلْمُؤْمِنْ

*"Maa wasi`anee laa Samayee, wa la ardee, laakin wasi'anee qalbi 'Abdee al Mu'min."*

*"Neither My Heavens nor My Earth can contain Me, but the heart of my Believing Servant." (Hadith Qudsi conveyed by Prophet Muhammad ﷺ)*

قَلْبَ الْمُؤْمِنْ بَيْتُ الرَّبّ

*"Qalb al mu'min baytur rabb."*

*"The heart of the believer is the House of the Lord."* *(Hadith Qudsi)*

## The Earth is Also Protected By Its Magnetic Core

Many times Mawlana Shaykh said that we are just like the earth. Divine is teaching that, 'I show you My signs upon the horizon and within yourself.'

سَنُرِيهِمْ آيَاتِنَا فِي الْآفَاقِ وَفِي أَنفُسِهِمْ حَتَّىٰ يَتَبَيَّنَ لَهُمْ أَنَّهُ الْحَقُّ ۗ ... (٥٣)

*41:53 – "Sanureehim ayatina fil afaqi wa fee anfusihim hatta yatabayyana lahum annahu alhaqqu, ..." (Surat Fussilat)*

*"We will show them Our signs in the horizons and within themselves until it becomes clear to them that it is the truth..."* *(Explained in Detail, 41:53)*

## The Magnetic Core Shields and Protects the Earth

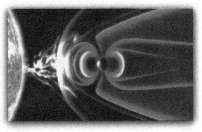

So then people who don't want to look at themselves, go study how the earth is protected. What is creating the shield of protection for the earth, so that everything in the stars and in the heavens doesn't fall upon our heads? A magnetic core. The heat and the core of the earth that moves, and the metal within that core, is a magnetic core, molten lead, molten iron, all within the center of the earth. The energy of that is what's creating an energy belt around the earth, and they describe layers of energy. So as things are trying to come and penetrate that earth, most of them burn before entering the atmosphere.

## Energy Attaches to the Iron in the Blood

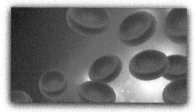

The Divine is teaching saying, 'You are no different.' If the energy within you is not developed, your heart is not developed. The core of your body is water; if it's not purified, the iron within your blood, if it's not polished and stamped with *zikrullah*, that iron becomes the source of your sickness.

They say most infection, staph infection, is from the rotting iron. It attaches itself to the iron and immediately increases the sickness. So the practice of *hijamah* (cupping) and taking away all the iron, they will pull the dirty blood from the body. And many different spiritual practices that when we chant, and when we are doing our spiritual practices, this *nazmah* and this *qudra* (power) of Divine Energy attaches itself to the iron within our body. It doesn't attach to the liquid. It attaches to the iron of the blood and moves and that iron within the blood begins to heat the moisture, begins to heat the water of the body and begins to change the whole being.

## The Blood is Purified Through Breathing and Divine Chanting

It can be a fiery being and as soon as something happens, you become angry and you are flush red. Or it could be a spiritual being where you have practiced and opened the energy within your heart. The energy within your heart is now *baytullah* (house of Allah). That every pump of blood when you are breathing,

the Divine Energy comes to the breath, that breath goes into the lungs and those lungs nourish the blood and the blood moves into the heart. As soon as it enters into the heart, it's going to be stamped. If it's from the house of Allah ﷻ it will be stamped by *Allah Hu*. It's stamped with the *zikr* of Allah ﷻ. Once that energy stamps upon the blood, the heart shoots it to the 11 essential organs of the body.

## Be Grateful to the Divine For Every Breath You Take

That is why they say that every step is based on the breath. Every spiritual order is based on the breath and consciousness of the breath because it is the Divine Blessing that is coming to us. Before you want this, you want that, you want money, you want jobs, you want a wife, you want a husband, you want children, the Divine is saying, 'You want so many things but did you thank Me for the *nafas*, the breath that you have? You have 24,000 gifts in one day and you don't thank Me once for those breaths.' So then we have all our wants and we have no thankfulness to the Divine. And that is the formula for depression and sadness; always sad because you want but you never thank.

لَئِن شَكَرْتُمْ لَأَزِيدَنَّكُمْ

*14:7 – "...La in shakartum la azeedanakum..." (Surah Ibraheem)*

*"...If you are grateful and thank Me, I will give you more (favours)..."*
*(Abraham, 14:7)*

So Divine is teaching that you always have to be thankful. Say, *"Alhamdulillah wa shukran lillah"* (All praise is to Allah, and Thanks be to Allah). *Alhamdulillah wa shukran lillah* because you have life. If God gets sick of you, He ends the breath and you are gone and all your complaints go with you. Divine is teaching that, 'You thank Me on a daily basis.'

*Hamd* (praise) is different than *shukr* (gratitude). *Alhamdulillah* is that everything *"yusabbihu bi hamdi"* (Holy Qur'an, 17:44), that everything is praising the Divine and I too, and with all my being, am praising you my Lord. So *Alhamdulillah, alhamdulillah, alhamdulillah,* for what you have given to me.

91

تُسَبِّحُ لَهُ السَّمَاوَاتُ السَّبْعُ وَالْأَرْضُ وَمَن فِيهِنَّ ۚ وَإِن مِّن شَيْءٍ إِلَّا يُسَبِّحُ
بِحَمْدِهِ وَلَـٰكِن لَّا تَفْقَهُونَ تَسْبِيحَهُمْ ۗ إِنَّهُ كَانَ حَلِيمًا غَفُورًا (٤٤)

*17:44 – "Tusabbihu lahus samawatus sab'u wal ardu wa man fee hinna wa in
min shayin illa yusabbihu bihamdihi wa lakin la tafqahoona tasbeehahum innahu
kana haleeman ghafoora." (Surat Al-Isra)*

*"The seven heavens and the earth and whatever is in them exalt [praises] Him.
And there is not a thing except that it exalts [Allah] by His praise, but you do
not understand their [way of] exalting. Indeed, He is ever Forbearing and
Forgiving." (The Night Journey, 17:44)*

## Be Thankful For Your Breath and Use It Wisely

*Wa shukran lillah* (thanks be to
Allah), because this breath, that my
breath is coming nicely. Go watch
people who suffer from breathing.
We have said many times before
this is Mawlana Shaykh's training.
When you think you have a hard
time because your sustenance is
short, go to the hospital where
children have asthma. They cannot
breathe and they cannot take air in and they gasp for breath. They are
small and they are innocent and they haven't smoked and they haven't
done stupid things to harm themselves. It's just what the cards have
been put out, what destiny was written.

So when we go to those situations and see the difficulty of breath, that
the hardship that they endure and what suffering really is, then we
should say *shukran lillah, shukran lillah, shukran lillah, shukran
lillah,* 1,000 times a day you make it and you still won't be enough.

The Divine is teaching you that is the key. That when we are thanking
and praising and being thankful for everything that we have, then they

begin to teach us this breath that's coming in, thanking the Divine. As this breath is moving through the body, be busy all day long with your chantings, whether asking for forgiveness, *astaghfirullah,* for all the things we have done wrong, known and unknown to us, or praising the Divine Presence, praising the prophetic reality.

It means that heart now becomes busy, it's like a factory in praise, constantly praising, constantly praising, constantly purifying. As the heart is purifying, it's now stamping with Divine Energy and every blood that's flowing through it, it's stamping with that praising.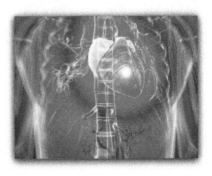
With that stamped blood it now begins to go to each organ and fight on our behalf.

## Negative Energy Attacks Our Organs – Kidneys and Liver

Where before all the organs were under attack. All of them are under satanic attack, under bad energy attack, and every organ begins to collapse. Every difficulty comes to the body. It's not a coincidence that the kidneys and the liver are the ones that collapse most in the world because bad energy is encouraging you, 'I want to take over your

being. I want to come and take over completely your heart; why don't you smoke. Because as soon as you smoke, you put all that horrible energy within your being and we get to move freely through your blood.'

So Prophet ﷺ described *Shaytan* moves through the blood. So *Shaytan* says, 'Why are you taking a long time? Smoke; I can come in very quick! I'll hit your heart, give you heart disease and a heart attack and from your heart I'll move with your blood and into your liver, into your kidneys, and into your lungs.'

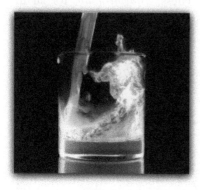

Then I'll inspire you to drink; drink and put spirits within your body. They don't call it heavenly names, they call it spirits. What spirits are coming into your body? These spirits; negative spirits. They want to dilute what you are made of, of pure water. The body is a pure water. We are asking to purify this water filled with chanting, filled with Divine Energy. And negative energy comes and says, 'No, no, dilute that water and make it to be like fire. Fill it with all sorts of spirits and that blood becomes like fire.' And that blood begins to move to all the organs and begin to shut down the entire body.

## Defend Your Kingdom and Focus on Your Inner Being

So we are under attack whether we know it or we don't. The reality of Sufism is to come and teach us how to defend our self until we regain a consciousness and become aware of what the Divine has guided us to. That, 'I thought I was just sitting on this carpet and chanting.' And Divine is saying, 'No, you are under an attack of negativity.' And this negativity is overtaking us, unless we begin to chant and begin to practice and begin to understand, begin to focus on the inside, focus on the heart, focus on the energy. As soon as we empower the heart, it means *nasrullah* (victory of Allah) is coming, that the Divine Energy is now coming within the heart for support.

إِذَا جَاءَ نَصْرُ اللَّهِ وَالْفَتْحُ (١)

*110:1 – 'Idha jaa a Nasrullahi wal Fath.'* (Surat An-Nasr)

*"When there comes the Divine Support of Allah and the Victory."*
*(The Divine Support, 110:1)*

If Divine Energy begins to come into the heart, again all the energy will change on all the organs of the body and now we are able to begin to secure the kingdom. This is a kingdom that the Divine has given to us. He says, 'Before I can open the reality of My Heavenly Kingdoms, you still don't know  your own kingdom and your kingdom is under satanic attack. How are you going to witness the grandeur of My Divinely Kingdom?'

So many people who are *zahiri* and do external practices only, they wonder why nothing is opening for them, why no understanding and reality is opening for them. Mawlana Shaykh is teaching that what Allah ﷻ wants to show you from this heavenly kingdom? When you don't know your own kingdom and you don't know who you are. You don't know what king is upon your throne, what king is sitting upon the heart? Is it a satanic king, the king of bad desires and bad actions and bad will, bad wants? Or is it the Divine King, 'Thy kingdom come, thy will be done on earth as it is in heaven'.

## We Need Guides of Manners and Purification – *Murshid Tarbiyah* and *Murshid Tazkiyah*

It means that the kingdom of the Divine must come into the heart. The light of the Divine must come into the heart and begin to push all want and desire down. Only by the energy of the internal begins to push and protect with energy of external.

That's why Mawlana Shaykh, under Naqshbandiya, under the levels of the *murshid*, (authorized spiritual guide), Mawlana Shaykh Hisham is all of those realities. But the Shaykh of *tarbiyah* (Guide of Manners) and *Shaykh ul Tazkiyah* (Guide of Purification), it's the same. They are going to give us from their *tarbiyah*, they are going to give us from their understanding. It means there has to be amongst you a Shaykh that teaches *tarbiyah*, manners, what's right and what's wrong, and what's the understanding of the self. As you begin to *tarbiyah*, discipline and provide yourself with an etiquette of understanding, the do's and don'ts, the right and wrong, so that you can begin the internal cleansing. There has to be a guide that teaches that *tarbiyah*.

*Tarbiyah* is a mannerism. We have the expression, 'Be *tarbiyah*,' which means a vulgar, rude person. So its opposite is that when there is no *tarbiyah*, how could there be *tazkiyah*? How could you have purification if you have no manners? So it is impossible. So then the guides of *tarbiyah*, they come and they teach right and wrong; *adab*, don't do, do; don't do, do, perfecting the manners. So that when you see them, they are the best of manners; loving and humbling and always seeking God's Support and seeking God's Mercy and Forgiveness.

## *Tarbiyah* (Mannerism) is a Requirement for *Tazkiyah* (Purification)

As soon as the *tarbiyah* comes, then the Shaykh begins to inspire from the reality of *tazkiyah* that now the *zikr* and the practices will hold onto you because your manners are at least working towards goodness. Then when they begin to give you *zikrs* and begin to give you from their *nazar* and their gaze, that that *zikr* is now housed within a beautiful vessel to hold it in. If you have no *tarbiyah* and you are asking for a *zikr*, it's like pouring liquid gold into a Styrofoam cup. As soon as that energy hits, it melts everything. The vehicle in which you are asking to place that is not yet purified and pure.

## When We Have Inner Purification, We Can Fight the Negativity

So they begin to teach us, then the same Shaykh of the reality of *tazkiyah* says that you follow all the *tarbiyah*, you follow all the right and wrong. When they have jumped you through all the hoops and the character is correct, and the manners are correct, then the *zikr* that they give to you will hold onto the soul. It brings a light and brings a tremendous energy. That energy on the inside begins to provide an energy on the outside that again stops *hawa* (desires), stops the desire of *dunya* (material world), stops the desire of the *nafs* (ego), and begins to fight against *Shaytan*. Without the inside, the outside is definitely under attack.

We pray that Mawlana Shaykh opens more and more understanding for us on how to build that inside energy, how to follow their *tarbiyah*, how to follow their *tazkiyah* and that the heart begins to open and that energy begin to shine within our hearts.

*Subhana rabbika rabbal 'izzati 'amma yasifoon, wa salaamun 'alal mursaleen, walhamdulillahi rabbil 'aalameen. Bi hurmati Muhammad al-Mustafa wa bi siri Surat al-Fatiha.*

# The Secret is in the Food – Come Hungry to Spiritual Associations

Allah ﷻ is our Creator and we are weak servants in need of Divine Mercy and Divine Grace. We are asking for Mawlana Shaykh's teaching on understanding of our self and an opening within our ears that directly connects to the opening of the heart. It means we say something but we don't really understand. It is to hear and to follow *"sami'na wa ata'na"* (Holy Qur'an, 2:285).

سَمِعْنَا وَأَطَعْنَا غُفْرَانَكَ رَبَّنَا وَإِلَيْكَ الْمَصِيْرُ (٢٨٥)

*2:285 – "…Sam'ina wa ata'na, ghufranaka Rabbana wa ilaykal masir."*
*(Surah Al-Baqarah)*

*"…We hear, and we obey: (We seek) Thy forgiveness, our Lord, and to Thee is the end of all journeys." (The Cow, 2:285)*

You can participate and attend and keep the company but we don't really hear and we don't really listen. Many years may go by and we look to ourselves and say, 'What did I gain? I gained nothing, and oh, maybe that group had no benefit for me.' There's no magic, because we are not magicians. It's a way of reality that teaches a reality to a people who are interested and hungry in reaching that reality.

## The Secret is in the Food

If we teach that the food has all the secrets and all the blessings, then the guides teach us it's best to come hungry. If you come hungry, oh you look at that table and you start to salivate. Your hunger, it's an analogy. They teach us if you keep yourself hungry, by the time you show up, 7 or 8 o'clock. We are eating around 9 o'clock. You try not to eat in the afternoon, famished, hungry, come meditate on an empty stomach and contemplate. Then when it's time to eat, you train your ego to enjoy. They teach us that in all spiritual associations, the secret is in the food because of the blessing of breaking bread with each other.

## Many Egos Reject the Blessings and Knowledge

At the angelic reality, our egos are taking different knowledges and many of the egos are rejecting. 'We hear you sir, but we are not listening.' There were many teachings from Prophet ﷺ that they were coming into his company and saying, 'We hear what you're saying but we don't listen and our hearts are locked.'

وَقَالُوا قُلُوبُنَا غُلْفٌ ۚ ...(٨٨)

*2:88 – "Wa qaloo qulobuna ghulfun..."*
*(Surat Al-Baqarah)*

*"And they said, "Our hearts are Locked..."*
*(The Cow, 2:88)*

'We enjoy it, but we are not listening to you and not opening my heart.' And because of that reality, like children, the Divine is teaching prophets and teaching the *awliya*, teaching the saints, that get to them and dress that reality. But it's going to be dressed through where our egos don't get involved. It is in the food and drink.

The ego is at the level of the mind and the mind rejects that these are different, these are foreign, these are things I'm not used to, I practice something else. So many of the realities we put a lock onto the heart and these realities don't absorb. So as a mercy for us, they begin to teach us they're going to dress us through a different way. They are going to dress us through our belly.

### *Awliya* Pray and Bring Out the Quantum Reality of the Food

The guides are going to make their prayers and ask from what

Sayyidina Isa, Jesus عليه السلام , was manifesting. He asked, 'Oh my Lord, send a table from heaven to feed the first of us and the last of us.' And a table from heaven is not a table from the material world. You can't say, 'Well I bought these doughnuts at Costco.' No no, we are talking about a spiritual realm. You bring them from Costco but they make a prayer that brings out the quantum reality of the food.

Everything is in structure and everything is a form. Every form breaks down to a light and every light is an energy. If you have the secret of that energy, which are *malaika*, which are angels. It means if your prayer and your recitations and your *du'a* and your connections are accepted, you unlock everything. So with their blessings, they unlock

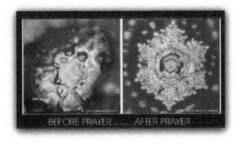

everything we eat and drink at its angelic reality where the angels say,

'Amen.' That, 'what you're asking for, we are without ego accepting,' because Divine Order is coming to that association, Prophetic order is coming, "*Ateeullah, atee ar Rasul wa Ulul amrin minkum*" (Obey Allah, Obey Prophet ﷺ, and those on Authority) that Allah ﷻ is telling them, 'They are coming from My Obedience.'

$$\text{أَطِيعُوا اللهَ وَأَطِيعُوا الرَّسُولَ وَأُوْلِي الْأَمْرِ مِنْكُمْ... (٥٩)}$$

*4:59 – "...Atiu Allaha wa atiur Rasola wa Ulil amre minkum..."*
*(Surat An-Nisa)*

*"... Obey Allah, Obey the Messenger, and those in authority among you."*
*(The Women, 4:59)*

They are people who are looking to be obedient to the Creator. They are coming to be obedient to the prophets and they are obedient to *Ulul amr;* open for them their realities.

So then those realities are in the food and drink. Those angelic realities at the quantum level begin to dress us. Where the ego was not allowing that dressing begins to come, begins to dress us, begins to change us. It's like going to a doctor's office and taking medicine. That medicine is in the food and drink.

## Come Hungry and Eat From the Heavenly Table

They teach us to come hungry. Physically make yourself hungry on that day. Come with the understanding that this is not a regular association. I'm asking and I'm making the most of it as a spiritual association. It means everyone has to have their level of faith, that, 'My Lord, I'm in need of a cleansing. I'm in need of your support. I'm in need of that table from heaven.'

When they were asking for that miracle from Sayyidina Isa, Jesus ﷺ, the ones who were asking, they had a lot of power. They were asking and asking and then Divine was communicating back with Sayyidina Isa ﷺ, 'If they ask and they don't eat, they are in big trouble,' because

that's a miraculous reality coming. Then human nature was, they are powerful, they are arrogant. They had a system, they had a level, they thought that they knew a lot. When that table immediately began to descend, they ran away. So who ate at the table? The poor.

## *Awliya* (Saints) Feed 3 Categories From Their Sustenance

These are the categories that Allah ﷻ says, 'These *Awliyaullah*, they feed you from their sustenance,' that you have to be *meskeen*, you have to be poor, you have to be *yateem* (orphan), and you have to be *asir* (captive).

وَيُطْعِمُونَ الطَّعَامَ عَلَى حُبِّهِ مِسْكِينًا وَيَتِيمًا وَأَسِيرًا (٨)

*76:8 – "Wa yu ta'imonat Ta'ama 'ala hubbihi miskeenan wa yateeman wa aseera." (Surat Al-Insaan)*

*"And they feed, for His love, the needy/indigent, the orphan, and the captive."* (The Human, 76:8)

These 3 categories *Awliyaullah* feed from their sustenance and they love their sustenance. They are not feeding you from what they don't like. You go to some people's house, they look at their refrigerator, the

garbage they have and say, 'You can have this.' Or they want to make a donation, they bring everything broken, used clothes with holes, used socks and say, 'Here, have some socks.' No, no, no.

When we talk about these saints, they give you from the

best of what they have. They give you from all their secrets and all the realities that they struggled all their life to achieve. Allah ﷻ is saying, 'They give you from the best of what they have.' They give it because of love of Allah ﷻ, love of the Creator. And they don't ask anything back from you. They're not expecting that when you eat you're going to write a big cheque and leave. They don't care. You make a cheque, you don't make a cheque, it was to the benefit of your own soul.

You always have to remember you don't affect *Awliyaullah*. You don't affect the association; we don't affect each other. You give for your soul. You give for your salvation. You bring and you eat for your salvation, for testimony of your faith.

## *Awliya* Don't Seek Paradise, They Want the Holy Face – *WajhaAllah*

Divine begins to teach us that they do it only to see the face of God.

$$ إِنَّمَا نُطْعِمُكُمْ لِوَجْهِ اللَّـهِ لَا نُرِيدُ مِنكُمْ جَزَاءً وَلَا شُكُورًا (٩) $$

*76:9 – "Innama nut'imukum liWajhillahi la nureedu minkum jazaa an wa la shukora." (Surat Al- Insaan)*

*"(Saying),We feed you for the sake of the Holy/Divine Face alone: We wish not from you reward or gratitude." (The Human, 76:9)*

It means the Divine begins to categorize these saints. They are not interested in paradise. If I throw them into paradise it's like Las Vegas for them; all these big things and shows. What do they care about them? They're not interested in these ups and downs and entertainment, and things moving and fruits coming. And

they are not fearful of hellfire. If Allah ﷻ wants them to be in suffering, they will be in suffering and they speak no different.

All they are asking for is that holy face. It means that Ocean of Power, that all power emanating from that. '*Ya Rabbi*, oh my Lord, I'm asking that, just put me in that Ocean of Power and emanate from Your Magnificence and Munificence upon us.'

## Do You Listen and Implement What You Hear?

It means that Mawlana begins to teach us in our associations that we have ears but do we actually hear? And when we hear, do we listen? You can hear but you don't listen to anything. When we listen, it means we take a reality and we start to move on it. We start to implement that reality in our lives. We take an action. Everybody can hear many things but how do you hear something and act upon it? It means how do you put it as a part of your life?

Say, 'I'm going to come and purify myself, I'm going to eat from these associations whatever they are.' These are tables from heaven. I'm going to drink from those associations. I'm going to take their teachings and I'm going to implement those teachings fiercely in my life. Otherwise why the Divine opened a seat at that school for me?

*Subhana rabbika rabbal 'izzati 'amma yasifoon, wa salaamun 'alal mursaleen, walhamdulillahi rabbil 'aalameen. Bi hurmati Muhammad al-Mustafa wa bi siri Surat al-Fatiha.*

105

# Reality of Water – Spiritual Understanding of *Wudu* (Ablution)

*A*lhamdulillah, we are asking to be nothing and to enter into the oceans of Allah's ✲ *Rahmah* and Mercy. *Alhamdulillah*, *Awliyaullah* (saints) come into our lives and expand everything. They expand the horizon, expand the understanding, expand the realities from Holy Qur'an, from holy *hadith* (traditions), from every aspect of our life, it begins an expansion in realities. That far beyond the world of form, to understand the world of light, to understand the world of energy, to understand the world of sound.

Every aspect of reality is far greater than just the physical. And they teach, that teaching towards that reality to be uplifting. If what we are learning is only the physical, it has a limited benefit for the physical body. But there must be a food; there must be reality that is affecting the soul. And that which you teach in regards to the soul is going to be an eternal dress on the body.

## *Wudu* (Ablution) According to Different Levels of Knowledge

The guides come into our lives and they teach us that from the *ilm al-Shari'ah* (knowledge of Jurisprudence), *ilm al-Tariqah* (knowledge of Spiritual Path), the *ilm al-Ma'rifah* (knowledge of Gnosticism), *ilm al-Haqiqah* (knowledge of Realities), *ilm al-Azemah* (knowledge of Determination). In every knowledge there must be *darajats* (levels) of the knowledge, whereas most people stay only on the outside at the *Shari'ah* and Jurisprudence level.

## Understanding of *Wudu* (Ablution) in Basic *Shari'ah*

Many times, from Mawlana Shaykh's teaching, we gave examples about *wudu* (ablution). Many teach the *shari'ah* aspect of *wudu*, that you have to wash. How much of the water to use so that it's clean. Then how to wash yourself so that your hands, your arms, your face, your ears, your feet, your nose, your mouth, everything is covered and washed. And this is from, and only an introduction of, *ilm al-Shari'ah* (knowledge of Jurisprudence).

## Understanding the Reality of Water

*Ilm al-tariqah, ilm al-ma'rifah, haqiqah, wal azemah*, begin to teach why you have to wash. You don't have the right to ask why, but as soon as you are patient in life and take a path towards realities, Allah ﷻ will begin to expand the heart and the teachers begin to teach.

They teach that water has a reality within it. And that water has an angelic force within it because Allah ﷻ described that, 'My Throne is upon that water'.

وَهُوَ الَّذِي خَلَقَ السَّمَاوَاتِ وَالْأَرْضَ فِي سِتَّةِ أَيَّامٍ وَكَانَ عَرْشُهُ عَلَى الْمَاءِ لِيَبْلُوَكُمْ أَيُّكُمْ أَحْسَنُ عَمَلًا ... ﴿٧﴾

*11:7 – "Wa huwal ladhee khalaqas samawati wal arda fee sittati ayyamin, wa kana 'arshuHu 'alal maa ye, liyabluwakum ayyukum ahsanu 'amalan, ..."*
*(Surat Hud)*

*"And it is He who created the heavens and the earth in six days - and His Throne had been upon water - that He might test you as to which of you is best in deed..."*
*(Prophet Hud, 11:7)*

'My Throne is upon that water' means they begin to teach that there is a *ma'rifah* of that *mai* مَاء (water), *meem* م *alif* ١. Everywhere you look must be *La ilaha illallah Muhammadun RasulAllah* ﷺ. Even in *mai* مَاء, *meem* م *alif* ١. And Allah ﷻ describes, 'My Throne is upon that water'. It means, Oh! There must be a secret, a *ma'rifah*, of that water.

## Water Has An Angelic Power

One basic understanding is its angelic power and because it's angelic, it's stable. If it was gas, it would be very difficult to work with in life. But because of *malaika*, it has a stable force and power. If you take 1 hydrogen away, it becomes explosive (HO – Hydrogen Monoxide). That's the degree of its power. All our oceans are that potential danger. So when you want to know how Allah ﷻ can bring an end to this *dunya* (earth), He merely  commands 1 of the hydrogen, 'Rise', and all the water itself is explosive. What is making it stable is the 2H in $H_2O$. If 1H (Hydrogen) leaves, it's explosive.

Then *awliya* (saints) come and teach us that water is very powerful. As soon as you leave the water for a certain amount of days, you see a green begin to form. That is the *malaika*. That is the angelic force that shows you that *mai* (water) brings life because the green in the mildew. It's a life force within that.

## Spiritual Understanding of *Wudu* (Ablution)

So then they begin to teach now the understanding of *wudu* begins to elevate because you're taught the element in which you're washing. You are washing with a very powerful force, an angelic force. And all the difficulty that you acquire throughout the day, your body is like a bus. We have a body and we have a soul. As soon as we move in the world, every subtle energy can move through you, from microwave, television wave, to all the different spiritual beings that Allah ﷻ has created. They all move through the physicality; they all either occupy the physicality or pass through the physicality.

So what Prophet ﷺ wanted for us was the perfection of energy, but he didn't have to describe it. He merely told the Companions; they understood the reality and they taught the *shari'ah* aspect of it, that you wash. And for deeper knowledge, they went into the *ma'rifah* of that; that when we're washing, there is an angelic force in that water, a life force within that water. As soon as we put it on, it begins to burn away all difficulty. It begins to wash away all fire and begins to dress you with an angelic light, a shield.

### *Salat al-Wudu* Shields Your Energy

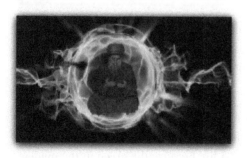

Then they come into our lives and teach that as soon as you wash, washing your mouth, your face, your hands, your feet, washing all the private parts if you had used the restroom; as soon as you wash, come out and pray *Salat al-Wudu* to seal yourself with your energies because as soon as you pray two *rakah Salat al-Wudu*, that water and angelic force becomes a shield that protects you until the next *wudu*.

Then they begin, because now you are going deeper into the *ma'rifah* of *wudu*, not that you just have to wash and that's it; there is a whole ocean of reality. Why are you washing with that; what power does that water have? Then the guides begin to teach as you are washing the body, you should be understanding the washing of the internal reality, and the importance of water and that your body is 70% water. So then the water within my being, how am I purifying that water?

## Purify the Blood and the Water Within

Then they go into the blood, that the body has 70% water. If we want healing and we want to build our energy, we have to understand why we are washing, dressing by these lights and these realities. As we are washing the outside, we have to be washing the inside. The water inside is the blood.

So how do you wash the blood? Prophet ﷺ describes *Shaytan*

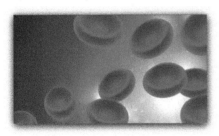 moves through the blood. That's why the fasting; that's why the importance of eating *halal* (permissible), drinking and breathing *halal*. It affects your breath, from your lungs, and is going to affect your blood. What you eat will go into your stomach and affect the blood. What you breathe will affect the blood. So then why are they only focusing on the outside washing and they don't teach the inside washing? The outside is the donkey that's going to be buried in the ground. Nobody is taking their body to Allah ﷻ. You're just making the body to be clean in *dunya* so that you can bring out the reality of your soul.

But *ahl ul-haqqa'iq* (people of realities) they come into our lives and begin to teach how to elevate beyond the kindergarten understanding. When you're washing, understand the reality of that washing, but begin your internal washing. Begin to understand that your blood has

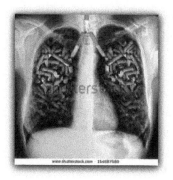

to be cleansed. When you begin to make *du'a* on your food and eating *halal*, your blood is now being washed. When you begin to be conscious of your breath and your breathing, don't put anything into your mouth that's going to contaminate your blood. Just as you are washing the body, you wouldn't take a feces and put it on your head.

## Shaytan is Attacking Your Heart Through the Blood

So imagine that whatever you put in your mouth and put in as a drink or food is going to affect the blood; then that blood is going to go and hit the heart, what they call a heart attack. It's attacking the heart and *'qalb al-mu'min baytullah'*.

قَلْبَ الْمُؤْمِنْ بَيْتُ الرَّبْ

*"Qalb al mu'min baytur rabb."*

*"The heart of the believer is the House of the Lord."* (Hadith Qudsi)

So it is *Shaytan* that is attacking the house of Allah ﷻ. *Shaytan* knows the system and knows that Allah ﷻ is not going to be occupying the mind; Allah ﷻ is going to occupy the heart. And he says, 'These Bani Adam, if he becomes powerful, he will be like 1,000 men. It's enough for me to begin to attack him. I'll influence what he eats, I'll influence what he drinks, I'll influence what he breathes and I will bring him down by contaminating and poisoning his blood.' And then he moves within that blood.

It means they begin to teach in our lives that it's far greater than just washing and somebody describing how to put their fingers and their hands. That's only washing of the outside. The reality of that water, the reality of the water within, the reality of purifying all the organs.

112

That when that blood is moving through the body, how the *zikr* (remembrance) and the breath is going to purify that blood.

## Importance of Breath and *Zikrullah* as it Purifies the Blood

Then you look at the physiology of breathing. Why is *zikr* so powerful? When they say the *nafas ar-rahmah* (breath of mercy). Why is it *nafas ar-rahmah*? Because everything is based on that breath. All *mashayikh* came and said that you have 24,000 secrets

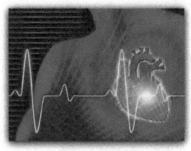

in one day; 24,000 pockets of life in one day. The quality of your life is from breath to breath. If Allah ﷻ doesn't grant a breath, the person dies. So each one is a secret of life.

So they make that breath in *zikrullah*, in remembrance, in a consciousness of Allah ﷻ. That, 'Ya Rabbi, before I try to ask for everything else in this *dunya* that I want, I have to be grateful for this breath that You gave me, this reality that You gave me. Then you begin to see the breath that we are breathing is going to the lungs, the lungs are producing the blood, the blood is shooting into the heart; and that is the house of Allah ﷻ. So if you want the house of Allah ﷻ within the heart, you have to sanctify and purify the breath.

What you eat through the mouth is going to affect the stomach and the belly; and that again is going to affect the blood that enters into the heart. So then there is a *wudu* inside the being, inside the body that is going to affect the heart. And that is the *wudu* of the inner reality. Now that begins to affect the soul.

## Within the Secret of Water is the *Zikr* of *Hu*

From the *azemat* they begin to teach that that breath and that air that you are breathing, it contains the elements of *mai* (water). Everything around us has from the secret of water; and within the secret of water is the *zikr* of *Hu*. And through the *zikr* of *Hu*, they are able to pull out the force of energy within everything. Every molecule that exists with its *hamd* (praise), "*yusabbiHu bi hamdi.*"

$$\text{تُسَبِّحُ لَهُ السَّمَاوَاتُ السَّبْعُ وَالْأَرْضُ وَمَن}$$
$$\text{فِيهِنَّ ۚ وَإِن مِّن شَيْءٍ إِلَّا يُسَبِّحُ بِحَمْدِهِ}$$
$$\text{وَلَٰكِن لَّا تَفْقَهُونَ تَسْبِيحَهُمْ ۗ إِنَّهُ كَانَ حَلِيمًا}$$
$$\text{غَفُورًا (٤٤)}$$

*17:44 – "Tusabbihu lahus samawatus sab'u wal ardu wa man fee hinna wa in min shayin illa yusabbihu bihamdihi wa lakin la tafqahoona tasbeehahum innahu kana haleeman ghafoora." (Surat Al-Isra)*

*"The seven heavens and the earth and whatever is in them exalt [praises] Him. And there is not a thing except that it exalts [Him] by His praise, but you do not understand their [way of] exalting. Indeed, He is Forbearing and Forgiving."*
*(The Night Journey, 17:44)*

With the *hamd* that Allah ﷻ gave that being, like you, whether it's yourself, your physicality, or your atom and molecules; the inner power within it, who's the "*bi hamdi*"? It's the *Hu*. It's the *zikr* of the *Hu* within that element which is its power. So then the guides begin to teach that the *wudu* of the soul is the *zikr* 'Hu'. And all *mashayikh* (guides), their *zikr* is '*AllahHu, AllahHu*'; to bring the purity of the soul.

## The Angelic Fire of Water Burns the Badness Within

As you are beginning to breathe, that you wash the outside, you understood the power of water, the importance of how this water is an angelic fire that burns all badness, *"Qul ja al-haqq wa zahaq al-batil."*

وَ قُلْ جَآءَالْحَقُّ وَزَهَقَ الْبَطِلُ، إِنَّ الْبَطِلَ كَانَ زَهُوقًا (٨١)

*17:81 – "Wa qul jaa alhaqqu zahaqal baatil, innal batila kana zahooqa."* *(Surat Al-Isra)*

*"And say, "Truth has come, and falsehood has perished. Indeed falsehood, [by its nature], is ever perishing/ bound to perish." (The Night Journey, 17:81)*

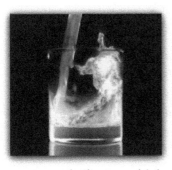

The *haqq* (truth) comes, the *Shaytans* move, but they go inside. You didn't scare them; they went inside to hide.

Then Prophet ﷺ came and taught all of the realities of the eating. That make the *wudu* inside because now they are hiding inside. So then your consciousness of your breath of what you eat and what you drink and what you put into your mouth, now the *wudu* is inside. You are fiercely fighting all the energies inside, where they can't find any safety. They are burning inside and they're burning outside with your *wudu* and they begin to leave.

Then they begin to teach that as you begin to breathe and make your *zikr*, that is now the force of energy upon the soul. And, *bi zikr Hu*, you can pull from that energy all around us. That *zikr 'Hu'* is from *Ikhlas* and Sincerity. It's the only *surah* (verse) that Allah ﷻ said, *"Qul"*, say, *"Hu"*. Forget the rest. *"Qul Hu..."*

قُل هُوَ اللَّـهُ أَحَدٌ ۚ (١)

*112:1 – "Qul huwal laahu ahad." (Surat Al-Ikhlas)*

*"Say, Hu (He) Allah is One." (The Sincerity, 112:1)*

*"Qul Hu"* قُلْ هُوَ, Allah's *Qaf* ق , *"Qaf, wal-Qur'an al-majid"* (Holy Qur'an 50:1) to the *lam* ل, *lisan al-haqq* (tongue of truth), that Allah's ﷻ *Azemat* and Order قل is upon that *Hu* هو.

ق ۚ وَالْقُرْآنِ الْمَجِيدِ (١)

*50:1 – "Qaf, wal Quranil Majeed." (Surat Qaf)*

*"Qaf. By the honoured Qur'an." (Qaf, 50:1)*

By imitating that *Hu*, you would be dressed from that reality, blessed from that reality and granted a dress of *Ikhlas* and Sincerity. It means that is the reality of *wudu*, not just how to wash your hands. And they make many different YouTube videos on how to wash your fingers, your hands and your toes. But what's the reality of the water? What's the reality within us? What's the reality of the blood within us, which is our water? How to combat the inside, the outside; and then the breath and how to take all the energy that's around us and bring it into the breath and purify and sanctify the soul.

*Subhana rabbika rabbal 'izzati 'amma yasifoon, wa salaamun 'alal mursaleen, walhamdulillahi rabbil 'aalameen. Bi hurmati Muhammad al-Mustafa wa bi siri Surat al-Fatiha.*

# Secrets of Water and *Wudu* – Levels of Knowledge

## Levels of Knowledge in Classical Islam

1. *Ilm al-Shari'ah* – Knowledge of Jurisprudence
2. *Ilm al-Tariqah* – Knowledge of Spiritual Path
3. *Ilm al-Ma'rifah* – Knowledge of Gnosticism
4. *Ilm al-Haqiqah* – Knowledge of Reality
5. *Ilm al-'Azemah* – Knowledge of Determination

## Reality of Circle and Levels of Knowledge

From Mawlana Shaykh's knowledges and realities they open for us very deep understandings. They teach us the difference between normal understanding, or what is in the books, or what is applied, in a normal environment; and they go into the realities of understandings. In every knowledge there must be *darajats* (levels) of the knowledge. For us, they are the levels of *ilm al-shari'ah*, the knowledge of *shari'ah* (Islamic Jurisprudence), the knowledge of *ilm ul-tariqa* (Spiritual Path), the way, the knowledge of *ma'rifah*, which is the knowledge of Gnosticism.

## *Shari'ah* (Jurisprudence) is the Circumference

The *ma'rifah* means that; when you are on the circumference, it is the *shari'ah*. It is the divine law of nature, that everything is based on that nature. That *shari'ah*, that divine law of nature, what the Divine has intended for creation, then it has a *tariq* (way). It has a radius to the

117

center, because everything is based on the reality of the circle. The circumference can expand infinite points on the circumference and can collapse to just one point which would be the *nuqt* (dot). And all the *ilm al-huroof*, everything will collapse into the *nuqt*. From that *nuqt* is the power that comes under and supports the *ba*; and from *alif ba*, all the *huroof* are born from those understandings.

Then they teach us, Mawlana Shaykh's teaching that, that *nuqt*, that dot, if you move towards that dot, it infinitely expands. And that's from a reality that Allah ﷻ can never be completely known. It means it's towards the understanding of realities and can never be fully encompassed. So as much as you move towards it, that reality, it expands; as much as you are away from it, it seems as one thing, maybe small. The way of reality is that we move into these oceans and they keep expanding. On the horizon, there is a new horizon; and at every horizon there must be

a new horizon, where Allah ﷻ describes, 'I am the Lord of the east and the west,' the Lord of two Easts and two Wests.

رَبُّ الْمَشْرِقَيْنِ وَرَبُّ الْمَغْرِبَيْنِ (١٧)

*55:17 – "Rabbul Mashriqayn wa Rabbul Maghribayn." (Surat Ar-Rahman)*

*"[He is] Lord of the two sunrises and Lord of the two sunsets."*
*(The Beneficent, 55:17)*

It means as much you are approaching, then Allah ﷻ again is expanding in these understandings.

## *Tariqa* (Spiritual Path) Teaches the Wisdom of the *Shàri'ah* Laws

How to understand and differentiate an *imam* or somebody teaching in a centre or somewhere, from a Spiritual Guide is that the guides come to teach us in our lifetime, deep realities of 'why'. You can't say why, because you can't ask Prophet ﷺ, 'Why', you can't ask the Divine 'Why', but the *hikmah*, the wisdom, on why we do what we do. Whereas if you go to a regular *imam* or go to a teacher somewhere and ask, 'Why I have to do that?' He will most likely yell at you and say, 'This is the rule; get out! You have to do it.'

## 1. Knowledge of *Shari'ah* Teaches to Make *Wudu* (Ablution) for Cleanliness

So many come and say, 'Why I have to make *wudu*? Why I have to make *wudu*?' At the *shari'ah* level, which means from Mawlana Shaykh's teaching, you make *wudu* because you have to clean yourself. You have to clean yourself, wash yourself, prepare yourself for a ritual purity to present yourself to Divinely Presence. Everything has to be clean and God is based on cleanliness; Allah ﷻ, the nearness to Divine is the nearness to cleanliness.

## 2. Knowledge of *Tariqa* (Spiritual Path) Teaches that Water Washes Away Negative Energy/Burden

The *tariqa* (spiritual path) comes and says, 'Oh, there is a much deeper reality than just you left it at washing'. This is Mawlana Shaykh's *barakah* (blessings) and the teachings of *Awliyaullah* (saints) of why their oceans are deep. And most people, when they hear these teachings, they realize that they have only been playing on the shore because every time they ask, they say, 'Why do I have to make *wudu*?

119

Why do I have to use water?' 'Because, you have to.' And then you find your knowledge and your level of understanding is very superficial.

*Tariqa* comes and teaches no, at the level of *tariq*, on the path, that *wudu* is based on water. We talked about *tayammum* (act of dry ablution); it is something different; that has its own reality. But in the reality of water, they begin to teach, no, that's just the basic knowledge of *tariq*, on the path, that that water takes away your burdens. That that water, it takes away fires of difficulty. That when we move within this earth and

everywhere we go and everyone we see, we are energy beings; and by our nature we are going to collect energy and give off energy. If your practices and your heart is positive, it means they are taking a path of improving the self, and you are radiating a positive energy.

So then they come and say, just the level of *tariq*, the way, the path, the most basic understanding is when you put out a positive charge, you are going to collect everyone's negative charge. You are just going to collect and collect and collect.

So then Prophet ﷺ is the master of energy, he is the owner of *Bahr al-Qudra* (Ocean of Power). Allah ﷻ created all creation for that reality. So instead of explaining the whole scientific detail that wouldn't make sense, he said, 'Just wash; use water'.

Then *Awliyaullah* (saints) come into our lives and say, 'No, no, the water has a reality'. They will go deeper into it and begin to say that, 'That water, it has a power and that power will wash off negative energy'. And everywhere you go, you're going to be loaded with negative energies. And if you use the water, it begins to burn away that negative charge.

## Protect and Fortify the Kingdom of Your Body for the Divine

As soon as you pray after washing, and washing all of the areas of the body, you seal the body with a seal of protection. They even tell you on the *tariq* that you are like a kingdom and God is asking to enter upon the throne. So then you must fortify the kingdom, seal the door, because anybody who has a home, you have got to be crazy if you leave your doors and windows open. Then you will be expecting a very nice looking person at the foot of your bed; somebody is going to break in! It's just common sense. You leave all your house open, there's going to be an intruder, especially if they know you have something, something worth taking.

## Don't Become Battery Source for Negative Energy and Evilness

So *wuquf al-qalb*, means the first level of understanding in *tariqa* is

vigilance of the heart. That you have a divine kingdom, divine palace, asking for divine lights to enter, then most definitely evilness, negativity, has their eye on us. If they have their eye on us, it means that all negative energy is going to be moving towards us. They are going to load us with a tremendous charge of negativity. It becomes like

these different movies that show these examples, like 'The Matrix'.

You are existing just for them to feed off of your positive energy. Because negative beings and negative energy, they don't have access to positive energy. It's not their creation. So then you become a battery source for them; they just cling onto you. They put all their devices onto you; you are the greater battery.

So we can never think that your mobile phone is actually using the charge from its battery; it's actually using the charge from your heart. It's draining you as well as that device. And as we plug in more in this world, plug into our ears, plug into our hands, plug in all over our being, everything is pulling our energy. Then as soon as we walk out, every negative energy comes to us.

## Negative Energy Enters Through Dirtiness

Then Prophetic reality makes it simplified; tell them to wash. As soon as you wash, that energy is washed away. As soon as you wash your private parts, you are sealing yourself. Because if you have a palace, they show in 'Lord of the Rings', when you have a palace, they are looking for a way to come in. And every criminal movie shows that when they want to rob a bank, they don't go through the front door, unless it's a very exciting movie; they usually go from the sewer! So Divine is showing they go through where it's dirty because they don't expect anybody to be there, and from the sewer they come up.

So then Prophet ﷺ was teaching wash your privates with water because these beings know where it's dirty and they know where they have quick access. When *Shaytan* saw the form of Sayyidina Adam عليه السلام, before the soul had entered, he came and he entered through the rear end and came out and went out. He said, 'Such a simple creation, I can easily attack this. It's not fortified.' He didn't understand the realities that Allah ﷻ was going to open for this creation. But this is just the *tariqa* level of understanding.

*Shari'ah* is, just you wash. *Tariqa* comes and says, 'Oh, but there's a tremendous secret in the water. That water is going to burn away negative energies; it's going to seal you for the kingdom.'

## 3. Knowledge of *Ma'rifah* (Gnosticism) Teaches That Water Has an Angelic Force

Now at the level of *Ma'rifah* (Gnosticism), it means you are now on a path of trying to go deep into knowledge. At the level of *ma'arif*, means every step on the *tariq*, on the path, is a *Ma'rifah*. *Ma'rifah* is Gnosticism. So every step that you make on the path towards knowledge, then more and more of its understanding opens.

 So then they begin to teach you why that water is going to burn away negativity, because that water is angelic force. And the angelic fire is much more powerful than satanic fire, *Shaytanic* fire, egoistic fire. That the secret of angelic power is in that H2O. So then scientists now come out and say, 'Oh, if you take one of these H (Hydrogen) away, it becomes Hydrogen Oxide; that is a hydrogen bomb. And all the oceans are explosive.' If the Divine wishes to make this world explode, He merely lifts the Hydrogen from the H2O; and that hydrogen oxide becomes extremely unstable and explosive, and explodes.

*Awliyaullah* (saints) come and teach us that is the angelic power. They are very powerful, but because of their stable nature, they are solid. They hold together by the Will of the Divine but they are tremendous angelic force, a fire that only Satan understands. So then if you look at people who are extremely possessed, they will not let water to touch them. If they drink and do too much drugs, and they are out, water burns them. When they want to wash, they scream, they cry, they go through many different difficulties, because this negative energy that overtakes them and rides them and is all-embracing around them, that angelic force will burn them.

## Power of *Du'a* (Supplication) on Water Molecules

So as soon as you make *du'a* on water, its angels, they don't say 'no';

they say, *'Ameen'.* That's why *Awliyaullah* (saints) and pious people who are following their teaching, their every prayer is on water. Because when we pray for each other, maybe the ego is saying, 'Oh who's he, who's she? Why should I do that?' And we reject that *du'a* (supplication). But the angels, they don't reject anything. As soon as we make *du'a* on water, the *malaika* (angels), it doesn't matter if the water was from Costco. It doesn't matter the price you paid for the water, because sometimes they say 'Oh Shaykh, this is the Costco water,' what's holy about it? It's not; it's the angelic force that is riding within that water and as soon as you make *du'a*, the angels say, *'Ameen'* and immediately that water is changed.

Now they have books on the science of water molecules. They recite things onto the molecule and the cell of the water and they see these amazing crystals. They say something bad and it

BEFORE PRAYER........AFTER PRAYER

becomes saddened and deformed. They say something good and love and divine, and they change to amazing crystals.

So then on the way of *ma'rifah* they begin to teach us the deep reality of water. It's not just the *wudu*; it's an angelic force and that angelic force has a tremendous power. Every time you're sad and every time you're upset and every time you're depressed, it's not just water that you are entering. This is a tremendous angelic force. Don't kill that water with chlorine; don't try to take the angelic force out of the water.

## Water Has a Force of Life

Then it sends its own proof for you because just put the cup of water on your counter. Two days, three days later it becomes green. It means it has the force of life. It's showing us that life is coming from that. Why Allah ﷻ says, 'My Divine Throne is upon the water?' Because He's saying, look, pay attention to the water. It has an angelic force.

وَهُوَ الَّذِي خَلَقَ السَّمَاوَاتِ وَالْأَرْضَ فِي سِتَّةِ أَيَّامٍ وَكَانَ عَرْشُهُ عَلَى الْمَاءِ ... (٧)

*11:7 – "Wa huwal ladhee khalaqas samawati wal arda fee sittati ayyamin, wa kana 'arshuhu 'alal maa ye..." (Surat Hud)*

*"And it is He who created the heavens and the earth in six days - and His Throne had been upon water - ..." (Prophet Hud, 11:7)*

So at the level of *ma'rifah* they begin to teach that this is an angelic force. Respect it, use it, wash with it, pray, seal yourself with it. As soon as you understand the external water, you begin to understand that you are 70% water. If you don't know 70% of yourself then how are you trying to approach the Divine Presence? Because with knowing the self, we know our Lord.

مَنْ عَرَفَ نَفْسَهُ فَقَدْ عَرَفَ رَبَّهُ

*"Man 'arafa nafsahu faqad 'arafa Rabbahu"*

*"Who knows himself, knows his Lord." Prophet Muhammad (ﷺ)*

I begin to know, oh, if the angelic forces are in the water, then what Allah  gave to me? He gave me the image of this earth, that 70% of my mass is water. So then what am I doing to purify that water within me? If it's an angelic force, then how I can put something into that that would threaten them and danger that energy? So that's why the spirits are so dangerous because it comes into that water and begins to attack them and then there's a battle for the water, the blood of the body.

## The Angelic Force of the Water Takes Away Depression

So at the level of *ma'rifah* they go deep into the understanding that this

is an angelic force, a tremendous reality that use it, wash with it; it takes away sadness, takes away difficulty, takes away many burdens. For those who are in energy lives where their energy is important for them, everyday they have to sit in a shower and meditate. They have to be near water to meditate and wash away difficulties, wash away burdens and see their soul moving in that water, because the soul will move in the water and release its burdens. And the angels will come and take these difficulties.

That's why they say if you're very sad and very depressed, go to the ocean. And every time the ocean collapses and the waves come, it's all billions of angels coming into existence. The angelic force of the ocean is unimaginable. It takes away sadness, takes away difficulties and gives us a tremendous amount of power. That is the level of *ma'rifah*.

## 4. Knowledges of *Haqiqa* (Reality/Truth) Decodes the Word of *Mai* (Water)

### *Mai* ماء = *Meem* م , *Alif* ا

At the level of *haqqa'iq* (realities), the guides now begin to open the reality of that angelic force. That angelic force is so powerful; why? What is *mai* (water)? What is the understanding of *mai* ماء, that the *meem* م *alif* ا. It means that Allah ﷻ is saying that this is the reality of Sayyidina Muhammad ﷺ upon that water; that the *mai* and the reality of that water, it opens up its *haqq*, it opens up its realities and begins to go into the greatness of the Divine Presence and what the Divine Presence has given to the reality of Sayyidina Muhammad ﷺ.

From *ilm al-haqqa'iq* and the realities of the *haqq*, the realities of truth, it begins to open up; why *mai?* Allah ﷻ put the *meem* and the *alif* because everything in our life is *La ilaha illAllah Muhammadun RasulAllah* ﷺ (There is no God but Allah, Sayyidina Muhammad ﷺ is the Messenger of Allah). Everything must exist in that reality.

### Allah's ﷻ Throne is Upon the *Mai* ماء (Water)

وَهُوَ الَّذِي خَلَقَ السَّمَاوَاتِ وَالْأَرْضَ فِي سِتَّةِ أَيَّامٍ وَكَانَ عَرْشُهُ عَلَى الْمَاءِ ... (٧)

*11:7 – "Wa huwal ladhee khalaqas samawati wal arda fee sittati ayyamin, wa kana 'arshuhu 'alal maa ye..." (Surat Hud)*

*"And it is He who created the heavens and the earth in six days - and His Throne had been upon water ... " (Prophet Hud, 11:7)*

Then Allah ﷻ is saying, 'Yes, My Throne is upon *mai* ماء', *meem* م *alif* ا; that reality is in that ocean and that ocean of reality is in the

ocean of Sayyidina Muhammad ﷺ. It means then at the level of *haqqa'iq*, there is nothing for us to be distracted with in *La ilaha illAllah*. Everything for us in *ma'rifah* is Muhammadun RasulAllah ﷺ. *La ilaha illAllah*, by its phrase is that there is no divinity, there is nothing but Allah ﷻ, so don't look there. Don't look to understand yourself in the *kalima*, *La ilaha illAllah* because Allah ﷻ says, '*La sharika la* (there is no partner with Allah), you are not like Me. You don't have to look there.' *La shabiha la*, there's no form like Me; there is nothing in this creation like the Divine Presence.

So it begins to open at the level of *haqqa'iq*, that this power, this reality, this energy that is existing for creation in creation. So where is creation? It is in the ocean of Muhammadun RasulAllah ﷺ.

So, *alhamdulillah*, it's much more than just *wudu*. Mawlana Shaykh's knowledge and *ilm* are like oceans. Depending upon who wants, and how they want, they can dive into that reality to pull out these pearls, pull out these gems. The guides can give the answers and understandings that most

people can't. They ask others a question, they get very basic surface information but not the depth of the reality of what Prophet ﷺ was bringing. And Prophet ﷺ was bringing tremendous realities for creation. It's like a seed that when you plant, at first, means

Prophet ﷺ planted the seed knowing that the tree of that reality was going to blossom. And that all those realities would come from what he has established on this *dunya* (material world).

*Subhana rabbika rabbal 'izzati 'amma yasifoon, wa salaamun 'alal mursaleen, walhamdulillahi rabbil 'aalameen. Bi hurmati Muhammad al-Mustafa wa bi siri Surat al-Fatiha.*

# Chapter Four

## Attune to the Masters of Light and Energy

### Seek the Real Guides, Attune to the Masters, and Accompany Them

يَا أَيُّهَا الَّذِينَ آمَنُوا اتَّقُوا اللَّهَ وَكُونُوا مَعَ الصَّادِقِينَ (١١٩)

9:119 – "Ya ayyuhal ladheena amano ittaqollaha wa kono
ma'as sadiqeen." (Surat At-Tawba)

"O you who have believed, have consciousness of Allah and be
with those who are truthful/pious (in words and deed)."
(The Repentance, 9:119)

وَاصْبِرْ نَفْسَكَ مَعَ الَّذِينَ يَدْعُونَ رَبَّهُم بِالْغَدَاةِ وَالْعَشِيِّ يُرِيدُونَ
وَجْهَهُ ۖ وَلَا تَعْدُ عَيْنَاكَ عَنْهُمْ تُرِيدُ زِينَةَ الْحَيَاةِ الدُّنْيَا ۖ وَلَا تُطِعْ
مَنْ أَغْفَلْنَا قَلْبَهُ عَن ذِكْرِنَا وَاتَّبَعَ هَوَاهُ وَكَانَ أَمْرُهُ فُرُطًا (٢٨)

18:28 — *"Wasbir nafsaka ma'al ladheena yad'ona Rabbahum bilghadati wal'ashiyi yureedona Wajhahu, wa la ta'du 'aynaka 'anhum tureedu zeenatal hayatid dunya, wa la ta'du 'aynaka 'anhum tureedu zeenatal hayatid dunya, wa la tuti' man aghfalna qalbahu 'an dhikrina wattaba'a hawahu wa kana amruhu furuta." (Surat Al-Kahf)*

*"And keep yourself patient [by being] with those who call upon their Lord in the morning and the evening, seeking His Face; And let not your eyes pass beyond them, desiring adornments/glitter of the worldly life, and do not obey one whose heart We have made heedless of Our remembrance and who follows his own desires and whose affair is ever [in] neglect."*
*(The Cave, 18:28)*

# Guides of Light/*Malakoot* and Sound Dress You From Their Souls

*A*lhamdulillah, always asking to be nothing and enter the oceans of Allah's 🕮 *Rahmah* and Mercy, and then to be dressed by that *Rahmah* and that Mercy. *Alhamdulillah*, a reminder always for myself of what they want us to concentrate on and the ocean of reality to be dressed with. It requires so much repeating because of the depth of that ocean and the depth of that reality, that the mind hears and goes through the ears and out. But for those that are contemplating, it's a constant contemplation, constantly contemplating that reality, to go deeper into that reality to understand, through the heart that reality.

## Everything is Based On These 3 – Form, Light, and Sound

The guides teach us, *"Atiullaha wa atiur Rasola wa Ulil amre minkum"* (Obey Allah, Obey the Messenger, and those in authority.)

يَاأَيُّهَا الَّذِينَ آمَنُوا أَطِيعُوا اللَّه وَأَطِيعُواْ الرَّسُولَ وَأُوْلِي الأَمْرِ مِنْكُمْ (٥٩)

*4:59 – "Ya ayyu hal latheena amanoo Atiullaha wa atiur Rasola wa Ulil amre minkum..." (Surat An-Nisa)*

*"O You who have believed, Obey Allah, Obey the Messenger, and those in authority among you..." (The Women, 4:59)*

Mawlana Shaykh Hisham is teaching that every reality is based on these three. *Ulul amr* are representing a physical guidance but containing all of it within them. And that the obedience to the Prophet ﷺ is the station of *iman* (faith). The obedience to Allah ﷻ is the station of perfection, *'maqamal ihsan'*. It is to be perfected in the belief. Moving towards that understanding, they begin to teach us that everything is going to be based on that body, the light, and the reality towards energy and sound.

It means that the secrets of guidance Mawlana Shaykh is always teaching is, 'Come to the oceans of guidance and leave that which is fake.' It means leave the fake fruit and leave the fake associations that cannot explain these realities and cannot go into these realities. You find that they are a waste of your time; they are a sense of entertainment for this self.

## For Every Form There Must Be a Light

But the reality that they want us to understand, for us at this time to understand, is that for every form and every guidance based on form, for every form, there must be a light. That there is going to be a guidance based on the form. That has one value. But for that form to be in existence, it has a light and what you are seeing is the light that is manifesting. It's atomic reality, its molecular reality; the reason you see the form is that there is a light.

## For Light to Exist There Must Be a Sound and Praise

That light has a guidance and the ocean of light has a guidance. That light, to be existing is coming from an ocean of  energy. And that energy to be existing must be coming from a sound. It must be coming from a praise and a resonance, what physics calls, or what quantum physics calls, string theory; what Allah ﷻ calls *"yusabbihu bihamdi".*

$$\text{تُسَبِّحُ لَهُ السَّمَاوَاتُ السَّبْعُ وَالْأَرْضُ وَمَن فِيهِنَّ ۚ وَإِن مِّن شَيْءٍ إِلَّا يُسَبِّحُ بِحَمْدِهِ وَلَـٰكِن لَّا تَفْقَهُونَ تَسْبِيحَهُمْ ۗ إِنَّهُ كَانَ حَلِيمًا غَفُورًا (٤٤)}$$

*17:44 – "Tusabbihu lahus samawatus sab'u wal ardu wa man fee hinna wa in min shayin illa yusabbihu bihamdihi wa lakin la tafqahoona tasbeehahum innahu kana haleeman ghafoora." (Surat Al-Isra)*

*"The seven heavens and the earth and whatever is in them exalt [praises] Him. And there is not a thing except that it exalts [Allah] by His praise, but you do not understand their [way of] exalting. Indeed, He is ever Forbearing and Forgiving." (The Night Journey, 17:44)*

That has its depth of ocean, that everything is in a praise. Allah ﷻ has

everything existing in a praise. What have they found in their string theory? That everything is moving, is resonating, and the resonating is from within itself. It has a sound, causing a vibration; that vibration produces an energy, that energy produces a light and that light produces a form.

In the material world people are busy with guidance of the form. And there are *darajat* (ranks) and understandings within the guidance of the form. That there are people who read something, teach you something, and only based on the form. They cannot reach into the depth of the light, into the reality of the energy, and definitely not producing the vibration of that sound. That which is based on the form has its value but, you must seek that which is based on the light.

## Three Stations of Religion:
## *Islam* (Submission), *Iman* (Faith), *Ihsan* (Moral Excellence)

So what Prophet ﷺ described for *Islam* (Submission) and for *Iman* (Faith) and *Maqamul Ihsan* (Station of Moral Excellence). It means that which is 'Islam' is related to the form and perfection of the form and the highest reality of the form is 'seek your Islam', which means submission. Submit your form to the reality of what Allah ﷻ wants to open within your *iman*, within your light.

That's why light that enters, and *Maqamul Iman*, the Station of Faith, is described by *noor* (light). The light of *iman* must enter into your heart so that you have been dressed with faith. It's not something that you just automatically have. The station of *iman* is that you will experience an energy and a light that opens within  the heart, and like a *khashf*, Allah ﷻ will grant a vision and many different experiences. That is *nurul iman* that begins to come and occupy the being and open the reality of the being.

Then the *Maqamul Ihsan* (Station of Excellence) and the oceans of perfection are going to be based on the reality of sound.

## Guides of Light Have an Unbroken Chain of Guidance

There is a guidance for the body, an understanding of the guidance for the body is on how to *tarbiyyah*, how to train the body, how to discipline the body. Then you keep the company of those who have an understanding of that *tarbiyyah*, of that discipline. How do I train my body and discipline my body so that I can reach the higher guidance?

The guides teach that this ocean of reality cannot come with a broken chain. Because for that light that they are going to begin to describe that is coming from the Prophetic presence, which means the heart of

136

the Divine presence that illuminates through the soul of the Prophet ﷺ. That light, to reach to us, is coming through a rope and a chain, where Allah ﷻ describes, 'Don't separate from that rope.'

$$وَاعْتَصِمُوا بِحَبْلِ اللَّهِ جَمِيعًا وَلَا تَفَرَّقُوا... (١٠٣)$$

*3:103 – "Wa'tasimo bihab lillahi jamee'an wa la tafarraqo..." (Surat Al-Imran)*

*"And hold firmly to the rope of Allah all together and do not separate..."*
*(Family of Imran, 3:103)*

These are the *turooqs* (spiritual paths), and *ahlal-haqqa'iq*, the 'people of reality'; they exist as a rope, to bring and to fulfill Allah's ﷻ command of *Ateeullah* and *atee ur Rasul* and the *Ulul Amr*. It means the *Ulul Amr* are that rope guiding us back into that reality.

That rope cannot be broken because we are now going to describe the guidance of the body is like an *imam* who tells you, 'Wash like this, clean your nose like this, give your *zakat* (charity) to this percentage.' They give all of the external understanding of Islam, and that has its limit and has its

capacity in which to perfect yourself. That guidance can be many places. Then they begin to describe that the higher level of guidance already takes that guidance; they guide the body.

But the guides of light, they have reached a state in which their light and their soul governs their reality. Allah ﷻ has opened for them their

137

soul, opened for them that light of their soul, and that light begins to interact with our being. That reality cannot come to anyone with a broken chain.

## There Must be a *Shajarah* (Family Tree) and Permission to Guide

So somebody says they read a book and now they are guiding based on

light? It's not the way. It's not the way and it's not the *adab* (manner) of Sayyidina Muhammad ﷺ. The Prophet ﷺ and his companions, *tabi'een* and *tabi' tabi'een*, (Followers and the followers of the followers), all of them kept the companionship and kept the rope to Prophet ﷺ.

So why then give it to someone that has no Shaykh? Somebody says, 'No, I'm a guide of light.' 'Ok, but who is your Shaykh?...' 'Ah, I don't have one.' 'And who's your Shaykh's Shaykh? And who's your Shaykh's Shaykh's Shaykh?'

There must be a *shajarah;* there must be a family tree in which you are taking that light that reaches to Prophet ﷺ like a wire, like an electrical cable. Like a *hubl*, a rope that is coming from Prophet ﷺ and was inherited down. And you are signed off, that now that cable comes to you. It is signed off by the Shaykh of

the Shaykh and any other Shaykh within that organization. They sign off that that cable has come from Allah ﷻ, and by authority of Sayyidina Muhammad ﷺ, and is reaching to you. Now you are a guide of light.

## Power of the *Ibadur Rahman* – The Guides of Soul

The guide of the body is the lowest. To tell you what to do on this earth is of the lowest dimension. It's like going before Allah ﷻ and ask, you know, 'Ya Rabbi, I am coming here to Divine Presence. I'd like to know how to get more gas from my gas station.' They will come to Mawlana Shaykh and ask for these types of prayers! That guidance is the lowest form of guidance. But what they are describing are the guides of light that they encompass the physical guidance. That is their kindergarten.

The harder and the bigger gift that Allah ﷻ has granted are the guides of light. These are from *Ibadur Rahman* (Servants of the most Compassionate). They have *nurul iman* (light of faith) and they are supported by the light of Sayyidina Muhammad ﷺ. Their light emanates around them and they merely release their light. The concept  of the soul is something we may not understand, that the soul is confined within the body, but those whose hearts are open, Allah ﷻ opens the reality of their soul. One understanding is their soul, if they release it, can hold all of *dunya* within its hand.

فَسُبْحَانَ الَّذِي بِيَدِهِ مَلَكُوتُ كُلِّ شَيْءٍ وَإِلَيْهِ تُرْجَعُونَ (٨٣)

*36:83 – 'Fasubhanal ladhee biyadihi Malakutu kulli shay in wa ilayhi turja'oon.' (Surat Yaseen)*

*"Therefore glory be to Him in Whose hand is the kingdom of all things,
and to Him you shall be brought back." (Yaseen, 36:83)*

## Everything is Created From One Soul *(Roh Wahid)*

The magnitude and the size of
the soul is not something we
perceive. But if you want to
understand the greatness of
the soul, look to the vastness
of this universe. All of this
universe with its infinite size is
all existing within Nur Muhammad ﷺ.

خَلَقَكُم مِّن نَّفْسٍ وَاحِدَةٍ ثُمَّ جَعَلَ مِنْهَا زَوْجَهَا (٦)

*39:6 – "Khalaqakum min nafsin wahidatin thumma ja'ala minha zawjaha..."
(Surat Az-Zumar)*

*"He created you (all) from one soul: then created, of like nature, his mate;..."
(The Troops, 39:6)*

All of its vastness, its unimaginable size must be in *La ilaha illAllah* or
*Muhammadun RasulAllah* ﷺ. *La ilaha illallah* (There is no God but
Allah), nothing, *'la sharik'*, there is no partner with Allah ﷻ. It means
everything is within that light of *Muhammadun
RasulAllah* ﷺ (Sayyidina Muhammad is the Messenger of Allah).

## The Guide's Soul Dresses the Atomic Reality of the Students

We keep repeating it to understand it and to really contemplate it. The
guidance of physicality? Very easy, that's nothing. But for Allah ﷻ to
open the reality of the guidance of light means they have trusted that
servant with the ability to use their soul.

With a little bit of studying of the atoms, you know that when the light
moves out, their atoms are moving, their *dhuriya*. When the *dhuriya* is

moving out, their atoms are moving out, their light is interacting with your light. Because light doesn't stay by itself; it's moving, it's connecting. Immediately their atoms are grafted onto your soul, and your soul is grafted onto their soul.

Whatever *zikr* they are doing, whatever practices they are doing, whatever lights from *Ateeullah, 'Ateeur Rasul, wa Ulul Amri minkum* (Obey Allah, Obey the Messenger, and those in Authority, Holy Qur'an 4:59). Whatever Allah ﷻ is dressing Prophet ﷺ, whatever

Prophet ﷺ is dressing those *Ulul amr*. The real *Ulul amr*, are 124,000 *awliya*. What Prophet ﷺ is dressing them, their *dhuriya*, their atomic reality is taking that dress. And because there is no ego, their atoms freely send to the level that the other atoms can take. They send it light, send it blessings, send it energy and *tajalli* (manifestation). It's sending it energies and frequencies. That atomic reality that you have is being dressed by their soul, blessed by their soul.

That's why they don't need you to do very much but just attend. As you attend, more light can be placed onto you and more of your light can be put onto them and they begin to carry that burden.

## Guides of Light Carry Your Atoms in Their Soul's Ship

What Allah ﷻ describes from the heart of Holy Qur'an because this guidance of light is based on *nurul iman*, the light of faith. *Nurul iman* has to do with love of Sayyidina Muhammad ﷺ. The heart of Holy

Qur'an is Sayyidina Yaseen ﷺ. So Allah ﷻ said, a sign for them, *"wa hamalna dhuriya'tuhum"* (We have carried their atoms, Holy Qur'an, 36:41).

$$ وَآيَةٌ لَهُمْ أَنَّا حَمَلْنَا ذُرِّيَّتَهُمْ فِي الْفُلْكِ الْمَشْحُونِ (٤١) $$

*36:41 – "Wa ayatul lahum anna hamalna dhurriyyatahum fil fulkil mashhooni."*
*(Surat Yaseen)*

*"And a sign for them is that we have carried their atoms in a loaded ship." (Yaseen, 36:41)*

## Conveyance of Energy From Guides' Atomic Reality

'We have carried them.' We talked about that before but to repeat it because people don't seem to be understanding the depth of what they are describing. When we say in *tariqa*, *'fana'* (annihilation), I'm in the *muhabbat* of my Shaykh and then entering the *fana* of my Shaykh, it's not your body and body are coming together. They want us to think out of the box, that your souls connect. And they don't need your approval. If you are in that attendance, it's enough for them and their light to begin to move and capture light.

The reality of the atom is if they take an atom from you and bring it out, physicists found you don't become something new. It's not a new creation. One out of your trillions of atoms, one of them, if they take out, all of them communicate back to you. It's not like you took something and it became something new. Quantum physics found that if we take an atom, there may be billions of atoms in this glass of water; if we take one atom, all of them communicate together.

So it's enough that they take one atom, *"wa hamalna dhuriyatuhum"* (Holy Qur'an, Yaseen, 36:41). Allah ﷻ says, 'We carry you, We have always carried you.' It's enough if they carry from one atom. The conveyance of energy from their atomic reality, from their light  reality, completely dresses that atom, completely blesses that atom. It means that there is something happening in the world of light here in these associations. We are not physical boxes and we're not couches and sofas sitting here.

## People of Reality Are Perfecting You From Inside Out

Allah ﷻ said, *"Wa laqad karramna bani Adama."* We have honoured the children of Adam.

$$ \text{وَلَقَدْ كَرَّمْنَا بَنِي آدَمَ ... (٧٠)} $$

*17:70 – "Wa laqad karramna bani Adama…" (Surat Al-Isra)*

*"Verily, We have honoured the children of Adam…" (The Night Journey, 17:70)*

You have a tremendous reality and a tremendous gift but you are so stuck on your physical understanding that you think this is a place where you come, you go, you eat and you use the facility. But there is an interaction and an event happening in the world of light, especially for those whose hearts are open and their light is emanating. Their light is grafting people's souls and they begin to change from within. They cook you from the inside, not outside. *Min ahle haqqa'iq.* They don't worry about perfecting your outside appearance and saying, 'You have got to look like you are perfect.'

You go to other associations and maybe they all look perfect on the outside. Because there is not a guide of light amongst them and they focus only on the *zahir*, only on the outside. That's like a clock that may not have an engine and if it has no engine you don't really know what time it is. It means the inside could be *khali*, could be empty; but they just focus on the outside. What the guides are teaching, the outside is the easiest. Do the outside, you can find that anywhere. If you have *ittibah* and follow, you will follow perfectly your outside, your *shari'ah* will be perfect if you follow the guides of light.

Real guidance is the guides of light. These are the guides of faith. These are the ones who represent Nur Muhammad ﷺ on this *dunya*. They are permitted to send their ship out. Why Allah ﷻ says *fulkil mashhoon*; why give the example of a *fulk* (ship) – because it carries.

$$\text{وَآيَةٌ لَّهُمْ أَنَّا حَمَلْنَا ذُرِّيَّتَهُمْ فِي الْفُلْكِ الْمَشْحُونِ (٤١)}$$

*36:41 – "Wa ayatul lahum anna hamalna dhurriyyatahum fil fulkil mashhooni."*
*(Surat Yaseen)*

*"And a sign for them is that we have carried their atoms in a loaded ship."*
*(Yaseen, 36:41)*

Their soul carries the light of everyone they come in touch with. They like it, they don't like it, it's not up to them. Allah ﷻ merely sends something into their presence and those atoms cling to that light.

## *Fana* (Annihilation) – Don't Be a Drop, Become One With the Ocean

Now, in the world of light, we begin to understand what is *fana*? What is the station of *fana* and annihilation is that if you can bring down your physical ego and your physical understanding. Annihilate your physical reality that, 'my form, *ya Rabbi*, is nothing. I'm not interested in my form. My form is going to go into the dirt. *Ya Rabbi*, let me to understand from the world of light.' As much as you annihilate your form, annihilate your form, you begin to reach your atomic reality. You begin to think that you are something greater than just this form; it means you realize there is an ocean and I'm keeping myself as a drop, and there's no power in a drop. As soon as the drop goes back into the ocean, it can begin to sense, it can hear everything.

That's from the *hadith*. Allah ﷻ said, 'Come to the ocean of voluntary worship.' It means, 'If I dress you from the oceans of love, I will be your hearing.' That is the ocean of power. We are not talking goofy stuff. You will find it all in the *hadith* (Sayings of Prophet Muhammad ﷺ)

... وَلَا يَزَالُ عَبْدِي يَتَقَرَّبُ إِلَيَّ بِالنَّوَافِلِ حَتَّى أُحِبَّهُ، فَإِذَا أَحْبَبْتُهُ كُنْت سَمْعَهُ الَّذِي يَسْمَعُ بِهِ، وَبَصَرَهُ الَّذِي يُبْصِرُ بِهِ، وَيَدَهُ الَّتِي يَبْطِشُ بِهَا، وَرِجْلَهُ الَّتِي يَمْشِي بِهَا، وَلَئِنْ سَأَلَنِي لَأُعْطِيَنَّهُ، وَلَئِنْ اسْتَعَاذَنِي لَأُعِيذَنَّهُ ( رَوَاهُ الْبُخَارِيُّ)

"..., wa la yazaalu 'Abdi yataqarrabu ilayya bin nawafile hatta ahebahu, fa idha ahbabtuhu kunta Sam'ahul ladhi yasma'u behi, wa Basarahul ladhi yubsiru behi, wa Yadahul lati yabTeshu beha, wa Rejlahul lati yamshi beha, wa la in sa alani la a'Teyannahu, ..."

"...My servant continues to draw near to Me with voluntary acts of worship so that I shall love him. When I love him, I am his hearing with which he hears, his seeing with which he sees, his hand with which he strikes and his foot with which he walks. Were he to ask [something] of Me, I would surely give it to him..."
(Hadith Qudsi, Sahih al-Bukhari, 81:38:2)

Allah ﷻ says, 'I'm going to dress you from My hearing.' That is the ocean of reality. Your ears don't hear beyond this because we are stuck in the form. The guides of light, when their souls touch, they are dressing the atomic reality of everyone, as they are being dressed by their Shaykh and their Shaykh by their Shaykh, and their Shaykh by their Shaykh; they have an internal structure. And that structure is a form of light and energy that moves across the earth. As their Shaykh is moving, their atomic reality been dressed by everything their Shaykh is being dressed by. As their Shaykh is moving on a *mi'raj* (ascension), they are moving on that *mi'raj*. All Shaykhs and all *ahle haqqa'iq* (people of reality) are moving in their *mi'raj*, in the *mi'raj* of Sayyidina Muhammad ﷺ. As they are moving, all light is moving.

## Guides' Light is Grafting Through Your Light and Vice Versa

It means, as they begin to dress us and bless us, they begin to teach us,

'Think from the world of light' and, 'Destroy your form, annihilate your form. Understand that the associations of light are not comparable to any other association.' You can sit a thousand years somewhere else, it doesn't mean anything. It's enough that every time you sit in that association, their light is grafting through your light, and your light is grafting through their light. They are able to dress and bless that atomic reality that will reach to you.

You begin to sense that energy, your love for Sayyidina Muhammad ﷺ increases. Because the identity of that light is the love of Prophet ﷺ, it's not their individual identity. Their identity died with the form; all there is, is the love of Sayyidina Muhammad ﷺ. The light we are talking about is the Muhammadan light that is moving out. When you begin to sense that in your soul, 'My love for Prophet ﷺ is increasing.' It's not from you. It's from their light that they have transplanted onto your light. You may begin to sense Prophet ﷺ, feel Prophet ﷺ, smell Prophet ﷺ and begin to see Prophet ﷺ, through your heart, through your light, but why? It's because the guides of light, they are moving their light into

146

your being. As much as you annihilate yourself out of the way, is as much as the Muhammadan reality can begin to move in.

## The Material World Uses Light for Destruction, Heavenly World Uses Light for Elevation

These are the guides of light. Then they describe above the guides of light, there are guides who have been granted the permission to guide through the oceans of sound. Again you have to study the physics, that for every form, there is a light; every light, there is an energy, and then a sound. In *dunya* (material world), because you are going to start seeing this from *Shaytan*, so you have to learn this from *Rahman* (the Most Compassionate). In *dunya*, *Shaytan* is going to release energies and weapons that are based on energies, weapons that are based on light. So it's not something that does not exist; it's now moving into this *dunya*. The Chinese have a laser that shot from *dunya* to 270 miles into space and they took out a satellite. This is the ocean of light. This is the reality of light.

The material world uses light for destruction. The heavenly world uses light for elevation. If the material world has it, you better believe that the spiritual world has it. By sitting in the associations, they are sending lasers onto the soul. And if you can shoot a satellite out of the sky, you don't think that they can take out your bad characteristics? It means the lights are coming like lasers and begin to burn all the bad

characteristics. But because it's from the heavens, it doesn't scar you and harm you but it merely replaces.

وَ قُلْ جَآءَالْحَقُّ وَزَهَقَ الْبَطِلُ، إِنَّ الْبَطِلَ كَانَ زَهُوقًا (٨١)

*17:81 – "Wa qul jaa alhaqqu wa zahaqal baatil, innal batila kana zahooqa."*
*(Surat Al-Isra)*

*"And say: Truth has (now) arrived, and Falsehood perished: Indeed is Falsehood*
*(by its nature) ever perishing." (The Night Journey, 17:81)*

*Zahooqa*, Allah ﷻ describes, 'it obliterates everything that's false.'
What? The *haqq* (truth) of Allah's ﷻ light, which is the *haqq* of Nur
Muhammad ﷺ. When that *haqq* comes, it destroys everything false
and begins to replenish your life back to its *haqq* and back to its reality.
But then we go out and sin, and we do bad things again and throw
more dirtiness upon that light. Those who succeed, they constantly try
to purify themselves, perfect themselves, lessen the amount of sins and
bad actions, so that their lights begin to change. The reality begins to
change.

## The Highest Ocean of Guidance is the Ocean of Sound

The highest ocean of guidance is the ocean of sound. So what is
*Shaytan* going to use now? He's going to send a sound and make things
to shatter. He sends a sound onto a glass, because everything has a
frequency, and that glass shatters. He sends a sound onto a building
and the building begins to move. Because everything has a frequency.
If you match its frequency, you can begin to make it to vibrate and fall
apart. What you think then from the oceans of sound, where Allah ﷻ
says, *"yusabbihu bihamdihi"* (Everything is in a praise).

تُسَبِّحُ لَهُ السَّمَاوَاتُ السَّبْعُ وَالْأَرْضُ وَمَن فِيهِنَّ ۚ وَإِن مِّن شَيْءٍ إِلَّا يُسَبِّحُ بِحَمْدِهِ
وَلَٰكِن لَّا تَفْقَهُونَ تَسْبِيحَهُمْ ۗ إِنَّهُ كَانَ حَلِيمًا غَفُورًا (٤٤)

*17:44 – "Tusabbihu lahus samawatus sab'u wal ardu wa man fee hinna wa in*
*min shayin illa yusabbihu bihamdihi wa lakin la tafqahoona tasbeehahum, innahu*
*kana haleeman ghafoora." (Surat Al-Isra)*

*"The seven heavens and the earth and whatever is in them exalt [praises] Him. And there is not a thing except that it exalts [Allah] by His praise, but you do not understand their [way of] exalting. Indeed, He is ever Forbearing and Forgiving." (The Night Journey, 17:44)*

That for everything is in a praise. When the guides are given permission to intercede, when they have been given from the reality and the guidance of sound, it means that they reached a level of annihilation in which they annihilate themselves back into the ocean of light. Then from the ocean of that light, they annihilate themselves back into the oceans of energy. And from the oceans of energy, they annihilate themselves back into the oceans of *Qul Hu*, (Holy Qur'an, 112:1), back into the ocean of sound.

## Guides of Sound Change Your Frequency

قُلْ هُوَ اللَّـهُ أَحَدٌ (١)

*112:1 – "Qul huwa Allahu Ahad." (Surat Al-Ikhlas)*

*"Say He is Allah, the One." (The Sincerity, 112:1).*

*Qul Hu*, from the 'Surah of Sincerity'. These are Allah's سُبْحَانَهُ sincere servants. That as soon as they enter the ocean of that *zikr*, they are annihilated back into a sound. If they are able to reach towards that reality of sound, it means that what is emanating out from them is a sound. And if that sound begins to hit your frequency, they begin to change your frequency. If they change the frequency in which you are operating at, you begin to change the light and the spectrum of the light of people. That is what's meant by intercession.

## The Flag of Praise and the Reality of Prophetic Intercession

When they describe Prophet ﷺ will be granted intercession on the Day of Judgment. Because the understanding is not yet ready to understand, they describe it as Prophet ﷺ would be making a *du'a* (supplication). He is *liwa wal hamd* ﷺ, which means he is the flag of Allah's ﷻ praise. He is the reality of Allah's ﷻ Divinely Word. He is the reality of Allah's ﷻ Divinely Tongue; that nothing can hear Allah ﷻ, and all that they can hear is the praise of Sayyidina Muhammad ﷺ.

Allah ﷻ says that, 'If I send My sound onto anything, it would be obliterated.'

لَوْ أَنزَلْنَا هَٰذَا الْقُرْآنَ عَلَىٰ جَبَلٍ لَّرَأَيْتَهُ خَاشِعًا مُّتَصَدِّعًا مِّنْ خَشْيَةِ اللَّهِ وَتِلْكَ الْأَمْثَالُ
نَضْرِبُهَا لِلنَّاسِ لَعَلَّهُمْ يَتَفَكَّرُونَ ...

*59:21 – "Law anzalna hadhal Qurana 'ala jabalin lara aytahu, khashi'an..."*
*(Surah Al-Hashr)*

*"Had We sent down this Qur'an on a mountain, verily, thou wouldst have seen it obliterated to dust (from its power)..." (The Exile, 59:21)*

That sound has to pass the reality of Prophet ﷺ to become cool and peaceful, as to not destroy and obliterate creation. So it means that Prophet ﷺ is going to make a sound but for people we say, 'Oh it's a *du'a*'. What's the reality of a *du'a*? They say a *du'a* that nobody has heard. It means

Prophet ﷺ merely begins to release a frequency.

## It Is But One Shout – "*Saihatan Wahidatan*"

That the *hamd* and the praise from Prophet ﷺ is such a powerful "*saihatan wahidatan*" (Holy Qur'an, 36:29), that it's but one shout, and they are destroyed.

$$ إِن كَانَتْ إِلَّا صَيْحَةً وَاحِدَةً فَإِذَا هُمْ خَامِدُونَ (٢٩) $$

*36:29 – "In kanat illa sayhatan wahidatan fa idha hum khamidoon."*

*"It was not but one shout, and lo! they were destroyed." (Surat Yaseen, 36:29)*

It means the sound that emanates from Prophet ﷺ will obliterate everything false. Everything that's standing on the Day of Judgment in its false realization, in its false character, not the way that Allah ﷻ wanted it. We are coming with all the animalistic form. It's but one shout from Prophet ﷺ, and everything false will be obliterated. But because it's heavenly, it's not destroyed. Every false will be obliterated and make another praise and everything will be brought back towards its reality.

$$ إِن كَانَتْ إِلَّا صَيْحَةً وَاحِدَةً فَإِذَا هُمْ جَمِيعٌ لَّدَيْنَا مُحْضَرُونَ (٥٣) $$

*36:53 – "In kanat illa sayhatan wahidatan fa idha hum jamee'un ladayna muhdaroon." (Surat Yaseen)*

*"It will be no more than a single Blast/Shout, when at once, they will all be brought up before Us!" (Yaseen, 36:53)*

That is, everything is already existing based on sound. It has a sound, based on the sound it has a light, based on the light it has a form. It means the intercession and the reality of intercession is going to be from the *hamd* حمد (praise) and the sound of Prophet ﷺ.

That's why the name Muhammad محمد is the reality of sound. *MuHamd* – the most, *meem* م of the *hamd* حمد, the most praised in Allah's ﷻ Divinely Presence. Ah, with the *alif* ا and *hamd* احمد means that he has even a Divinely praise from Allah ﷻ, granting the reality of the name of Sayyidina Ahmad احمد *(alaihis salatu wa salaam)*.

## The Praise and *Zikr* (Divinely Remembrance) Raises Your Frequency and Light Spectrum

We pray for more understanding, to understand and open the heart and to leave the world of form and not be locked into the box of the form. That the greatness is in the oceans of light, and from light there's the energies and sound. Then we begin to understand the importance of the *zikr*, the importance of *salawat* (praisings) on Prophet ﷺ.

Everything that the guides are teaching us from the ocean of the soul is based on sound. Every *durood shareef*, every *salawat*, every *zikr* that you are making is affecting the sound and the vibration in which we are vibrating at. If we change that frequency and raise it and raise it and raise it, you will see a difference in the light that you emanate. If no frequency, the light spectrum is low. If you raise and elevate the frequency in which you are praising, your light should reflect that frequency.

That's why the two, they don't meet. Angels and demons, they don't meet because the frequency is such a high frequency and the one is so low that there's no meeting point; they basically obliterate. If the angel comes and the angelic frequency comes, it obliterates everything that's false, and destroys it and will re-raise it to something that is true.

We pray that Allah ﷻ grant us an understanding, grant us more understanding of annihilation, annihilating ourselves and entering into the oceans of light and guidance of light, guidances of sound and the importance of sound.

*Subhana rabbika rabbal 'izzati 'amma yasifoon, wa salaamun 'alal mursaleen, walhamdulillahi rabbil 'aalameen. Bi hurmati Muhammad al-Mustafa wa bi siri Surat al-Fatiha.*

# Attuning to the Masters of Energy Through Light and Sound

*"Ateeullah wa atee ar rasool wa ulil amrin minkum"* (Obey Allah, Obey the Messenger, and those who are in Authority, Holy Qur'an)

يَاأَيُّهَا الَّذِينَ آمَنُوا أَطِيعُواللَّهَ وَأَطِيعُواْلرَّسُولَ وَأُوْلِي الْأَمْرِ مِنْكُمْ (٥٩)

*4:59 – "Ya ayyu hal latheena amanoo Atiullaha, wa atiur Rasola, wa Ulil amre minkum..." (Surat An-Nisa)*

*"O You who have believed, Obey Allah, Obey the Messenger, and those in authority among you..." (The Women, 4:59)*

Always a reminder for myself that, by the Grace of Allah ﷻ, we are still in existence. That we took a path of trying to be nothing, and by Allah's ﷻ *Rahmah* and Mercy, we find ourself in existence. *Alhamdulillah*, we wanted to share for ourselves always about energy and the importance of energy and sound, and to open that reality of the importance of sound for our self.

It means that in the understanding of attunement, we are talking in reference to energy and people put it into the understanding of Holy Qur'an and holy *hadith* (traditions of Prophet ﷺ). That these are from the world of *malakoot* (heavenly realm). These are from the oceans of *iman* (faith) and *maqam al ihsan* (station of excellence) and above.

155

## Actions Produce Energy, Everyone Drums to Their Own Beat

That *Ahlul Turuq*, the People of *Haqqa'iq* (realities), teach that what Allah ﷻ wants, *"Wa kunu min as sadiqin."* (Be with those who are truthful).

$$\text{يَا أَيُّهَا الَّذِينَ آمَنُوا اتَّقُوا اللَّه وَكُونُوا مَعَ الصَّادِقِينَ (١١٩)}$$

*9:119 – "Ya ayyuhal ladheena amano ittaqollaha wa kono ma'as sadiqeen."*
*(Surat At-Tawba)*

*"O you who have believed, have consciousness of Allah and be with those who are truthful/pious (in words and deed)." (The Repentance, 9:119)*

*Itaqullah* means have a consciousness and keep the company of these *Sadiqeen*. They are going to dress you and bless you. And in the understanding of attunement, they have to break you down and build you back up.

It means everybody in their life is vibrating and playing their own drum to their own beat. The expression is 'you drum to your own beat'. It doesn't matter what somebody else is playing, you ding ding, ding ding, ding ding to yourself. Everybody is happy with what they are doing and the level in which they are resonating and vibrating. What you eat, what you breathe, what you drink, what you do, how you do; every action is creating an energy. That energy is bringing out lights, these lights are what cause our manifestation.

## Vibration of Sound Determines the Quality of Light

It means that this manifestation is manifesting, you are only seeing this

world of form because there is a light. That is the quantum, the atoms and the molecules. Those lights, the colour and the spectrum and the quality of those lights are going to be based on sound. If they vibrate high, the spectrum, the quality of the light is very high. As they begin to emanate lower, the quality is lower. The light and the spectrum of the light is lower.

Now, *MashaAllah,* we live in a time where they have so many proofs, they even have the physics of sound. I recommend everybody to Google and go watch YouTube on the physics of sound, so you get the whole course in the understanding of sound. They can resonate a sound and it begins to vibrate and make forms. They can play a sound and a machine and a device that picks up that this wood has a certain frequency.

## Everything Praises at the Atomic Level

Allah ﷻ says, "*Yusabihu bi hamdi,*" for 'Verily everything is in My Praise.'

تُسَبِّحُ لَهُ السَّمَاوَاتُ السَّبْعُ وَالْأَرْضُ وَمَن فِيهِنَّ ۚ وَإِن مِّن شَيْءٍ إِلَّا يُسَبِّحُ بِحَمْدِهِ وَلَـٰكِن لَّا تَفْقَهُونَ تَسْبِيحَهُمْ ۗ إِنَّهُ كَانَ حَلِيمًا غَفُورًا (٤٤)

*17:44 – "Tusabbihu lahus samawatus sab'u wal ardu wa man fee hinna wa in min shayin illa yusabbihu bihamdihi wa lakin la tafqahoona tasbeehahum innahu kana haleeman ghafoora." (Surat Al-Isra)*

*"The seven heavens and the earth and whatever is in them exalt [praises] Him. And there is not a thing except that it exalts [Allah] by His praise, but you do not understand their [way of] exalting. Indeed, He is ever Forbearing and Forgiving." (The Night Journey, 17:44)*

Everything, not just the birds, is praising, everything. The wood is praising; otherwise you would not see it manifesting. The table, the glass, me, you, our clothes; everything has atoms. These atoms are moving, these molecules are forming, from what? From a *zikr* and a praise that Allah ﷻ gave to it, what they call string theory, something is moving.

157

When they look into the atoms with their microscopes, they found that there is a vibration. That is *"bi hamdi"*; Allah ﷻ said, 'Verily everything is in My Praise'. Everything has a *zikr* which gives it its manifestation. Then Allah ﷻ says, 'You won't know except the people

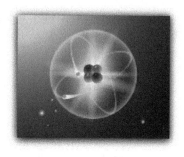

of *tafakkur* (contemplation). You haven't the ability to hear it.'

## Guides of Light Can Hear the Praises

People of *tafakkur* (contemplation), when Allah ﷻ opens their heart, their eyes, their soul; the *hadith* where Allah ﷻ is describing, 'They come, they finish their *fard* (obligatory), they did their voluntary act and I gave them from My Hearing, I gave them from My Seeing.'

قَالَ رَسُولُ اللهِ صلى الله عليه و سلم إنَّ اللَّهَ تَعَالَى قَالَ :وَمَا تَقَرَّبَ إِلَيَّ عَبْدِي بِشَيْءٍ أَحَبَّ إِلَيَّ مِمَّا افْتَرَضْتُ عَلَيْهِ، وَلَا يَزَالُ عَبْدِي يَتَقَرَّبُ إِلَيَّ بِالنَّوَافِلِ حَتَّى أُحِبَّهُ، فَإِذَا أَحْبَبْتُهُ كُنْت سَمْعَهُ الَّذِي يَسْمَعُ بِهِ، وَبَصَرَهُ الَّذِي يُبْصِرُ بِهِ، وَيَدَهُ الَّتِي يَبْطِشُ بِهَا، وَرِجْلَهُ الَّتِي يَمْشِي بِهَا، وَلَئِنْ سَأَلَنِي لَأُعْطِيَنَّهُ، وَلَئِنْ اسْتَعَاذَنِي لَأُعِيذَنَّهُ." [ رَوَاهُ الْبُخَارِيُّ]

*"Wa ma taqarraba ilayya 'Abdi bi shayin ahabba ilayya mimma aftaradtu 'alayhi, wa la yazaalu 'Abdi yataqarrabu ilayya bin nawafile hatta ahebahu, fa idha ahbabtuhu kunta Sam'ahul ladhi yasma'u behi, wa Basarahul ladhi yubsiru behi, wa Yadahul lati yabTeshu beha, wa Rejlahul lati yamshi beha, wa layin sa alani la a'Teyannahu, wa la in asta'adhani la u'yidhannahu."*

*Hadith Qudsi narrated by Abu Hurayra, that Prophet Muhammad (pbuh) said that "Allah (AJ) said, 'My servant does not draw near Me with anything I love more than what I have made obligatory for him. My servant continues to draw near to Me with voluntary acts of worship so that I shall love him. When I love him, I am his hearing with which he hears, his seeing with which he sees, his hand with which he strikes and his foot with which he walks. Were he to ask [something] of Me, I would surely give it to him He will become Rabbaniya and say be and it will be. I do not hesitate about anything as much as I hesitate about [seizing] the soul of My faithful servant: he hates death and I hate hurting him." (Sahih al-Bukhari, 81:38:2)*

## Reality of Herbal Medicine is Based on Praise of the Plants

It means from Allah's ﷻ Dress and *Sifat* (attribute) upon their hearing, they can hear the praise of what Allah ﷻ wants them to. They direct themself to a tree, they can hear the praise of the tree. They direct themself to a plant, they can hear the praise of the plant and the plant would tell them what its benefit is for, why Allah ﷻ created it. That becomes

what they call herbal medicine. Not that they found something, they read something on the Internet and they put it together and then they poisoned ten people. But the actual herbs and plants talk to them. They have a vibration and a *zikr*. And if that *zikr* is known into the heart, they'll begin to understand from what Allah ﷻ wants them to understand.

## Reality of Attunment – Real Guides Raise the Frequency of People

The attunement on how to reach these *haqqa'iq* is that you come with how you are resonating and what you are thinking. The responsibility of *Ibad ar Rahman* and these guides – not everybody calls themself a *murshid* (spiritual guide) and say, 'I have *murshid*, this one is a *murshid*, this one is a *murshid*.' No, this is a title now everybody uses. These guides are from *Ibad ar Rahman*, which Allah ﷻ gives them a very specific light and a very specific responsibility. And one of these responsibilities is on raising the frequency of *insaan* (human being). Many are known, many are unknown; many I never even hear them speak, it's not necessary. We'll go into that. They are the Bluetooth *awliya*; they don't need to say anything. We have the *awliya* (saints) who speak and they vibrate and the frequency in which they are vibrating.

It means they begin to teach attunement is that they have to bring down and break down that person, not physically, but through all their testing and teaching, completely re-change. How you think it's not important. What you want is not important. All of those are creating a resonance, in which you are vibrating at a different frequency.

## Everything is Manifested by the Sound – 7 Notes, 7 Verses of *Fatiha*

So they gave an example. There is a master violinist. He makes every violin with his own hand and as a result of making everything precise, he is a master. He makes everything precise, then when he puts the cords; and sound has a tremendous reality. There are 7 notes; there are 7 verses of *Fatiha* (first chapter of Holy Qur'an), there are 7 *tawafs* (circumambulation) around the *Ka'bah*. Why Allah ﷻ created these 7 notes? Because within this sound, everything is resonating. Everything is manifesting by sound. If Allah ﷻ takes the sound, everything collapses.

So it has a tremendous reality, because as soon as you say sound, then people say, 'Oh Shaykh, we pray, that is enough for us.' No, no! These are *haqqa'iq* and realities for us to understand where Prophet is teaching, 'Who knows himself will know his Lord.'

مَنْ عَرَفَ نَفْسَهُ فَقَدْ عَرَفَ رَبَّهُ

*"Man 'arafa nafsahu faqad 'arafa Rabbahu"*

*"Who knows himself, knows his Lord." Prophet Muhammad (pbuh)*

That which governs him, if he knows himself. Not to know himself that he likes tacos and he likes kebabs, 'I know myself Shaykh, I like tacos on Tuesday night and I like kebab on Saturday'. What is knowing yourself is very deep! To know yourself, you have to go into all the realities with your guide about yourself and your whole physiology of how Allah عز وجل created you.

## The Character Must Break Down To Rebuild Better

Then everything that you think and you want and you want to do is making you vibrate at a different beat. The Guides responsibility is to break down. So when Allah عز وجل gave the *daleel* (proof) of Nabi Musa (Moses) عليه السلام and Sayyidina Khidr عليه السلام. It doesn't mean you are bad. One is *Kalimullah* (speaks to Allah) and the other one is a beloved servant of Allah عز وجل, whom Allah عز وجل gave a *rahmah* (mercy) and then he attained a knowledge.

فَوَجَدَا عَبْدًا مِّنْ عِبَادِنَا آتَيْنَاهُ رَحْمَةً مِّنْ عِندِنَا وَعَلَّمْنَاهُ مِن لَّدُنَّا عِلْمًا (٦٥)

*18:65 – "Fawajada 'abdan min 'ibadinaa ataynahu rahmatan min 'indina wa 'allamnahu mil ladunna 'ilma" (Surat Al-Kahf)*

"*And they found a servant from among Our servants to whom we had given mercy from us and had taught him from Us a [certain] knowledge.*" *(The Cave, 18:65)*

But what Allah عز وجل wants for this reality is to break him down. Nabi Musa عليه السلام is coming to Sayyidina Khidr عليه السلام, he is breaking him down. He says, 'Me and you, we are not going to be able to do this. You are not going to have patience with knowledge that is not complete.' Why to say that, to *Kalimullah*? To break now his frequency.

161

قَالَ لَهُ مُوسَىٰ هَلْ أَتَّبِعُكَ عَلَىٰ أَن تُعَلِّمَنِ مِمَّا عُلِّمْتَ رُشْدًا (٦٦)

*18:66 – "Qala lahu moosa hal attabi'uka 'alaa an tu'allimani mimma 'ullimta rushda." (Surat Al-Kahf)*

*"Moses said to him: "May I follow you, on the footing/ condition that you teach me something of the (Higher) Truth which you have been taught?" (The Cave, 18:66)*

قَالَ إِنَّكَ لَن تَسْتَطِيعَ مَعِيَ صَبْرًا (٦٧) وَكَيْفَ تَصْبِرُ عَلَىٰ مَا لَمْ تُحِطْ بِهِ خُبْرًا (٦٨)

*18:67-68 – "Qala innaka lan tastatee'a ma'iya sabra. (67) Wa kayfa tasbiru 'ala ma lam tuhit bihi khubra.(68)" (Surat Al-Kahf)*

*"(The Other) said, "Verily you will not be able to have patience with me! (67) And how can you have patience for what you do not encompass in knowledge? (68)" (The Cave, 18:67-68)*

## *Tasleem* – Surrender All Your Doubts and Concerns

What you want of this knowledge and the thought pattern you have, the understanding you have; the responsibility of that guide is to break everything down. Everything in his testing to confuse everything so that you begin to surrender all of that. All of the busy thoughts, all of the questioning, all of the doubt, all of these concerns that you have, *tasleem* (submit). 'Pray upon your Lord and submit', and everything of Islam is submit.

فَصَلِّ لِرَبِّكَ وَانْحَرْ (٢)

*108:2 – "Fasali li rabbika wanhar." (Surat Al-Kawthar)*

*"So pray to your Lord and Sacrifice/ Submit." (The Abundance, 108:2)*

How you can submit to Allah ﷻ if you can't even submit to yourself first? You are still struggling with yourself. So then they teach, submit. Why you have to doubt, why you have to have so many questions? Why you have to say something? Just submit, submit. And you begin to fight and struggle with yourself; no, no, I want to say something, I want to do something different. I don't want to be like them. If they are all wearing white, I'm going to wear yellow and if they are all wearing yellow I'm going to wear red. Just completely keep changing and fighting the self until you can *tasleem*, and *tasleem*, until you begin to shut off all your faculties.

## Attune to the Masters of Light and Energy

Then that master violinist, once he puts these strings, he tunes every

string with his own hands. As a result of tuning every violin, then they show him put like 30 violins on the shelf. As soon as he plays one violin, they all vibrate, because he made them, he tuned them, he perfected them. As soon as he 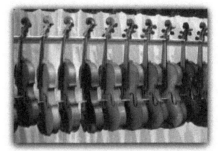 plays one cord, they are all resonating on the same cord. As soon as he plays the next cord, they are all resonating. He can play 30 to 40 of them with one he is playing and they are all vibrating.

It is just an analogy, that when they break down the character, break down the ego, break down all of that identity, then you begin to *tasleem* in the Ocean of *Tasleem* (submission). Then they begin to build the student back up.

## Real Masters Feed You Like Mother From Knowledge and Wisdom

They build the student back up with that *muhabbat* and with that love that the student has. He begins to take from the Shaykh *ilm al laduni wa hikmati bis salihin.* (Heavenly Knowledge and the Wisdom of the Righteous). It means he is now being breastfed by that reality. When he is taking from his Shaykh, he is taking from the two. They say that the mother cannot feed from one side; you would be an oppressor to the body. You have to feed from both sides. In *ruhaniyat* (spirituality), you are taking from the milk and the reality of the Shaykhs. Milk represents heavenly knowledges and realities that are coming.

Just like the *shari'ah* (Islamic Jurisprudence) in *dunya* that if you put your child onto another woman to drink, that woman becomes a mother for the child and your children cannot marry from that family. It means Allah ﷻ want us to understand. When Allah ﷻ doesn't care the wing of a mosquito for *dunya*, there must be a deep reality. That if that child takes the milk and drinks from her, she is responsible now like a mother. She is a mother for him. So it carries all of its motherly responsibility.

What do you think then about the spiritual reality? That once you've been brought down, the ego has been brought down, all of the business is brought down, they are going to begin to feed you. And it has to be a balanced feed, where they don't just throw out knowledges but there has to be training on *hikmah, hikmati bis salihin* (wisdom of the Righteous).

Which now you don't see anywhere because you hear and see people speak with absolutely no *hikmah* (wisdom). They just say things that are irrelevant to the crowd, irrelevant to the audience. They don't care how the heart of those people are going to be affected. The knowledge could be hard and immediately shock everybody in the room and want to leave Islam; or it could be so crazy, beyond the capacity of the person to understand because they take a book and they read it.

## Inherit From the Tongue of the Truthful, Most High

So then Allah ﷻ says, 'No, whom We gave *ilm al laduni wa hikmati bis salihin*, he has been granted the greatest gift of the Heavenly Presence, because he inherits from *lisan as-sidiq al aliya*.' (Holy Qur'an, 19:50)

وَوَهَبْنَا لَهُم مِّن رَّحْمَتِنَا وَجَعَلْنَا لَهُمْ لِسَانَ صِدْقٍ عَلِيًّا ﴿٥٠﴾

*19:50 – "Wa wahabna lahum min rahmatina wa ja'alna lahum lisana Sidqin 'Aliya." (Surat Maryam)*

*"And We bestowed of Our Mercy on them, and We granted them lofty honour from/on the tongue of truth." (Mary, 19:50)*

In *Surat Maryam* Allah ﷻ describes, 'To inherit from the tongue of the *sidiq al Aliya*.' The tongue of the *siddiqs* most high, because that tongue gives *ilm al la duni wa hikmati bis salihin*. It means you'll be given divinely knowledges and the wisdom and the character on how to use it so that that knowledge never harms anyone, never causes a confusion to anyone, but is a means in which to uplift and to raise people.

## Hold Tight to the Rope of Allah – *Habl* حبل

The guides begin to teach that when Allah ﷻ, these are all from Holy Qur'an and *hadith*, when Allah ﷻ is saying, 'Hold tight to the rope of Allah ﷻ.'

$$وَاعْتَصِمُوا بِحَبْلِ اللَّهِ جَمِيعًا وَلَا تَفَرَّقُوا ۚ (١٠٣)$$

*3:103 – "Wa'tasimo bihab lillahi jamee'an wa la tafarraqo." (Surat Al-Imran)*

*"And hold firmly to the rope of Allah all together and do not separate."*
*(Family of Imran, 3:103)*

*Habl* حبل – *ha* ح , *ba* ب , *lam* ل. Hab and *hub* حُبْ، حَبْ , are written the same way in Arabic. What is *hablillah*? One understanding from their understandings, the rope of Allah ﷻ is a *hab*, is a *hub*, and the *hub* points to the *lam*. It means accompany these people who are lovers of Sayyidina Muhammad ﷺ and they are inheriting from this *Lisan al Haqq* (Tongue of Truth).

165

*Habl* حبل (Rope) = *ha* ح, *ba* ب , *lam* ل

*Habl* حب ل = (hab and hub) حب + *Laam* ل *(Lisan al Haqq)*
       = Love + Tongue of Truth

Allah ﷻ says, 'Hold tight to them and don't ever separate.' They carry *hub*, they carry from the *ha*, the Oceans of *Hayat;* they carry from the *ba* = *Bahr al Qudra*. Where all of Qur'an is in 30 *juz* (parts), all 30 *juz* in *Fatiha*, all of *Fatiha* in *Bismillahir Rahmanir Raheem*, all of *Bismillahir Rahmanir Raheem* is in *ba*.

*Habl* حبل – Rope

=*ha* ح, *ba* ب , *lam* ل

*Ha* ح = *Hayat* حياة – Oceans of Ever Living

*ba* ب = *Bahr ul Qudra* بحر القدرة – Ocean of Power

Those *Awliyaullah* (saints), they carry that *ba* ب ; they carry the secret and the reality of Holy Qur'an. Allah ﷻ dressed them from the *ha* ح because they are the people of *hayat*, dressed them from the Oceans of *Hayat* (ever-living). These are *Ahbab an Nabi* ﷺ (lovers of Prophet ﷺ) and they are the lovers of that *lisan al Haqq*, the tongue of Sayyidina Muhammad ﷺ. As a result they are the ropes of Allah ﷻ on this earth, *Hablilallah*.

## The Masters Attune You to Their Vibration and Raise Your Light's Frequency

And Allah ﷻ says, 'Hold tight to them and never separate.' As a result of holding tight to their reality, whatever they are reciting, once they broke your frequency down, they build back your frequency. It means every association with them is building back your frequency to their frequency, not to your frequency.

So when you empty your cup, they begin to transmit, whether they are vibrating from their tongue and their teachings or in their *zikr*. When they make a *zikr*, the vibration and the energy of their *zikr* is not the

same as your *zikr*. Their vibration is at a speed that is not imaginable. We gave that example in *Laylat al Qadr* (Night of Power). If you just take one of these people of *Ahl al Qadr* (People of

Power), Allah ﷻ multiplies their *amal* (deed) by 30,000. Their 'Allah' is 30,000 of your 'Allahs', if you meet one of these *Ahl al Qadr* from *Laylat al Qadr*.

So it means every *zikr* they are doing is changing the frequency of your light. So people who have their little brain and they see that in science. They see that you can change a frequency and things begin to change. They can take a frequency and they find the frequency of this wood, they play the frequency and this wood shatters. In the old days they had an opera singer who would sing a high note and the glass

went pow and shattered! We have to understand the science of this because the science of it is proving it to you.

## The Truth Shatters the False Level of Your Energy

So everything has a sound and a frequency. Those whom their lives are emanating at angelic frequencies, as soon as they are reciting, everything is being shattered. Every falsehood, when Allah ﷻ describes, 'When the truth comes, falsehood, *zahuqan*, is perishing.'

وَ قُلْ جَاءَالْحَقُّ وَزَهَقَ الْبَطِلُ، إِنَّ الْبَطِلَ كَانَ زَهُوقًا (٨١)

*17:81 – "Wa qul jaa alhaqqu wa zahaqal baatil, innal batila kana zahooqa." (Surat Al-Isra)*

*"And say, "Truth has come, and falsehood has perished. Indeed falsehood, [by its nature], is ever perishing/ bound to perish." (The Night Journey, 17:81)*

It means that the false level of your energy, that which you listen to, that which you build yourself, that which you are emanating in, in their presence, *zahuqan* (perishing).

## The Power of Vibration of Prophetic Praise and Intercession

We were reading the *salawat* of Prophet ﷺ that he is *muhyil qulubi wa mahyi dhunubi* (O' Reviver of the hearts, O' Eraser of the Sins).

يَا مُحْيِي الْقُلُوْبِ، يَا مَاحِي الذُّنُوْبِيْ ، سَلَامٌ عَلَيْك

*"Ya Muhyil qulubi Ya Mahidh dhunubi Salaam 'Alayk"*

*"O the reviver of the hearts, O the eraser of the sins, Peace be upon you."*

That in the presence of Prophet's ﷺ energy, *Mahyi* مَاحِي means that he is going to devastate every incorrectness. He crushes it with his light as a grand intercession for all creation because the frequency is what controls. When the frequency and the *hamd* (praise) and why Prophet ﷺ is *MuHamd* (most Praised) is when the *hamd* of Prophet ﷺ comes, the vibration of that *hamd* annihilates everything. Right, the science of it, that if Prophet's ﷺ *hamd* comes upon you, it means make one *salawat*, Prophet ﷺ said, 'I'm going to make ten *salawats* upon you.'

عَنْ أَنَسِ بْنِ مَالِكٍ رَضِيَ اللهُ عَنْهُ، قَالَ: قَالَ رَسُولُ اللهِ ــ صلى الله عليه وسلم ـ:
" مَنْ صَلَّى عَلَيَّ صَلَاةً وَاحِدَةً، صَلَّى اللهُ عَلَيْهِ عَشْرَ صَلَوَاتٍ، وَحُطَّتْ عَنْهُ عَشْرُ
خَطِيئَاتٍ، وَرُفِعَتْ لَهُ عَشْرُ دَرَجَاتٍ "

*Qala RasulAllah (ﷺ): "Man Salla `alaiya Salatan wahidatan, Sallallahu
`alayhi `ashra Salawatin, wa Huttat `anhu `ashru khaTeatin, wa ruf`at lahu
`ashru darajatin."*

*Prophet Muhammad (pbuh) said: "Whoever sends blessings [Praises] upon me,
God will shower His blessings upon him ten times, and will erase ten of his sins,
and elevate [raise] his [spiritual] station ten times." (Hadith, recorded by Nasa'i)*

So, *Durood Shareef* (praising on
Prophet Muhammad ﷺ) is
heavy; it is going to put you to
sleep this energy, so try to stay
awake. When this energy hits
you, upon your being,
everything about your frequency

will shatter and be rebuilt back up, shattered and be rebuilt back up,
rebuilt back up, rebuilt back up.

## The Transmission of Light Between Remote and TV

Now the reality is whether the guides praise physically or they praise
through their heart, Allah ﷻ wants us to know through technology.

They say, 'Shaykh how is this
possible? How is it possible that
you have a television remote and
with this remote you click and
you change all the channels of
your TV?' You can do it because
this television remote is an
infrared light, a specific spectrum
of light on the red; and the TV

has the same device inside of it so the two can communicate. If Toshiba can build that, you don't think Allah ﷻ builds better?

## Guides Build Within You a Specific Frequency of Their Own Light

When you resonate at the frequency of the Shaykh and they build you up with these *murshids* and these guides, they build it within you, a specific frequency of light that they are resonating in. They have the ability to begin to flip the switches, flip the switches inside. They are more powerful than the TV remote; TV remote you change, I can change it to 7, I can change to 13 and don't need the permission of the TV, just, click, click, click, click. What you think then about what Allah ﷻ gives to the heart of His believers? And those who have control of their energies and their lights; that is the attunement.

If you are switching constantly on a different channel because your thought is always going in a different place, that is why the breakdown. Break it down until the person is in *tasleem;* they are like the TV waiting for the channels to be changed. Then the frequencies of the Shaykhs are coming out. So don't say and don't think it's far too difficult. How the remote is sending a frequency?

Their frequencies and their powers are much more powerful. And they are reaching into the heart of people, not only in their presence, but they can reach them anywhere on *dunya* (earth). Their light communicates beyond even *dunya*, beyond space, and time cannot confine their energy because they are in the Oceans of Love. They can talk to those who passed away thousands of years ago. Because the light and the power of light is something that is unimaginable.

## Transmission of Energy Like the Bluetooth Technology

So it means not only do they begin to change your frequency, then even in their presence, they don't need to speak and this is what Allah ﷻ wants us to understand from Bluetooth. Bluetooth technology is that your telephone could be 30 feet away on a speaker but, because the device inside the speaker has an ability through that blue light and blue light technology, through your phone, you click like this on  your phone. All of a sudden this sound from your phone is in the air, nobody can hear it. The speaker hears it and begins to recite.

What do you think then about *awliya*? They are rebuilt by Allah 🕌 with Bluetooth technology, one on themselves and one on all their  students. The one from their self is then from their Shaykh. Their Shaykh is playing the *suhbat* (discourse) at that time. He looks through his inventory, 'We are going to talk about this, click, ding,' and the Shaykh here starts talking, right? You are the speaker. When you are in *tasleem* because he is teaching the student because he has been taught. When he is in *tasleem*, his ears are submitting, his eyes are submitting, his breath is submitting, his tongue is submitting. Everything is submitting; he is like a speaker for them. They merely pick the playlist and when they play it, that speaker is playing.

And at the same time, they are training all the students that are in their association be in *tasleem*, submit, submit. The more you submit, the more that light can come to you, the more that energy can come to you and they don't even have to say anything. The energy and the frequencies that are  emanating from the heart and from their soul are by Bluetooth going and hitting onto your speakers. You may hear it and nobody in the room heard a sound.

## Technology Gives Us a Glimpse of Heavenly Technology

Isn't that what happens with the speaker? If I play it, nobody heard the *salawats* going through the phone and going out. But as soon as the speaker heard it, it begins to play it. With these technologies Allah ﷻ is not saying that you become *bud parast* (idol worshiper) and you're worshipping these speakers and these technologies and you walk around with all your phones and all your devices.

أَلَمْ أَعْهَدْ إِلَيْكُمْ يَا بَنِي آدَمَ أَن لَّا تَعْبُدُوا الشَّيْطَانَ ۖ إِنَّهُ لَكُمْ عَدُوٌّ مُّبِينٌ (٦٠) وَأَنِ اعْبُدُونِي ۚ هَـٰذَا صِرَاطٌ مُّسْتَقِيمٌ (٦١)

*36:60-61 – "Alam a'had ilaykum ya bani Adama an la ta'budosh Shaytan. Innahu lakum 'aduwwun mubeen. (60). Wa ani'budoni, hadha Siratun Mustaqeem. (61)" (Surah Yaseen)*

*"Did I not caution you, O children of Adam, that you should not worship Satan - Indeed, he is your clear enemy (60.) And that you worship [only] Me? This is the Straight Path [Muhammadan Way]. (61)" (Yaseen, 36:60-61)*

These devices were meant for us to reach our realities. Allah ﷻ can, when you see this device, do you see how much power you have, what realities you have? Don't worship Toshiba that made this; worship me, Allah ﷻ, *"Wa laqad karamna Bani Adam."*

وَلَقَدْ كَرَّمْنَا بَنِي آدَمَ...(٧٠)

*17:70 – "Wa laqad karramna bani adama..." (Surat Al-Isra)*

*"And We have certainly honoured the children of Adam..."*
*(The Night Journey, 17:70)*

This donkey form, it has a tremendous power from the world of light but if you are only using this body to eat, drink and to produce waste, that life has been wasted. But if you reach to the reality of the soul and understand from *malakoot* that these lights are powerful. That attendance into their association is not like attendance anywhere else. The frequency in which they are emanating and resonating changes the whole association and they can do it by *lisan* (tongue) or by *khafi*, by *qalb* (heart); by *khafi* much more powerful. The full force of their soul is moving out like Bluetooth.

## Importance of Following and Loyalty to the Guides For Attunement

Those that attune themselves, that is why Allah ﷻ and the Ocean of *Itibah* (obedience) and to follow. When you are following loyally and you are in submission, you don't go left and you don't go right; otherwise your speaker is not ever going to be attuned to the right Bluetooth, you are going everywhere. That is why the *turooqs* (spiritual paths), they teach that; that is why we asked about the breastmilk, is that when you take from somebody you are responsible to that one that you took that knowledge from. That one is like a mother. You have a responsibility, you now have a relationship. That is why we don't sit in 50 different associations taking from 50 different mothers; you won't know who is your mother and who is your father.

But that loyalty that they want and what they want to teach from us is that it's going to bring the attunement. When you are loyal and you are in *tasleem* and submitting and you are taking from that milk and from only that reality, you are now being attuned, you're becoming like a

173

speaker. So every frequency that's coming from the Shaykh is then dressing and you are picking up the frequency and all its realities.

We pray that Allah ﷻ dress us and bless us from these lights and from these nights, *InshaAllah*.

*Subhana rabbika rabbal 'izzati 'amma yasifoon, wa salaamun 'alal mursaleen, walhamdulillahi rabbil 'aalameen. Bi hurmati Muhammad al-Mustafa wa bi siri Surat al-Fatiha.*

# Etiquette of Accompanying the Guides and Seeking Heavenly Knowledge

## How to Accompany *Ibadullah* –
## The Ones Whom Allah ﷻ Has Dressed and Taught

*A*lhamdulillah, that the guides are teaching of *Shamsi wal Qamar* (The Sun and the Moon), the way of following and *itibah* (obedience), the way of and reaching towards knowledges. That Allah ﷻ shows us the real way. It means to follow the *shams* (sun) and be like a *qamar* (moon), and efface yourself and be nothing, be nothing, and keep staring at that sunshine, *shamsud duha*.

لَا الشَّمْسُ يَنْبَغِي لَهَا أَن تُدْرِكَ الْقَمَرَ وَلَا اللَّيْلُ سَابِقُ النَّهَارِ ۚ وَكُلٌّ فِي فَلَكٍ يَسْبَحُونَ (٤٠)

*36:40 – "La ash shamsu yan baghee la haan tudrika al qamara wala allay lu sabiqu an nahari wa kullun fee falakin yasbahoon." (Surat Yaseen)*

*"It is not permitted to the Sun to catch up/ reach the Moon, nor can the Night overtake the Day: Each (just) swims along in (its own) orbit (according to Law)." (Yaseen, 36:40)*

It means all the *naats* (praises) that we are reciting, they knew that reality. It is nice to be taught the reality then recite the *naat* and begin to understand that their whole way was the way of the moon. To be a moon, to be nothing. Don't be like the Earth with all of its buildings and its structures. The way of nothingness is to be nothing and to efface.

175

## Reality of Number 18 = 8 Holds the Throne of One King

The relationship that Allah ﷻ wants for us is based on the secret of the nine. That from the ninth chapter of Holy Qur'an, *Surat At-Tawba* the fortieth verse in which Prophet ﷺ describes that he entered into the cave with Sayyidina Abu Bakr as Siddiq ؏.

إِذْ أَخْرَجَهُ الَّذِينَ كَفَرُوا ثَانِيَ اثْنَيْنِ إِذْ هُمَا فِي الْغَارِ إِذْ يَقُولُ لِصَاحِبِهِ لَا تَحْزَنْ ...
إِنَّ اللَّهَ مَعَنَا ۖ فَأَنزَلَ اللَّهُ سَكِينَتَهُ عَلَيْهِ وَأَيَّدَهُ بِجُنُودٍ لَّمْ تَرَوْهَا ... (٤٠)

*9:40 – "...thaniya ithnayni idh huma fil ghari idh yaqolu lisahibihi la tahzan inna Allaha ma'ana, fa anzalAllahu sakeenatahu, 'alayhi wa ayyadahu, bi junodin lam tarawha ..." (Surat At-Tawbah)*

*"... as one of two, when they were in the cave and he said to his companion, "Do not grieve; indeed Allah is with us." And Allah sent down his tranquility upon him and supported him with angels you did not see ..." (The Repentance, 9:40)*

From that 9:40 it opens for us that in the month of *Safar* (second Lunar month) in the power and reality of the *sultanat* of nine; that eight will uphold the throne and there is a *Malik* (King).

وَالْمَلَكُ عَلَىٰ أَرْجَائِهَا ۚ وَيَحْمِلُ عَرْشَ رَبِّكَ فَوْقَهُمْ يَوْمَئِذٍ ثَمَانِيَةٌ (١٧)

*69:17 – "Wal Malaku 'ala arjayeha, wa yahmilu 'Arsha Rabbika fawqahum yawmaidhin thamaniyatun." (Surat Haqqah)*

*"And the angels will be on its sides, and eight will, that Day, bear the Throne of thy Lord above them." (The Reality, 69:17)*

That *Malik*, cannot be described as Allah ﷻ, *laa Sharik*, nothing can hold Allah ﷻ. There is no angel created to hold Allah ﷻ, then you will be saying the angel is more powerful than Allah ﷻ. So that *Malik* and the one who sits upon the seat of authority is Sayyidina Muhammad ﷺ.

## We Are Stamped with 18 = ١٨

That eight and one ١٨ is our whole life and we are stamped with that

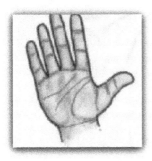

one and the eight on our hands (left palm and right palm) and Allah created perfect symmetry of that reality.

From that understanding of eighteen we look to *Ashaab al Kahf* in *Surat Al-Kahf* (Chapter 18 of Holy Qur'an) and begin the understanding and dress of *atiullah*. Allah wants from us *atiullah, ati ur Rasul* and then how it is taught to us by *Ulul amr*.

يَاأَيُّهَا الَّذِينَ آمَنُوا أَطِيعُوا اللَّه وَأَطِيعُوا الرَّسُولَ وَأُوْلِي الأَمْرِ مِنْكُمْ (٥٩)

*4:59 – "Ya ayyu hal ladheena amanoo Atiullaha wa atiur Rasula wa Ulil amre minkum..." (Surat An-Nisa)*

*"O You who have believed, Obey Allah, Obey the Messenger, and those in authority among you." (The Women, 4:59)*

What Allah wants for us is to be like My *Qamar*, be like the moon and follow the sun. Your eyes should always be upon the light of Prophet ﷺ, the love of Sayyidina Muhammad ﷺ and that is all that should occupy your existence. Don't look left or right.

## Sayyidina Musa ﷺ Wanted to Reach Where the Two Rivers Meet

The guides begin to teach from Nabi Musa (Moses) ﷺ. Why Nabi Musa? Because he is *kaleemullah*, the one who speaks to Allah ﷻ. The example is set so high, from teaching of *Shamsi wal Qamar*, Allah ﷻ begins to teach that I will show you now from the one who speaks to Me, speaks to My Divinely Presence that he is also in need of these realities. Nabi Musa ﷺ wanted from these

realities. That what he had from realities had a '*had* حد', a limit.

حد وَإِذْ قَالَ مُوسَىٰ لِفَتَاهُ لَا أَبْرَحُ حَتَّىٰ أَبْلُغَ مَجْمَعَ الْبَحْرَيْنِ أَوْ أَمْضِيَ حُقُبًا (٦٠)

*18:60 – "Wa idh qala Mosa lefatahu laa abrahu hatta ablugha majma'a al bahrayni aw amdiya huquba." (Surat Al-Kahf)*

*"Behold, Moses said to his attendant, "I will not give up until I reach the junction of the two seas or (until) I spend years and years in travel." (The Cave, 18:60)*

## The Two Rivers Meet at Two Bow Length or Nearer – 'Qab Qawsaini aw Adna'

What he wanted, from what he saw when he asked to see Allah ﷻ, he saw the *ruhaniyaat* of Sayyidina Muhammad ﷺ. And he said this is what I want, this power, this light, this authority. Then I am going set my life to meet where the two rivers meet.

We said the two rivers meet between *laa ilaaha ilAllah Muhammadan RasulAllah sallallahu alayhi wa sallam* because Allah ﷻ doesn't care for *dunya* (material world). It is not the Tigris and Euphrates. What they want is from *malakoot*, the heavenly realm, from the oceans of these realities. It means where *la ilaha ilAllah Ha* ه, *Waw* و, *Meem* م connects and become *Muhammadun RasulAllah sallallahu alayhi wa sallam*. These are Allah's ﷻ ancient realities.

لَا إِلَٰهَ إِلَّا اللهُ مُحَمَّدُ رَّسُولُ اللهِ

*"La ilaha illAllahu Muhammadu RasulAllah."*

*"There is no God but Allah, Muhammad is the Messenger of Allah."*

It means that the secret between *Ha* ه, *Waw* و and *Meem* م, is *Qaba Qawsaini aw Adna*. Where *laa ilaha illAllah* is *la Sharik*, nothing from that ocean of *la ilaha illAllah* but with a *Waw* and the secret of love, it brings *Muhammadun RasulAllah* صلى الله عليه وسلم. It means *laa ilaha illAllah* (on one side) and *Muhammadun RasulAllah* (on the opposite side); this is *Qaba Qawsaini aw Adna*. *"Aw Adna"* أَوْ أَدْنَىٰ is the *Waw* و, that this Creation is the creation of love.

فَكَانَ قَابَ قَوْسَيْنِ أَوْ أَدْنَىٰ (٩)

*53:9 – "Fakana qaaba qawsayni aw adna." (Surat An-Najm)*

*"And was at a distance of two bow lengths or nearer." (The Star, 53:9)*

## ه is for *Hidayat* – Guidance That is Inside the Cave

Where the *Ha* ه comes with *hidayat* هداية directing and pointing to us that the *Ha* of *laa ilaha illAllah*. There is a hidden *Waw* inside the Ha ه; when you make the *Ha* you put the *Waw*

179

within and that is the cave. So the *hidayat* هداية (guidance) is inside the cave and inside the cave are the *Ahlul Muhabbat*, the People of Love, the people of realities that Allah ﷻ dressed them from the oceans of *hayat* (ever-living).

$$إِنَّ الَّذِينَ آمَنُوا وَعَمِلُوا الصَّالِحَاتِ سَيَجْعَلُ لَهُمُ الرَّحْمَٰنُ وُدًّا (٩٦)$$

*19:96 – "Innal ladheena Amano wa 'amilos salihati sayaj'alu lahumur Rahmanu Wudda." (Surat Maryam)*

*"Indeed, those who have believed and done righteous deeds - the Most Merciful will appoint/ bestow/ grant for them Love." (Mary, 19:96)*

## Souls Come to Life in the Presence of *Ibadur Rahman*

Nabi Musa ﷺ wanted that reality. We said it before that he was going in search of that reality and the sign of where he reached was a dead fish that he had to eat for lunch, came to life and jumped into the water. There must be a secret of *hayat* (eternal life) and these are *Ibadur Rahman* (Servants of the Most Compassionate) that Allah ﷻ mentions, *"Alamal Qur'an. Khalaqal insaan."* (Holy Qur'an, 55:2-3).

$$عَلَّمَ الْقُرْآنَ (٢) خَلَقَ الْإِنسَانَ (٣)$$

*55:2-3 – "Allamal Qur'an. Khalaqal Insaan." (Surat Ar-Rahman)*

*"It is He Who has taught the Qur'an. He has created Man."*
*(The Beneficent 55:2-3)*

They carry the lights and the realities and secrets of Holy Qur'an. They have been granted a light from Allah ﷻ that worshipness cannot achieve. It is a grant from Allah ﷻ. Allah ﷻ then describes that things come to life in their presence. The fish is symbolic of the soul and all souls come to life in their reality and in their presence. And he said *ajaban*, the one accompanying Nabi Musa ﷺ saw a dead fish come to life and jump into the water.

قَالَ أَرَأَيْتَ إِذْ أَوَيْنَا إِلَى الصَّخْرَةِ فَإِنِّي نَسِيتُ الْحُوتَ وَمَا أَنسَانِيهُ إِلَّا الشَّيْطَانُ أَنْ أَذْكُرَهُ ۚ وَاتَّخَذَ سَبِيلَهُ فِي الْبَحْرِ عَجَبًا ﴿٦٣﴾

*18:63 – "Qala araayta idh awayna ilas sakhrati fa-innee naseetu alhoota wa ma ansaneehu illash Shaytanu an adhkurahu, wat takhadha sabeela hu fee al bahri 'ajaba." (Surat Al-Kahf, 18:63)*

*"He said, Did you see when we retired to the rock? Indeed, I forgot [there] the fish. And none made me forget it except Satan – that I should mention it. And it took its course into the sea amazingly." (The Cave, 18:63)*

It means these are the realities of the soul. That if the soul dried up and is hopeless and giving up any chance of mercy or swimming in the oceans of *ma'rifah*, Allah ﷻ says, 'No, no, what We have dressed of Our servants,' and that was just one of the servants, that *tajalli* and that light and that dress is upon them and Nabi Musa ﷺ wanted that knowledge.

### *Ibadur Rahman* Are Servants of Allah ﷻ Who Attained Mercy and Heavenly Knowledge

فَوَجَدَا عَبْدًا مِّنْ عِبَادِنَا آتَيْنَاهُ رَحْمَةً مِّنْ عِندِنَا وَعَلَّمْنَاهُ مِن لَّدُنَّا عِلْمًا ﴿٦٥﴾

*18:65 – "Fawajada 'abdan min 'ibadinaa ataynahu rahmatan min 'indina wa 'allamnahu mil ladunna 'ilma" (Surat Al-Kahf)*

*"So they found one of Our servants, on whom We had bestowed Mercy from Ourselves and whom We had taught knowledge from Our own Presence..."*
*(The Cave, 18:65)*

What Nabi Musa عليه السلام wanted was these knowledges and realities. This is an *isharat* (sign) that wherever there is knowledge, Divinely knowledge, *ilm Ladunee wa hikmati bis Saliheen* (Divinely Knowledge and Wisdom of the Righteous). Not people who memorize books, not people who make a translation of one language to the next. They take the Arabic and give the Holy *Hadith* and tell it to you in Urdu and English and people are astonished. They

are astonished because these are the Holy *Hadith* of Sayyidina Muhammad صلى الله عليه وسلم. What the guides are talking about is the realities of these Holy *Hadith* and realities of Holy Qur'an. These Servants of Allah جل جلاله attained mercy, then Allah جل جلاله taught them in their hearts through their *murshids* (spiritual guides).

## The Etiquette of Seeking Divinely Knowledge According to Holy Qur'an

Then Allah جل جلاله begins to describe, 'If you are seeking knowledges like Nabi Musa عليه السلام there is an entire way to achieve that reality; it is not easy to achieve.' It means if you are seeking these knowledges and wish to sit with those who have been dressed by heavenly knowledges, there is an entire *adab* (etiquette) in their company.

### 1. *Itibah* (Follow) – Admit That You Want to Be His Follower

The first thing that Nabi Musa عليه السلام is teaching us is that, 'As soon as I am going, I am admitting to that teacher that I want to be from your *tabi'een* (followers).'

قَالَ لَهُ مُوسَىٰ هَلْ أَتَّبِعُكَ عَلَىٰ أَن تُعَلِّمَنِ مِمَّا عُلِّمْتَ رُشْدًا (٦٦)

18:66 – *"Qala lahu moosa hal attabi'uka 'alaa an tu'allimani mimma 'ullimta rushda." (Surat Al-Kahf)*

*"Moses said to him: May I follow thee, on the footing that thou teach me something of the (Higher) Truth which thou hast been taught?" (The Cave, 18:66)*

I want to follow you, means immediately I am going to take my rank off, anything that distinguishes me of any hierarchy. That in the presence of that teacher, there is no permission to show any hierarchy. This is Nabi Musa ﷺ, this is something that people do not make up, but this is what Allah ﷻ wants.

## Above Every Knower is a Knower

Above Every Knower is a Knower with Higher/More Knowledge. Even Nabi Musa ﷺ was asking for The Muhammadan Reality. Allah ﷻ says, this knowledge and its *azemat* requires certain characteristics. From the one who speaks to My Divinely Presence, how difficult it is that he immediately humbled himself and said, 'If you grant me permission to follow you, *itibah.*' That implies that he could not use his prophecy and he could not use whatever Allah ﷻ had given him in accompanying that one. (It means I cannot use whatever Allah ﷻ has given me in accompanying you.)

It means you cannot tell your dreams to the Shaykh to influence the Shaykh; you cannot tell stories, you cannot have discussions, you cannot give *suhbats* (lectures)*;* you cannot do anything that is going to use your signal with the signal of that guide. There are many different realities in that. There are many different ways that people's egos try to control the guide and teachers. They tell them stories and events and begin to use their connection in the presence of that one. It is not allowed. It is going to block everything and makes everything difficult.

The bar that Allah ﷻ is setting is that My *Kaleemullah/Nabi Musa* ﷺ came and said, 'Let me to be your student. *InshaAllah,* you find me to be patient with you and be taught from what you know of knowledge and *adab* (manners) and characteristics.'

قَالَ لَهُ مُوسَىٰ هَلْ أَتَّبِعُكَ عَلَىٰ أَن تُعَلِّمَنِ مِمَّا عُلِّمْتَ رُشْدًا (٦٦)

18:66 – *"Qala lahu moosa hal attabi'uka 'alaa an tu'allimani mimma 'ullimta rushda." (Surat Al-Kahf)*

*"Moses said to him: May I follow thee, on the footing/condition that thou teach me something of the (Higher) Truth which thou hast been taught?" (The Cave, 18:66)*

## 2. Be Patient – Accompanying These Guides Requires Patience

Then Sayyidina Khidr ﷺ clarifies for us that you are not going to be able to be patient.

قَالَ إِنَّكَ لَن تَسْتَطِيعَ مَعِيَ صَبْرًا (٦٧)

18:67 – *"Qala innaka lan tastatee'a ma'iya sabra." (Surat Al-Kahf)*

*"(The Other) said, Verily you will not be able to have patience with me!"*
*(The Cave, 18:67)*

It means then the biggest characteristic of this path, not the smallest, is *sabr* (patience). Because he knows this is a great prophet of God. Allah ﷻ is giving us an example because this is the highest level to set the standard of the character. There is another secret in why Nabi Musa ﷺ humbled himself. Maybe he was testing Sayyidina Khidr ﷺ? That is for a different time, but tonight they set the standard so high that to be nothing and to approach in that ocean of nothingness that I want to be granted from the knowledges that you have and they begin to teach that it requires a tremendous *sabr, wa ta*

*wa saw bil haqqi wa tawa saw bi-sabr.* The way is based on *haqq*, its bricks are *sabr*, and *sabr* is patience.

$$وَالْعَصْرِ (١) إِنَّ الْإِنسَانَ لَفِي خُسْرٍ (٢) إِلَّا الَّذِينَ آمَنُوا وَعَمِلُوا الصَّالِحَاتِ وَتَوَاصَوْا بِالْحَقِّ وَتَوَاصَوْا بِالصَّبْرِ (٣)$$

*103:1-3 — "Innal insaana lafee khusr. Illal ladheena aamano wa `amilos salihaati, wa tawaasaw bil haqi wa tawaasaw bis sabr." (Surat Al-Asr)*

*"By al 'Asr (the time)! Verily, Mankind is in loss. Except for those who have believed and done righteous deeds and advised each other to truth and advised each other to patience." (The Declining Day, 103:1-3)*

## You Can't Be Patient With What You Don't Know

The next *ayah* (verse) Sayyidina Khidr ؏ tells Sayyidina Musa ؏, who is *kaleemullah.*

$$وَكَيْفَ تَصْبِرُ عَلَىٰ مَا لَمْ تُحِطْ بِهِ خُبْرًا (٦٨)$$

*18:68 — "Wa kayfa tasbiru 'ala ma lam tuhit bihi khubra." (Surat Al-Kahf)*

*"And how can you have patience about things which your understanding is not complete?" (The Cave, 18:68)*

For anyone who is following and trying to take a path of realities and constantly trying to hear something and make a comment; they think they saw something and make a comment. They think they had a dream and make a comment. Many different variables, everybody is at different levels. This way requires everything to be shut off in the pursuit of that knowledge. It teaches that how can you have patience with something where your knowledge is incomplete with it. It means I am going to teach you from a knowledge you don't have. If you don't have it, you are going to be impatient in trying to pursue it. So again established that a tremendous amount of patience that is required.

185

## 3. Do Not Ask Any Questions

If you follow, no questions about anything until I myself speak to you about it.

قَالَ فَإِنِ اتَّبَعْتَنِي فَلَا تَسْأَلْنِي عَن شَيْءٍ حَتَّىٰ أُحْدِثَ لَكَ مِنْهُ ذِكْرًا (٧٠)

*18:70 – "Qala fa ini ittaba'tanee fala tasalnee 'an shay-in hatta ohditha laka minhu dhikra." (Surat Al-Kahf)*

*"[Khidr] He said, Then if you follow me, do not ask me questions about anything until I myself speak to you concerning it." (The Cave, 18:70)*

What you learn in college and schools today is the worst of manners. What you learn in school is to constantly ask the professor, challenge the professor, and examine the professor, which is *tark al adab* (leaving manners) and the worst of manners.

## *Iman* (Faith) is Blind Like Love

Because faith is blind, it is like love. They make fun of this, 'Oh, blind faith, blind faith!' Yes, it is an oxymoron statement. Faith has to be blind because you are not seeing *Iman. Iman* is an action based on love, they don't see love either. Faith has to be and is required to be blind. It means that you believe in your heart the actions are correct, the understanding is correct and when you act on faith Allah ﷻ grants you the *darajats* of *Iman* (Station of Iman). If you have to prove it, that is no longer your *iman*, this is now your *aql* (reasoning). That (*iman*) is involved with something in your heart which is superior and then begin the path.

186

### 4. Be Patient and Don't be Disobedient

Sayyidina Musa ؑ said, *InshaAllah* you will find me to be patient with you, I will accompany you. Everybody knows the story that they came across three tests and each test Nabi Musa ؑ had something to say.

$$قَالَ سَتَجِدُنِي إِن شَاءَ اللَّهُ صَابِرًا وَلَا أَعْصِي لَكَ أَمْرًا (٦٩)$$

18:69 – *"Qala satajidunee in shaa Allahu sabiran wa la a'see laka amra."*
*(Surat Al-Kahf)*

*"[Moses] said, You will find me, if Allah wills, (truly) patient, and I will not disobey you in [any] order." (The Cave, 18:69)*

# The Eternal Tests in the Pursuit of Heavenly Knowledge

### 1. Sayyidina Khidr ؑ Sinks the Boat – Earning *Rizq* (Sustenance)

They came across the boat that the fisherman had and we won't go into depth about that. But the importance is that they came across a

boat and that boat symbolizes *rizq* and sustenance. It means the way in which you are going to achieve your *rizq* or sustenance, there is going to be an issue with it. Sayyidina Khidr ؑ had involvement with that sustenance to lower the boat and not to destroy it, and Nabi Musa ؑ had an issue with it. 'Why are you doing that?'

It means there is going to be an importance in that guidance that is going to deal with our *rizq*, our sustenance. It means how you interact with that teacher and guide, and the knowledges they are conveying, that they are going to be directly involved in your sustenance. They give advice on how to achieve your sustenance. How to lower the importance of that sustenance, how to take it out of your eyes because it is going to block you. Then the *ayah* becomes clear of why that happened.

## Fear of Poverty Blocks From the Pursuit of Spiritual Realities

When Nabi Musa ﷺ asked, 'Why did you break the boat?' because that boat that he was earning his income with, *Shaytan* was after it. It means that your income and money is under the influence of *Shaytan*. It is never going to move towards *Rahman*, because *Shaytan* is going to keep coming to you and whisper, 'It is going to finish, it is going to finish' and you begin to save it, save it, save it. It means that *rizq* is going to be a direct (link). That is why Allah ﷻ is saying that in pursuit of these knowledges these three tests are eternal tests. It was not only for Nabi Musa ﷺ. The pursuit of money is going to block us from the pursuit of realities and the fear of poverty is also going to block us. So already they had a difficulty at that test. 'Why did you have to break that boat?' He described later why they had to break that boat. Again he said, 'I will be patient, I will be patient, please bear with me.'

أَمَّا السَّفِينَةُ فَكَانَتْ لِمَسَاكِينَ يَعْمَلُونَ فِي الْبَحْرِ فَأَرَدتُّ أَنْ أَعِيبَهَا وَكَانَ وَرَاءَهُم مَّلِكٌ يَأْخُذُ كُلَّ سَفِينَةٍ غَصْبًا (٧٩)

*18:79 – "Amma assafeenatu fakanat limasakeena ya'maloona fee albahri faarattu an a'ebaha wa kana wa ra-ahum malikun ya khudhu kulla safeenatin ghasba." (Surat Al-Kahf)*

*"As for the ship, it belonged to poor people working at sea. So I intended to cause defect in it as there was after them a king who seized every [good] ship by force." (The Cave, 18:79)*

## 2. Sayyidina Khidr ﷺ Made the Boy *Zabiha* (Sacrifice)

The next test that the people of knowledges will be involved in your life. And we saw it in our own lives and we see it every day with everything that transpires. They came across a boy and the boy was ordered by Allah ﷻ to be slain. And Sayyidina Khidr عليه السلام slayed the boy and Nabi Musa عليه السلام said, 'That's it, why did you do an extreme injustice against such a pure *ghulam* (servant)?

$$فَانطَلَقَا حَتَّىٰ إِذَا لَقِيَا غُلَامًا فَقَتَلَهُ قَالَ أَقَتَلْتَ نَفْسًا زَكِيَّةً بِغَيْرِ نَفْسٍ لَّقَدْ جِئْتَ شَيْئًا نُّكْرًا ﴿٧٤﴾$$

*18:74 – "Fantalaqa hatta idha laqiya ghulaman faqatalahu qala aqatalta nafsan zakiyatan bighayri nafsin laqad jita shay-an nukra." (Surat Al-Kahf)*

*"So they set out, until when they met a boy, al Khidr killed him.*
*[Moses] said, "Have you killed a pure soul for other than [having killed] a soul?*
*You have certainly done a deplorable thing." (The Cave, 18:74)*

It means here is a big time to *tafakkur* (contemplate) that, in this way of relates everything about us has to be destroyed, there cannot be two in that presence. What they want is everything to be brought down so that that light of Allah's ﷻ Divine Presence, the light of Sayyidina Muhammad ﷺ to shine within us. So what is blocking is 'us'. What is blocking is my 'I-ness', my 'Me-ness', as much as 'I am there', I am distant from that reality.

# Relevance of the Three Tests in Our Spiritual Path

## 1. Don't Run after *Dunya*, Build your *Iman* (Faith)

First we pursued a *rizq*, a sustenance that becomes my whole focus in life. We say like running constantly in the *bazaar* looking for where is the money is. We are the people of being spider, *ankaboot*. You build your web, do your *zikr*,

do the things that Allah ﷻ finds to be beautiful and Allah ﷻ sends the sustenance. There are many who live like that as a *daleel*, as a proof. They do what Allah ﷻ wants them to do and Allah ﷻ sends them and can send from ways you never imagined.

## 2. Get Rid of Your Bad Characteristics/Ego

Then the boy, and it is *nafs al amarah*, the very bad characteristic that constantly is in a naughty condition. Then when Nabi Musa ﷺ complained but he attributed it in words of Arabic that, 'This is a very purified *ghulam*. Why did you do that?' It means it is an *isharat* (sign) for us everybody thinks themselves to be great, that I am very pure, I am very wonderful, why is it that I am coming under attack? Why is it that I am having testing in my life? Why am I constantly under difficulty, I am a very wonderful person.

Sayyidina Khidr ﷺ told Nabi Musa ﷺ about the naughty boy.

وَأَمَّا الْغُلَامُ فَكَانَ أَبَوَاهُ مُؤْمِنَيْنِ فَخَشِينَا أَن يُرْهِقَهُمَا طُغْيَانًا وَكُفْرًا (٨٠) فَأَرَدْنَا أَن يُبْدِلَهُمَا رَبُّهُمَا خَيْرًا مِّنْهُ زَكَاةً وَأَقْرَبَ رُحْمًا (٨١)

*18:80-81 – "Wa amma alghulamu fakana abawahu muminayni fakhasheena an yurhiqahuma tughyanan wa kufra."*
*"Faaradna an yubdi lahuma rabbuhuma khayram minhu zakatan wa aqraba ruhma."*
*(Surat Al-Kahf)*

*"And as for the boy, his parents were believers, and we feared that he would overburden them by transgression and disbelief. (80) So we intended that their Lord should substitute for them one better than him in purity and nearer to mercy (81)." (The Cave, 18:80-81)*

The dialogue that Sayyidina Khidr ﷺ was teaching about the boy, 'No, no, that naughty one is going to be blocking. If you let it to die,

Allah ﷻ will replace it with a *rahmah*, a mercy, something that will be merciful to you.' It means the new reality that is born within somebody is a pure reality that guides us and assists us in reaching towards our realities. It means now the sustenance is going to be after it. The pureness of the inner character and that we stick to it thinking it is a pure *ghulam* and they are teaching from Allah ﷻ that 'No, no, put that down and make a *zabiha* (sacrifice). That character was to be purified.'

## 3. Live a Life of Service and *Khidmat*

Then the last test was the building of the wall. The building of the wall is living the life of service, of *khidmat* and open the reality of *khidmat*. That is why you have to build the wall and you didn't charge? It means everything we do we have to get money for it, you have to live a life of money. But when you look at these *mukhlis* (sincere people), they don't live a life of money, they live a life of service. They serve Allah ﷻ

and money flows from every direction possible, that is not the issue.

$$اتَّبِعُوا مَن لَّا يَسْأَلُكُمْ أَجْرًا وَهُم مُّهْتَدُونَ (٢١)$$

*36:21 – "Ittabi`o man la ya salukum ajran wa hum Muhtadon." (Surat Yaseen)*

*"Obey/Follow those who ask no reward of you (for themselves), and who have themselves received Guidance." (Yaseen, 36:21)*

The issue that Nabi Musa ﷺ was complaining to Sayyidina Khidr ﷺ that, why we didn't charge? He said, 'That is where we are having problems now.'

فَانطَلَقَا حَتَّىٰ إِذَا أَتَيَا أَهْلَ قَرْيَةٍ اسْتَطْعَمَا أَهْلَهَا فَأَبَوْا أَن يُضَيِّفُوهُمَا فَوَجَدَا فِيهَا جِدَارًا يُرِيدُ أَن يَنقَضَّ فَأَقَامَهُ ۖ قَالَ لَوْ شِئْتَ لَاتَّخَذْتَ عَلَيْهِ أَجْرًا (٧٧)

18:77 – *"Fantalaqa hatta idha ataya ahla qaryatin istat'ama ahlaha faabaw an yudayyifoo huma fawajada feeha jidaran yureedu an yanqadda faaqamahu, qala law sheta lat takhadhta 'alayhi ajra." (Surat Al-Kahf)*

*"So they set out, until when they came to the people of a town, they asked its people for food, but they refused to offer them hospitality. And they found therein a wall about to collapse, so al Khidr restored it. [Moses] said, "If you wished, you could have taken for it a payment." (The Cave, 18:77)*

It means this reality of doing something for Allah ﷻ and not asking anything in return for it. Live a life of *khidmat* means serve Allah ﷻ, serve Sayyidina Muhammad ﷺ, do what you have to do and Allah ﷻ will sustain you. Allah ﷻ will take care of you. And at that point Sayyidina Khidr عليه السلام was the first to say that, 'This is enough. I am going to free you from these responsibilities so that Allah ﷻ won't be angry with you.'

قَالَ هَٰذَا فِرَاقُ بَيْنِي وَبَيْنِكَ ۚ سَأُنَبِّئُكَ بِتَأْوِيلِ مَا لَمْ تَسْتَطِع عَّلَيْهِ صَبْرًا (٧٨)

18:78 – *"Qala hadha firaqu baynee wa baynika, saonabbioka bitaweeli ma lam tastati' 'alayhi sabra." (Surat Al-Kahf)*

*"[Al-Khidhr] said, This is parting between me and you. I will inform you of the interpretation of that about which you could not have patience." (The Cave, 18:78)*

## We Must Go Through These Three Tests to Get Our Amanat (Trust)

Sayyidina Khidr عليه السلام said, 'This is where we can go no more.' They open a reality for us that why the *adab* (etiquette) is like that. It means that when we want to achieve what Allah ﷻ wants to grant us of our *amanat*, it is a trust that has been set aside for ourselves. And these three tests are the way to our own *amanat* and if that relationship is

192

built on doubt and constant questioning, it is no longer *iman* (faith). They can give you all the answers, every time you question them and have doubt, they give you an answer, you didn't get granted anything from *iman*. You just got granted a satisfaction in your mind. Allah ﷻ will still test again.

## Faith Requires Patience – Know That Allah's ﷻ Hand is in Everything

It means the way of *Iman* is not something that is needed through the head but through *sabr* (patience). That is why it was clarified at the beginning of the relationship. That, 'Are you sure you want these realities? These are the realities of the Paradises not the knowledges of *dunya*.' The way of Paradise requires *sabr*, an extreme level of faith where whatever is done to you, be patient, because Allah ﷻ knows best. Allah's ﷻ hand is complete *tawheed*.

1. Allah's ﷻ hand is in everything. If He lowers your sustenance don't be distracted by it. As much as you are distracted by it is as much as your attachment to it. Once it loses its attachment from your house all the wealth of the world can be put in front of you and *Shaytan* won't have a share in it because you do everything for the sake of Sayyidina Muhammad ﷺ with it.

2. The second is if you don't allow the character to be *zabiha* (sacrificed) and cleaned then you will always have that bad characteristic, that naughty characteristic which will always be rebellious against Allah ﷻ, rebellious against Sayyidina Muhammad ﷺ and rebellious against *Ulul amr* (saints).

3. If those two characteristics are met the third becomes perfected;

they live a life of service. They do everything, they may work but they eagerly await to serve Allah ﷻ, to serve Sayyidina Muhammad ﷺ and they live a life of *khidmat* (service). So much so that for the people in *khidmat* the people outside keep coming to them asking, 'Why did you do that? Why are you always going there? Why are you always serving there? Why are you doing like this? Who is paying you? Why are they not doing like this?' Because *dunya* (worldly) people do not understand *khidmat*. They only understand that you do something and you get $20 and you do this you get $20, you do this you get $20 but to be paid by Allah ﷻ, that requires a high level of faith, a level of *tasleem*, and submission.

It means that is what was being conveyed and the understanding of the conveyance that when Sayyidina Khidr ؑ said, 'This is enough for us,' that (it is) the way of patience, the way of *itibah* and following guidance and how to take away the bad characteristic of doubt. As much as there is doubt and as much as there is questioning, there is no more a relationship of these realities and that is when the student and the guide part their ways. Because any more time in that will actually be written against the student, because it is no longer faith. It is constant questioning, constant questioning; it is no longer any *Iman* (faith). If there is no *Iman* involved in it, then it becomes detrimental to the growth of that student and that is why at that time they part their ways. You are free to go in your direction and we go back to our direction.

We pray that Allah ﷻ open for us these understandings from this holy month of *Safar;* opens the holy month of *Rabbi al Awwal* and the full sun shining of Sayyidina Muhammad ﷺ that Allah ﷻ grant us more and more understanding, more and more *adab* (manners), more and more love for Sayyidina Muhammad ﷺ and love for *Awliyaullah* (saints) and all of that love to be dressed with patience and *sabr*, *InshaAllah*.

## Three Tests Reflect Nabi Musa's ﷣ Life

The three tests, with a trust for that reality that Nabi Musa ﷣ wanted, means that when you look at the miracle of the path what they test you on is for your *amanat* (trust). It is not a test from the Shaykh. That is what Sayyidina Khidr ﷣ was trying to convey to Nabi Musa ﷣ that, 'This test Allah ﷻ is sending you on is so miraculous; it is a reflection of your life, not my life because:

1. You were thrown into the water in a basket so if you have a

problem of throwing ships and drowning ships, your mom threw you in a basket.' You see this ship this has to do with how your mom threw you in the water. What was the *hikmah* and the wisdom of that? That you will be saved by that basket because Allah ﷻ is great, you have nobody to fear. Allah ﷻ raised you in the hands of your enemy, who wanted and slayed many thousands of children looking for you. Allah's ﷻ greatness is that I am going to make you feed him, clean him, wash him and raise him, because Allah ﷻ is great.

2. 'You have a problem with this boy, but weren't you the one who hit

the guard with your hand to save one from your community? Allah ﷻ wants to show you your own *ma'rifah* within the way of *ma'rifah* because it is your *amanat* that you want, it is your trust, your characteristics that

Allah ﷻ wants to show to you.' It is not about the Shaykh's characteristics; he is merely a guide taking you, be patient, be patient.

3. 'The wall that you were so upset about, you gave the well of Mad'een, you gave water to the ladies that you wanted a wife from one of them.'

It means every test that Allah ﷻ sent was a reflection of your own life. And if we are patient to understand, patient to take the way, we will find that the *amanat* that they set aside for us is the *amanat* that was our inheritance. It means you inherit the pen of realties and then you will be tested all the way to reach towards that reality, to be dressed by that reality. And we pray that Allah ﷻ grant us from these realities and what we were promised on the Day of Promises, *InshaAllah*.

*Subhana rabbika rabbal 'izzati 'amma yasifoon, wa salaamun 'alal mursaleen, walhamdulillahi rabbil 'aalameen. Bi hurmati Muhammad al-Mustafa wa bi siri Surat al-Fatiha.*

# Chapter Five

## How to Acquire Positive Energy

وَ قُلْ جَآءَالْحَقُّ وَزَهَقَ الْبَطِلُ، إِنَّ الْبَطِلَ كَانَ زَهُوقًا (٨١)

17:81 – *"Wa qul jaa alhaqqu wa zahaqal baatil, innal batila
kana zahooqa." (Surat Al-Isra)*

*"And say, Truth has come, and falsehood has perished. Indeed
falsehood, [by its nature], is ever perishing/ bound to perish."
(The Night Journey, 17:81)*

# Control the Five Senses to Open the Soul

The gift of life is such a precious gift, and what the Divine wants for us is to achieve the reality of this life that was given. And many choose the lower existence and the pursuit of the physical desires. And then there are some whom the Divine inspires within themselves that there is a higher reality. That, by a means of coming into this world, you are to discipline yourself to see the majesty, magnificence, and munificence of the Divine soul, the Divine lights that the Divine has created upon the soul.

Then the spiritual paths come and begin to teach the reality of the religious orders and the religious understandings. By disciplining your physicality and bringing the physicality and the physical desires down, they begin to teach us how to bring out the spiritual reality. As much as we listen to the physical ears and take enjoyment from the physical hearing, spiritual hearing can't open. So they begin to train to control what you're hearing and don't let unnecessary sounds occupy the ear because it's going to be a direct effect to the heart.

They begin to teach us in Sufism that everything is based on the heart. Even the physiology of the body has an effect onto the heart. This was from the knowledge of the prophets, then inherited by knowledge of *Awliyaullah* (guides). That's the inheritance of the Prophet ﷺ. Now in science they know that based on what you hear, aggressive loud noises can actually cause an agitation into the heart. They know that certain sounds, when they are beating and the repetition of that sound, begins to cause a difficulty within the heart.

## Discipline the Physical Hearing to Open Spiritual Hearing

They begin to teach us that if you want spiritual hearing to open, then begin the disciplining of your physical hearing. It means all the bad

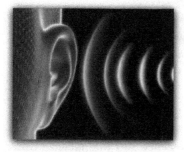

sounds and all the bad gossips and unnecessary noises, those are all *zikrs* (chantings) that are coming into the heart. If it's an agitating sound, it has a direct effect into the heart. If it's nasty, then the soul and body will be accountable for what it is hearing. It will be written on and transcribed into the heart; that the negative and the very vile chanting that people listen to, it's moving into the heart.

It's not by coincidence that the negative and the evil ego comes up with this, because the ego and egoism, *Shaytan* and all the negativity, it doesn't want us to reach our reality. It doesn't want us to reach the goal of our existence here because that's not its goal. Its goal is to play and enjoy the physical world.

The soul comes from above, comes from the heavens. There's no up or down. It comes from the heavens and returns to the heavens.

$$ إِنَّا لِلَّـهِ وَإِنَّا إِلَيْهِ رَاجِعُونَ ﴿١٥٦﴾ $$

*2:156 – "Inna lillahi wa inna ilayhi raji'oon." (Surat Al-Baqarah)*

*"Indeed we belong to Allah, and indeed to Him we will return."*
*(The Cow, 2:156)*

The ego and bad desires, they stay here. Their only interest is in entertainment and playing. And they know that when the power of the soul comes, they are in trouble and they are going to be burned by the power of the soul. So at every stop, it says, 'Listen to this' and begins to put iPods and music and sounds that will directly darken the heart. Then the fasting of the ears and the beginning of the practices of, 'I'm going to listen to spiritual sounds that bring about an enjoyment in my soul that bring about a pleasure and an energy in my soul; and that those other sounds I will be accountable'. They are a chanting from very negative forces that are being chanted upon and trying to darken the soul.

## Control the Physical Eyes

Then they begin to teach control your eyes. If you want the soul to open, then when you look with your physical eyes and your eyes become hungry and they eat and absorb everything. They teach then keep a path of closing your eyes. The  insatiable appetite of the eyes never end. If everything in our lives is based on eyes and what we see we want, it will never end. So then they teach keep a path in which you keep closing your eyes, that what we are looking for is not through the physical eyes.

## Each Sense Has a Dual Nature

As soon as we close each sense, each sense has a dual nature, like the moon. There is a side you see and a side that you don't. You have the outer ear, the physiology of the self, and you have the inner ear. As soon as you close the outer ear, the inner ear becomes more fine-tuned. It means the inner ear begins to hear not the voices of angels first, but the voices of the conscience. The lower conscience locked within us, the higher conscience is in Divinely Presence. And the Divinely lights are telling that conscience, 'Teach them. He came down to earth and he forgot what he has promised Me.' (He or she, it doesn't make a difference.)

It means we have a reality always in Divinely Presence. Only a small part of that light was sent into the physicality. So then the higher reality is always trying to communicate with the lower reality that's locked behind the egoism of the body.

Then they begin to teach that as soon as you close your eyes, then your outer vision stops so that the inner vision of the heart can begin.

It means that with every abstinence and every fasting, its reality will be born. But as much as we indulge in it, that reality will never be born. In old times they would go to the Shaykh and the Shaykh would show a seed. Have you ever seen an avocado seed? It's like a baseball. They take the seed and say, 'Look at the seed. Is it ever going to become anything if I just hold it like this?' They would say, 'No, it's actually going to be a very hard piece of wood. You can use it for baseball, you can throw it at somebody.'

That seed, it can become a tree, which is amazing in itself that where the sprout comes from, that big seed. So then they teach by taking that seed and putting it into the soil. And the reality of the soil is the reality of the physicality because we are made from soil.

## Importance of *Khalwah* (Seclusion)

So Allah 🕉 says, 'You put your sense back in. Go into your soil; put the seed in,' and that becomes the concept of seclusion and *khalwah*. We can make a seclusion in our daily life just by isolating ourselves at times. Having a discipline that at certain times in which, 'I'm going to isolate, not to see and speak to anyone, and just be with myself; thinking of my reality so that the seed can one day be a tree.'

If it becomes a tree, it can one day bear fruits. And those fruits become eternal gifts upon the soul because people are now benefiting from the fruits of your tree. Versus the Divine teaching that most come into this world with the capability; they have the seed and they leave with the seed. They didn't take the time to plant it. And they become immensely saddened by the reality that is lost, because you show up to the Divine with a seed. It didn't become a tree and it bore no fruit.

So all the discipline of the spiritual order, it is not hocus pocus. It's a very defined science and matches the science that is known in this *dunya* (earth), not their hypothesis that they keep guessing and hope one day that they'll be right, but the proven ones.

Then abstaining in the hearing to open real hearing; abstaining in the vision to open the real vision of the soul. What we are seeing is an illusion. All these atoms are moving and none of it is real. As soon as you witness with the soul, the soul can witness what Allah 🕉 wants it to witness.

## Control the Breath

Then they begin to teach to control your breath. That make with your

breath the chanting of the Divinely Presence. Your life is based on breath. The extent and the time of your life is based on how many breaths you have. So no need for all the life insurance and all the big plannings. It is better to sit and make *zikr hadra* (Hay, Hay, Hay (Name of Allah 'ﷻ)). That is why they call *Nafas ur Rahmah* – the Breath of Mercy. Because Allah's 'ﷻ saying, 'Before you make big plans and how long you're going to live here, how you're going to spend your money, you still haven't thanked Me for the breath you have. And you may have 1 breath left, 10 breaths left, 70,000 breaths left; so make them in My remembrance.'

Then you have energized and opened the reality of your breath. So then all the *tariqas* (Islamic spiritual paths), they are all based on breathing; consciousness of the breathing, importance of the breath, the power that's coming in with the breath. Then when you look to the lungs, you see it is a tree upside down, and that is the tree of life. Before you can reach the lote tree of the furthest boundary, Allah 'ﷻ

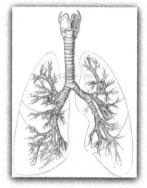

says, 'Before you can make the external *mi'raj*, you have to make your internal pilgrimage.'

Before you can find that bodi tree and that reality, the Divine says, 'It exists within you.' The tree that are the lungs. What is happening when we are breathing is that energy and that light is coming in, nourishing the blood and the first place that blood goes is to the heart. It doesn't go to any of the other organs. That breath comes in and stamps the blood. It takes all of the energy it needs from the breath and then that blood goes to the heart.

Then *tariqa* and Sufism says, everything is based on the heart. If the heart is pure, it takes that blood and then stamps it with 'Allah', with the *zikr* (remembrance) of the Divine, and then moves to 11 essential organs. If the heart is dirty, and the breath coming in contaminated, all of the being is going to be then made dirty from all the dirty blood flowing. It means if the reservoir is filthy and filled with *najas* and dirtiness, whatever you pour into it will sicken everything that comes in contact with it.

Then *tariqa* comes and says, that is the reservoir of your entire being. Why you want to focus on your leg and your head and your back and this chakra and that chakra? The main reservoir of your physiology, not hocus pocus of your physiology, is your breath coming in, going into your lungs, your blood into your heart. If that heart is sick, Prophet ﷺ described from holy *hadith*, 'If one part of you is sick, all of you will be sick' and said, 'that one part is the *qalb* (heart).'

أَلَا وَإِنَّ فِى الْجَسَدِ مُضْغَةً إِذَا صَلَحَتْ صَلَحَ الْجَسَدُ كُلُّهُ، وَإِذَا فَسَدَتْ فَسَدَ الْجَسَدُ كُلُّهُ، أَلَا وَهِى الْقَلْبُ

*"Ala wa inna fil Jasadi mudghatan idha salahat salahal jasadu kulluho, wa idha fasadat fasadal jasadu kulluho, ala wa heyal Qalb."*

*"There is a piece of flesh in the body, if it becomes good (reformed) the whole body becomes good but if it gets spoiled the whole body gets spoiled and that is the heart."*
*Prophet Muhammad (pbuh)*

205

And that same part, the heart, if it's purified, the Divine says, 'Then I'm not in heavens and I'm not on earth; but I'm in the heart of the one who believes in Me.'

*"Maa wasi`anee laa Samayee, wa la ardee, laakin wasi'anee qalbi 'Abdee al Mu'min."*

*"Neither My Heavens nor My Earth can contain Me, but the heart of my Believing Servant." (Hadith Qudsi conveyed by Prophet Muhammad (pbuh))*

*"Qalb al mu'min baytur rabb." Ka'bah – Heart of Believer*

*"The heart of the believer is the House of the Lord." (Hadith Qudsi)*

It means *"qalb al mu'min baytullah."* The Divine's saying that's such an important organ that if your purify it, you wash it, you cleanse it, you circumambulate around it, it will become My Divinely house within your being. It means you will have a 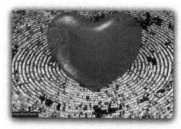 *Ka'bah* within your soul, your very own *Ka'bah* that you wash, you clean, you purify and you begin to make your *tawaf* (circumambulation) around your heart; because Divinely light is now like rays of sun dressing your heart.

## Open the Taste of the Reality

So then hearing with reality, begin the seeing of reality, the breathing of reality and then opening up now the touch and the taste of reality. That if everything is working on the level of the soul, that it's now hearing its conscious orders, because of discipline, it can hear what it's supposed to do and it doesn't keep making crazy choices. When we want to see our life, how out of whack we are, is that when we listen to our self, how we are always falling short and making very crazy choices and seem to have a very chaotic life.

206

Then they begin to teach that as you begin to discipline, discipline, discipline, you are hearing now the co-ordinance and those co-ordinance are coming from the Divine. As you are abstaining with your vision and looking for the vision of the soul, your lights are going on and you begin to be inspired within your heart. And the real vision and the real purpose of our being here becomes more and more clear. 'I'm not being sent here to be in a doughnut shop'. We have not been sent here to do all these different jobs we do. But once we are inspired and understand what is the reality of the soul, what is the mission and the purpose that I have been sent here. And then I open the ability to hear, to see and to breathe with reality; then I begin to taste the reality.

## *Zikr* (Divine Chanting) Empowers the Soul

At the level of the soul then opens the reality of light; and the reality of light is different from the reality of physicality. In the physical world, we see this room with 60 people sitting around doing their best to chant. In the world of light, these are 60 souls and millions of other lights. And as soon as they begin their chanting, the energy that begins to dress their souls, begins to dress all the souls.

All those energies, they have no boundaries. We have our boundaries – you can't sit on somebody's lap; he's not going to appreciate it. Physicality has boundaries. But once you begin to open from the reality of the soul, your light is everywhere. And the light of many beings are present because it's a holy association gathering for chanting. And as soon as they begin chanting, there is a fierce Divine light that begins to dress the souls and they begin to wash and cleanse and bathe within that light, purify themselves, dress from realities that are unimaginable in their dressing.

الَّذِينَ آمَنُوا وَتَطْمَئِنُّ قُلُوبُهُم بِذِكْرِ اللَّـهِ ۗ أَلَا بِذِكْرِ اللَّـهِ تَطْمَئِنُّ الْقُلُوبُ (٢٨)

*13:28 – "Alladheena amano wa tatma'innu Qulobu hum bidhikrillahi, ala
bidhikrillahi tatma'innul Qulob." (Surat Ar-Ra'd)*

*"Those who believe, and whose hearts find satisfaction in the remembrance of
Allah. for without doubt in the remembrance of Allah do hearts find satisfaction."
(The Thunder, 13:28)*

And then when the chanting and the program ends, those souls go
back fully loaded, fully energized, fully dressed with an ability to
empower themselves more to conquer themselves of all the desires
we've already talked about.

فِي بُيُوتٍ أَذِنَ اللَّـهُ أَن تُرْفَعَ وَيُذْكَرَ فِيهَا اسْمُهُ يُسَبِّحُ لَهُ فِيهَا بِالْغُدُوِّ وَالْآصَالِ (٣٦)

*24:36 – "Fee buyotin adhina Allahu an turfa'a wa yudhkara feeha ismuhu
yusabbihu lahu feeha bil ghuduwwi wal asal." (Surat An-Noor)*

*"(Lit is such a Light) in houses, which Allah hath permitted to be raised to
honour; and that His name be mentioned therein: In them He is glorified in the
mornings and in the evenings, (again and again)." (The Light, 24:36)*

But if the soul doesn't take from that energy, it is virtually impossible
to come against all the other desires of the body. Because the hearing
desires are so overwhelmed by negative surroundings. We are talking
about 1,000 negative sounds versus one holy association for a nice
sound. We are talking about millions of negative visions and images

that everything is popping up to us versus sitting and meditating. Most people can't do that for five minutes, versus how many minutes a day you look at negative and horrible images? It means the overwhelming tide of negativity is to darken all the senses.

## With Energy of *Zikr*, Soul Controls 5 Senses & Fights Back Negativity

So then they begin to teach, by these associations, an immense energy is released. The soul becomes loaded with that energy and goes back and now has more ability to fight against its desires. And again, to push down the negative desires so that it can come out, it can come out, it can come out until enough of those associations and the tide flips; where the power of the soul is enough to begin to push down and take control.

Then it has control and abstains from hearing negativity. It has control and abstains from seeing negativity. It has control and abstains from breathing in negativity. And begins to harness the reality of the breath, of pulling every energy out of that breath and igniting it to its reality. And then abstaining with the tongue and not speaking negativity and purifying to represent the reality of the soul.

## Pray for Gift of Faith and Coming to *Zikr* Associations

It means then *tariqa* (spiritual path) comes and spirituality comes with a big reality for the lights and for the reality of the soul. And we pray that on these nights and on these days that the biggest gift the Divine can give us, is the gift of faith. That to create that love and that yearning within our heart, to keep coming and to keep doing. For a day may come when the Divine takes that and we find ourselves not wanting to do and not wanting to go. It's not our cleverness that not wanting to go and not wanting to do.

اسْتَحْوَذَ عَلَيْهِمُ الشَّيْطَانُ فَأَنْسَاهُمْ ذِكْرَ اللَّهِ ۚ أُولَٰئِكَ حِزْبُ الشَّيْطَانِ ۚ أَلَا إِنَّ
حِزْبَ الشَّيْطَانِ هُمُ الْخَاسِرُونَ (١٩)

*58:19 – "Istahwadha 'alayhimush Shaytanu fa ansahum Dhikra Allahi,
Olayika hizbush Shaytani, ala inna hizbash Shaytani humul khasiroon."
(Surat Al-Mujadila)*

*"The Evil One has got the better of them: so he has made them lose the
remembrance of Allah. They are the Party of the Evil One. Truly, it is the Party
of the Evil One that will perish!" (The Pleading Woman, 58:19)*

It is a gift and a *ni'mat* from the Divine (to go to these associations).
It's a gift that somebody gives you a diamond and if you know the
value of it, you are constantly thanking God that, 'Don't let that faith
to go from me; don't let that love to go from me. Don't let that
yearning that you placed into my heart to be taken by the thieves of
the heart.' And then I find myself cut from that line and cut from that
blessing.

So always, always asking that, 'Please don't lift that mercy from me and
increase my yearning to move towards Your Divinely oceans and to
open the reality of the soul.'

*Subhana rabbika rabbal 'izzati 'amma yasifoon, wa salaamun 'alal mursaleen,
walhamdulillahi rabbil 'aalameen. Bi hurmati Muhammad al-Mustafa wa bi siri
Surat al-Fatiha.*

# Energy Meditation – Timeless Reality – Control Faculty of the Head

### The Journey Doesn't End at Physical Purification

We want to achieve a rank of purification for the physicality. The journey doesn't end with the purification of the physicality; it is merely a beginning, in which to reach towards our timeless reality. The timeless reality is the soul and that soul is governed by, and its energy, is going to be love. The guides teach us that how to open that reality is what is important. Then heart and love, the seed of love is the heart. So every direction you look, you have to come back to the heart. What they want for us to understand is the spiritual and the physiology of the body. That is because you are trying to achieve a rank by disciplining the physicality, to open the reality of the heart, the spirituality, the base of the soul which is based off of love.

### The Testimony of Oneness – *Shahada*

Then the guides teach because it is an eternal loop. In the beginning phase the head has to be in submission. So the first *zikr* is *laa ilaha ilAllah* (there is no God except Allah). *Laa* ﻻ – you bring your energy to the forehead, *ilaha* ﺍﻟﻪ – to the right (side of chest) *ilAllah* ﻻ / ﺍﻟﻠﻪ to the left (the heart). It means the energy is

coming in and moving that energy to the head. Head is *laa*. Then to the right, *ilaha*. And then bringing all the focus of the energy into the heart, *ilAllah.*

# La ﻻ

### الله اله ﻻ IlAllah

### ﻻ Ilaha

So *laa ilaha ilAllah* (energy from forehead, to right side, then towards the heart on the left). So then it is the testimony of Oneness, 'there is nothing but God, there is nothing but Allah.' You can't even say God because they have gods and goddesses. Allah ﷻ has no plural, Allah ﷻ is the Arabic word for the Divinely Presence. It has no plural, no masculine, no feminine. So *laa ilaha ilAllah* (forehead, right, left) to bring into Oneness.

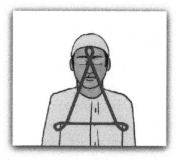

## The Ego Partners with Satan and Hijacks the Head

The guides begin to teach that the only way to open the heart is to

bring the head into submission. So then they begin to teach us, the focus of what we are trying to learn is that the head has to submit. The head is the governing entity of this body, incorrectly. That kingdom that the head has claimed, is through the ego and the partnership of Satan. There can be no partnership with Allah ﷻ, with God, so there is no *sharik* (partner) with Allah ﷻ. What Allah ﷻ

212

is warning us is that your ego is becoming a partner with Satan. And the two of you are coming against My Heavenly Kingdom. My light should be within your heart and My Kingdom should be in your heart, as it is in Heaven. As you want it to be in Heaven and you want to be under My Dominion and in My Kingdom in Heaven, then you must be a mini kingdom of that reality. We must have that light in our heart and the dominance of the Divinely Presence within the heart.

So they begin to teach that Satan and they are in partnership to bring us down. They have hijacked the head. So then our first goal is to decapitate the head, in spiritual terminology not the physical. So by saying, "*Laa ilaha ilAllah,*" it means you are trying to teach yourself there is no importance in my head, that my head is confusing everything. My head is confusing my path. I am contemplating through my head who my Shaykh is, who Allah ﷻ is, *audhubillah*, *astagfirullah*, who Prophet ﷺ is, who my Shaykh is, who my teacher is? Who is everyone? I am putting it through my head. And the head does not have the faculty to know anything.

## 1. Ears Are the First Thing to Discipline

Then the guides begin to teach, if you want to open the heart, focus on the head. Know that the first thing that has to come into discipline is the ears. The ears have to be, 'I heard and I obey, I heard and I obey.'

سَمِعْنَا وَأَطَعْنَا غُفْرَانَكَ رَبَّنَا وَإِلَيْكَ الْمَصِيْرُ (٢٨٥)

*2:285 - "…Sam'ina wa ata'na, ghufranaka Rabbana wa ilaykal masir."*
*(Surat Al-Baqarah)*

213

*"...We hear, and we obey: (We seek) Your forgiveness, our Lord, and to You is
the end of all journeys." (The Cow, 2:285)*

Then we begin to realize how difficult that process is. That is a lifelong
process. It means it doesn't come complete, you have mastered it, and
now you go on. No, because even Allah ﷻ was asking us, 'Don't talk
to Prophet ﷺ by saying, 'listen to me,' but ask Prophet ﷺ to look
at you,' because his ﷺ hearing is in perfection for God, for Allah ﷻ.

...يَا أَيُّهَا الَّذِينَ آمَنُوا لَا تَقُولُوا رَاعِنَا وَقُولُوا انظُرْنَا وَاسْمَعُوا (١٠٤)

*2:104 – "Yaa ayyuhal ladheena aamano, laa taqolo ra'yina wa qolu unzurna
wasma'o; ..." (Surat Al-Baqarah)*

*"O you who believe! Do not say (to Prophet Muhammad (saws)) Raina, listen to
us, and say Unzurna (gaze upon us) and you listen (to him (saws), ..."
(The Cow, 2:104)*

## If You Listen to Yourself, You Submit to Your Ego

Then they are teaching the perfection of hearing is to reach that level
of perfection. So then my focus is on my ears, my ears have to be in
submission. So then how are they going to be in submission if I don't
accompany a guide? Then I am listening to myself and submitting to
myself. It is impossible! That is the *sharik* and that is what God said,
'Watch out for.' How can you be submitting if you are only submitting
to yourself? Your self is already partner with bad desires and what they
call Satan; the bad desires and bad characteristics. So it means you
have to find and seek a guide, a teacher. By listening and trying our
best to submit to their teachings, to their understandings, I am able to
calibrate myself.

## By Speaking, You Negate the Teachings

The most important to listening is not talking. The more you talk, the
less you listen. The ego becomes so big, that as soon as it hears

something, it is going to say five things back as a rebuttal. Because the ego is saying inside, 'Don't tell me anything, I know everything.' So then in the formula for this energy to work, is to open the ears to listen, to listen, to submit. Not where you forcefully submit, but you take the teaching and then you put it upon yourself and say, 'I am going to try my best to submit to that teaching, to take that understanding, to take what is being said for me.' Why? Because I am in need to show my humility to my Lord so that my heart can open, so that my soul can reach its timeless and eternal reality.

Then the guides begin to teach and teach, and interact with them. So as much as that energy is coming to the ears, they said then, 'Put a rock in your mouth,' because as you are hearing, you are going to try to speak. Why? Because your speech is going to negate what he (teacher) just said. So then you didn't go forward and you are going backwards. That is why everything in the way and on the path has tremendous secrets.

## The Ego Makes Us Talk, Not the Soul

Why did Sayyidina Abu Bakr as-Siddiq ☬ put a rock in his mouth? He

is teaching us that as the message is coming, these realities are coming is the father of our way. He says, 'Put a rock in your mouth so as to not speak.' Because the energy that comes, who is going to want to speak? Not your soul, but the bad characteristics, the ego, and Satan within us. The ego and Satan wants for us not to achieve the rank but to fall from grace as he fell, as Satan fell. So it means as much as we are hearing, as much as we are hearing, as much as we are hearing, they recommend, don't speak, don't speak. Take it into your heart. Take it in and digest it, digest it, digest it, and bring that reality into your being.

Then you have to have your internal fight. Now this knowledge and this information comes into your ears and now moves. Who is waiting inside there? The ego and Satan saying, 'What did he just say? No way.' Here we go, *waooo waooo waooo*, like the cartoons, all the different beings are now talking and fighting. We are going to see who comes above. Information comes and you are going to see who came out victorious. You see them the next day, did they come out victorious or the other one won, and the soul was put down and crashed? So then that path is very real, the battle is very real and we experience it on a daily basis.

## The Spiritual Guide Has a Specific Curriculum to Teach

Then hear and don't speak. The guides are not interested in any knowledge or information that you have. Keep it for yourself. This is not a collective resource academy where you bring two things that you know, you bring two things that you know, you bring two things you know, and we put it together like a *kallepache*, a soup with the head; the eyes and ears in one soup and say, 'Ok this is now our reality.' No! They don't care for it.

The guides have a curriculum, a lesson and teaching to be taught for anyone who has the ability to learn. They don't care about any other curriculum; they don't care about any other book and they don't care about any other website. They don't care about anything other than what their Shaykh (teaches them), through their *sami'na wa atanaa* (we listen and we obey).

It means they achieve what they achieved by exactly what they are teaching; they achieved it by reaching a station of listening and obeying. So as the guides listen, they listen only to their Shaykhs; they don't listen to anybody else. If they listen to anybody else that would not be a guide. That would be sort of a political system, everybody votes and puts their opinion and based on the greater opinion then everybody will do something. No, they have a curriculum of spirituality that has to be achieved.

## 2. Keep the Eyes Closed

The guides begin to teach that discipline the ears, and stay silent. As they begin to teach to discipline your ears and begin to understand the teaching, you submit your eyes. Keep a path in which your eyes are

closed. Negate the vision, negate the importance of what you eyes are seeing. Your eyes are seeing everything as an illusion, everything as a deceit. Keep a path in which your eyes are closed and don't fall for all the allurements of this *dunya* (material world).

## Reality of Prophet Yusuf (Joseph) ﷺ and Material World

This was the reality of Sayyidina Yusuf ﷺ that when Sayyidina Yusuf ﷺ was put into the kingdom, and Zulaikha kept running after him. Zulaikha represents the love of *dunya* (material world). Because his beauty was a heavenly divinely beauty. That *dunya* keeps running after and is going to entice him. So what did he ask from Allah ﷻ? 'I think it is better that You put me into jail.'

قَالَ رَبِّ السِّجْنُ أَحَبُّ إِلَيَّ مِمَّا يَدْعُونَنِي إِلَيْهِ ۖ وَإِلَّا تَصْرِفْ عَنِّي كَيْدَهُنَّ أَصْبُ
إِلَيْهِنَّ وَأَكُن مِّنَ الْجَاهِلِينَ (٣٣)

*12:33 – "Qala rabbis sijnu ahabbu ilayya mimma yad 'oonanee ilayhi, wa illa tasrif 'annee kaydahunna asbu ilayhinna wa akum minal jahileen." (Surat Yusuf)*

217

*"He said: O my Lord! The prison is more to my liking than that to which they invite me: unless you turn away their plan from me, I might (in my youthful folly) feel inclined towards them and join the ranks of the ignorant"*
*(Prophet Yusuf, 12:33).*

Not that he was running after her, because she was running after him, scratching him from the back. It means they are going to teach this is a *barakah*, there is tremendous *barakah* (blessing).

قَالَ هِيَ رَاوَدَتْنِي عَن نَّفْسِي ۚ وَشَهِدَ شَاهِدٌ مِّنْ أَهْلِهَا إِن كَانَ قَمِيصُهُ قُدَّ مِن قُبُلٍ
فَصَدَقَتْ وَهُوَ مِنَ الْكَاذِبِينَ (٢٦) وَإِن كَانَ قَمِيصُهُ قُدَّ مِن دُبُرٍ فَكَذَبَتْ وَهُوَ مِنَ
الصَّادِقِينَ (٢٧)

*12:26-27 – "Qala hiya rawadatnee 'annafsee, wa shaheda shaahedum min ahlihaa in kana qameesuhu qudda min qubulin fasadaqat wa huwa minal kadhibeen. (26) Wa in kana qameesuhu qudda min duburin fakadhabat wa huwa minas sadiqeen. (27)" (Surah Yusuf)*

*"He said: It was she that sought to seduce me from my (true) self." And one of her household saw (this) and bore witness, thus "If his shirt is torn from the front, then her tale is true, and he is a liar!"(26) But if his shirt is torn from the back, then she is the liar and he is telling the truth!(27)" (Prophet Joseph, 12:26-27)*

This reality is real; begin the practice of keeping the eyes closed, that nothing from this world is of any benefit for us. As soon as you meditate and keep your eyes closed you are asking Allah ﷻ to go inside.

## Brain Meditation is Hallucination

This is all the way of opening the heart. We said that how could that be popular today? Heart meditation? No, everything is brain meditation; they don't teach you to shut anything off. They teach to hallucinate and visualize

anything you want. They go and spend a thousand dollars and become a master in a weekend, or spend three or five thousand dollars just to open the faculty of the head and hallucinate.

But to come and say, 'No, no, you have to discipline your ears.' Why the ears? Because it is the door to the soul. You have to discipline the eyes because it is the window to the soul. It means for me to pull your soul out it is going to be through sound. That is why as soon as they play the *salawat* (prophetic praising) and begin to meditate, they are able to pull the souls out. The soul comes out like butter because it loves the *salawat*. It loves the praising upon Allah ﷻ and like butter to a knife it begins to move towards that presence because they have that secret.

They teach us then discipline your eyes, begin to take a path of keeping the eyes closed and what I want is not from here, *ya Rabbi* I want from the eternal reality.

## 3. Guard Your Breath, Your Existence Depends On It

Discipline the breath and the importance of the breath, and our whole way is built upon the breath. That my existence is based on the breath. As soon as I am disciplining myself and I understood the importance of hearing, trying my best to hear, try my best to stay quiet. Try my best to not be under the allurement of my eyes, keeping myself closed. Then beginning to listen to these beautiful sounds and praisings upon the Divinely Presence, praising upon

Prophet ﷺ and then breathe.

That when I breathe, then asking to breathe with *Zikr Hu*, where Allah ﷻ says, *Qul Hu* قُل هو, say, "*Hu, Allah*," and everything coming in *Hu, Hu, Hu* [Shaykh demonstrates with saying *Hu* in his breathing] with the *zikr* of Allah ﷻ in the heart and everything is saying, "Allah,

Allah, Allah...."

قُلْ هُوَ اللَّـهُ أَحَدٌ (١)

*112:1 – "Qul Huw Allahu Ahad." (Surat Al-Ikhlas)*

*"Say, He is Allah, The One and Only." (The Sincerity, 112:1)*

All of that to open the power of the breath. It means our reality is based on that breath, our being is based on the breath. The soul's energy is the breath. If you energize the breath, the soul, like a rocket, moves into that Divinely Presence. So then you begin to master the breath, that every breath is with a *zikr*, every breath with a consciousness.

## Your 5 Senses Directly Affect the Heart

If the breath is being mastered, then from these seven openings, the last opening is the tongue. The guides begin to teach that was the tongue that had to be closed because the ears have to be in submission. So keeping a path of silence and silence and silence because they want the focus of this head, for you to begin to understand your heart. Because everything coming through your ears is affecting your heart, we don't know it. As soon as you hear the words, oh, oh, you feel an agitation in your heart.

You start looking at all these different things and you find your heart now leaving Allah ﷻ and running after *dunya* (material world). It is coming from your eyes. If Allah ﷻ took your eyes away, what would you be doing? If tomorrow, God forbid, that Allah ﷻ took your eyesight away there is no more hope of *dunya*, you can't even comb your hair. You will be sitting on your *sajada* (prayer carpet) crying and praying to Allah ﷻ that it is time to go, I don't want to be here anymore.

They are teaching us our psychology that that hearing is directly affecting your heart. Your eyes are directly affected to your heart. Your

220

breath is going to be the consciousness of your heart. If you don't care for your breath, what are all the other things that you are not grateful for? Allah ﷻ says, how many of My Signs are you not grateful for?

$$ فَبِأَيِّ آلَاءِ رَبِّكُمَا تُكَذِّبَانِ (٣٠) $$

*55:13 – "Fabi ayyi alayi Rabbikuma tukadhdhiban." (Surah Ar- Rahman)*

*"Then which of the favours of your Lord will you deny?" (The Beneficent, 55:13)*

So then it opens up gratefulness; it opens up what we call the Breath of Mercy, it is Allah's ﷻ *Rahmah. Ya Rabbi*, thank You for the breath that You gave me, that I breathe it in with a consciousness.

## 4. Most Powerful Opening is the Mouth

All of that is now teaching me in my heart, then they say that now because you are understanding, the last and most powerful opening, is your mouth. If the mouth really has a rock and you try to hold back your mouth from talking back to what he says, and what you have heard, and what you have learned, because everything you are going to nag about it. 'Why is this Shaykh like this? Why this Shaykh said like this? Why that Shaykh said like this?' It is not coming from the soul. It is coming from the ego.

## What You Say Shows What is in Your Heart

As soon as you put a rock in your mouth, now you are becoming conscious of your heart because they begin to teach you when Allah ﷻ says in Holy Qur'an, 'What is in their heart is far greater and far worse than what is manifesting from their tongue.'

$$ ...وَدُّوا مَا عَنِتُّمْ قَدْ بَدَتِ الْبَغْضَاءُ مِنْ أَفْوَاهِهِمْ وَمَا تُخْفِي صُدُورُهُمْ أَكْبَرُ ۚ قَدْ بَيَّنَّا لَكُمُ الْآيَاتِ ۖ إِن كُنتُمْ تَعْقِلُونَ (١١٨) $$

*3:118 – "...wad doo ma 'anittum qad badatial baghdao min afwahihim wa ma tukhfee Sudooruhum Akbaru, qad bayyana lakumul Ayaati, in kunum ta'qiloon." (Surat Al-Imran)*

*"...Hatred has already appeared from their mouths, and what their hearts conceal is far worse. We have made plain to you the signs, if you have wisdom."*
*(Family of Imran, 3:118)*

So now your volcano, they are showing, the fire is within the heart. What is coming from people's mouth is the lava. People think they have a bad mouth and Allah ﷻ says, 'Wait, what is in their hearts is far worse.' So as much as you allow your mouth to erupt, the volcano is becoming stronger and stronger. So here in western philosophy they say, 'Shout, get it out, go and yell at people.' Well, your volcano will become more fierce. The guides want you to shut it, destroy it, suffocate the oxygen from it so that it burns no more. It doesn't give up.

## Working on the Heart through Faculty of the Head

So now we understand that we are actually working on the heart through the faculty of the head. This is the Crown of Creation, if that crown cannot imitate God's Kingdom and He says bring it into submission. As soon as you focus on your mouth and you keep your mouth quiet, you begin to see how much your heart is boiling. Keep silent, keep silent, keep silent, make *sajda* (prostration) and cry to Allah ﷻ, cry that I am frustrated, cry to Allah ﷻ that this is like this, this is like this. Then Allah ﷻ says, *"qul ya naru bardan wa salaamun alaa ibrahim."*

قُلْنَا يَا نَارُ كُونِي بَرْدًا وَسَلَامًا ... (٦٩)

*21:69 – "Qulna ya Naaru, kuni Bardan wa Salaman ..."*
*(Surat Al-Anbiya)*

*"We said, "O fire, be cool and Peaceful upon Abraham." (The Prophets, 21:69)*

Allah 🕮 wants us to know from all the prophets that Sayyidina Ibrahim
🕮 was being thrown into the fire. He 🕮 comes and teaches us that at
this level of what you want, is ask Allah 🕮 that give me a coolness
from this fire. I am angry at everyone and whatever they say to me, I
am very angry from it. I am just a volcano in Your Creation, hurting
everything and everyone. Allah 🕮 says, that is not what I want from
you of Paradise. Hurt no one, stay silent, cry onto Me until I begin to
send that fire down and down and down. Once that is moving, they
are registering and seeing that the ears are reaching submission, the
eyes are leaving the love of *dunya* (material world).

## The Four Enemies That Block the Soul

### *Dunya* (Material World), *Hawa* (Desires), *Nafs* (Ego), and *Shaytan* (Satan)

They say that you have the four enemies that are blocking the soul.
That the love of *dunya* is blocking the soul. The soul has been
quartered into four sections. Why the soul is not whole because of the
four enemies, which are the *dunya* – the love of the material world, the
*hawa* – the seeking of physical pleasure and physical entertainment, *nafs*
(ego) and *Shaytan* (Satan). These four enemies have quartered the soul,
not to be whole. When we begin to focus on these realities we begin to
understand that when the head is submitting, that these realities are
being worked on, it is actually working on the heart. As soon as we
begin to work on the heart, we begin to see if I can keep silent, the
flame and the fire and the agitation within my heart begins to go
down, to go down, to go down, using always the reality of *wudu*
(ablution).

## Make *Wudu* (Ablution) to Wash Away Anger

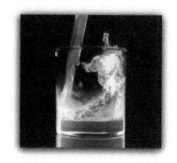

Why Prophet ﷺ said, 'To wash,' is to take the fire. As soon as you are feeling angry go make another *wudu*, go wash and ask, *ya Rabbi*, let the water put away this fire, *qul ya naru konee bardan wa salaamun alaa Ibrahim.*

قُلْنَا يَا نَارُ كُونِي بَرْدًا وَسَلَامًا ... (٦٩)

*21:69 – "Qulna ya Naaru, kuni Bardan wa Salaman ..."*
*(Surat Al-Anbiya)*

*"We said, "O fire, be cool and Peaceful upon Abraham." (The Prophets, 21:69)*

Then the reality of the water begins to take fire away. More important is that every action provides a reaction from Divinely Presence, that as you wash with that intention on your physical being, Allah ﷻ sends a *rahmah* (mercy) on to the soul. Because you can't wash the soul with water, but you provide the action and the *niyyat* (intention) that I am washing with this water to take away the anger that is coming upon my heart. It is not allowing my heart to open.

*Subhana rabbika rabbal 'izzati 'amma yasifoon, wa salaamun 'alal mursaleen, walhamdulillahi rabbil 'aalameen. Bi hurmati Muhammad al-Mustafa wa bi siri Surat al-Fatiha.*

# *Wudu* of the Blood, Heart, and Soul
## The Angelic Force of Water

*lhamdulillah, Awliyaullah* (saints) come into our lives and expand everything. They expand the horizon, expand the understanding, expand the realities from Holy Qur'an, from holy *hadith*. From every aspect of our life, it begins an expansion in realities, that far beyond the world of form, that to understand the world of light, to understand the world of energy, to understand the world of sound. Every aspect of reality is far greater than just the physical, and teaching towards that reality is to be uplifting. If what we are learning is only the physical, it has a limited benefit for the physical body, but there must be a food, there must be a reality that is affecting the soul. And that which you teach in regards to the soul is going to be an eternal dress on the body.

### There Are Different Levels in Every Knowledge

The guides come into our lives and they teach from the Knowledges of *ilma ash-shari'ah, ilmat tariqa*, the *ilma ma'rifah, ilma haqiqa, ilma azema*, (Knowledge of Divine Law, of the Spiritual Path, of Gnosticism, of Reality, and of Allah's Might and Majesty). That in every knowledge there must be *darajats* (ranks) of that knowledge, where most people stay only on the outside.

## 5 Levels of Knowledge in Islam

1. *Shari'ah* (Jurisprudence)
2. *Tariqa* (Spiritual Path)
3. *Ma'rifah* (Gnosticism)
4. *Haqiqa* (Reality)
5. *Azema* (Dedication)

## Knowledge of *Shari'ah* Teaches – How to Make *Wudu* (Ablution)

We gave the example many times, from Mawlana Shaykh's teaching, about *wudu* (ritual washing/ablution). That many teach the *shari'ah* (legal) aspect of *wudu* that you have to wash. How much of that water to use so that it's clean. Then to wash yourself, how to wash yourself so that your hands, your arms, your face, your ears, your feet, your nose, your mouth, everything is covered and washed. And this is from only an introduction of *ilm ash-Shari'ah* (Knowledge of Jurisprudence).

## Other 4 Levels of Knowledge Teach the Angelic Reality of Water

*Ilm at tariqa, ilm al ma'rifah, haqiqa, wal azema* (knowledge of the Divine Law, the spiritual path, Gnosticism, reality, Allah's Greatness), begin to teach that why you have to wash. Because you don't have the right to ask why, but as soon as you are patient in life and take a path towards realities, Allah ﷻ will begin to expand the heart and the teachers begin to teach the reality. That water has a reality within it and that water has an angelic force within it, because Allah ﷻ described that, 'My Throne is on that water.'

## The Divine's Throne is Upon the *Mai* ماء (Water)

وَ هُوَ الَّذِي خَلَقَ السَّمَاوَاتِ وَالْأَرْضَ فِي سِتَّةِ أَيَّامٍ وَكَانَ عَرْشُهُ عَلَى الْمَاءِ لِيَبْلُوَكُمْ أَيُّكُمْ أَحْسَنُ عَمَلًا (٧)

*11:7 – "Wa huwal ladhee khalaqas samawati wal arda fee sittati ayyamin, wa kana 'arshuhu 'alal ma ye liyabluwakum ayyukum ahsanu 'amalan, ..."*
*(Surat Hud)*

*"And it is He who created the heavens and the earth in six days - and His Throne had been upon water - that He might test you as to which of you is best in deed..."(Prophet Hud, 11:7)*

'My Throne is upon that water.' It means they begin to teach that there's a *ma'rifah* (spiritual reality) of that *mai* ماء (water). For the people that know Arabic, *mai* ما is *meem* م, *alif* ا. Everywhere you look must be *La ilaha ilAllah Muhammadur RasulAllah* ﷺ, even in *mai*, there is *Meem* (Muhammad) + *alif* (Allah's *izzat*).

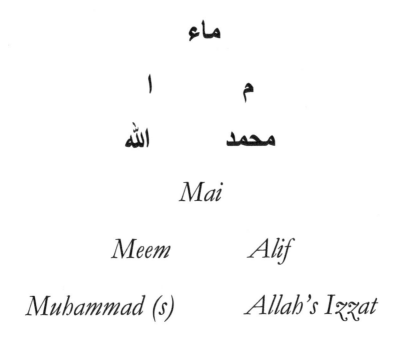

Mai

Meem      Alif

Muhammad (s)      Allah's Izzat

## Water Has an Angelic and a Life Force

Allah ﷻ describes, 'My throne upon that water,' which means, ooh! there must be a secret, and a *ma'rifah* of that water. One basic understanding is its angelic power, and because it's angelic, it's stable. If it was gas, it would be very difficult to work with in life but because of *malaika* (angels), it has a stable force and power. But if you take one hydrogen away, it becomes explosive. That's the degree of its power! All our oceans are

that potential danger. So when you want to know how Allah ﷻ can bring an end to this *dunya* (material world), He merely commands one of the hydrogen, 'Rise,' and all the water itself is explosive. But making it stable is the two hydrogen atoms. If one hydrogen leaves, it's explosive.

So then *awliya* (saints) come and teach us, 'Water is very powerful'. As soon as you leave the water for a certain amount of days, you see a green begin to form. That is the *malaika*, that is the angelic force that shows you that *mai* (water) brings life because the green is the mildew, it's a life force within that.

## *Wudu* (Ablution) Washes Away Burdens and Shields You From Difficulties

Then the guides begin to teach, that now the understanding of *wudu* begins to elevate because you're taught the element in which you are washing. You're washing with a very powerful force, an angelic force. All the difficulties that you acquire throughout the day, because your body is like a bus. We have a body and we have a soul. As soon as we move in the world, every subtle energy can move through you; from microwave, television wave to all the different spiritual beings Allah ﷻ created. They all move through the physicality. They all either occupy the physicality or pass through the physicality.

So what Prophet ﷺ wanted for us was the perfection of energy. But he ﷺ didn't have to describe it, he merely told the Companions. They understood the reality and they taught the *shari'ah* of it, that, 'you wash'. Then for deeper knowledge they went into the *ma'rifah* (spiritual realities) of that. That when we're washing there's an angelic force in that water, a life force within that water; as soon as we put it on, it begins to burn away all difficulty. It begins to wash away all fire and begins to dress you with an angelic light, a shield.

Then they come into our lives and teach that, as soon as you wash, washing your mouth, your face, your hands, your feet, washing all the private parts if you had used the restroom. As soon as you wash, come out and pray *salatul wudu* (prayer of ablution) to seal yourself with your energies.

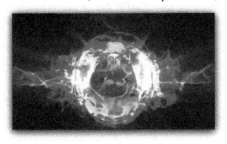

Because as soon as you pray two *rakah* (cycle) *salatul wudu*, that water and angelic force becomes a shield that protects you until the next *wudu*.

## As You Wash the Outside, You Need to Wash the Inner Being

Then they begin, because now you're going deeper into the *ma'rifah* (spiritual reality) of *wudu*, not just, you have to wash and that's it; there are whole oceans of reality. That, why are you washing with that, what power does that water have? Then they begin to teach, as you're washing the body you should be understanding the washing of the

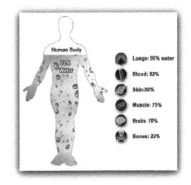

internal reality. The importance of water and that your body is 70% water. So then the water within my being, how am I purifying that water? Then they go into the blood. That the body has 70% water. If we want healing and we want to build our energy, we have to understand why we are washing, dressing by these lights and these realities. As we're washing the outside, we have to be washing the inside. The water inside is the blood. So how do you wash the blood?

## How to Purify the Water Within – The Blood

Prophet ﷺ describes, '*Shaytan* moves through the blood.'

قَالَ رَسُولُ اللَّهِ صَلَّى اللَّهُ عَلَيْهِ وَسَلَّمَ: إِنَّ الشَّيْطَانَ يَجْرِي مِنْ الْإِنْسَانِ مَجْرَى الدَّمِ." صحيح مسلم

*Qala Rasulallah ﷺ: "Innash Shaytana yajri minal Insaani majrad dami."*

*The Prophet (pbuh) said, "Satan circulates in the human being as blood circulates in the body." (Sahih Muslim, 2174)*

That's why the fasting is important. That's why the importance of eating *halal* (permissible), drinking and breathing *halal*. What you breathe is going from your lungs and affects your blood. What you eat will go into your stomach and affect the blood. What you breathe will affect the blood. So then why are they only focusing on the outside washing, and they don't teach the inside washing? The outside is the donkey that going to be buried in the ground, nobody is going to take their body to Allah ﷻ. You are just making the body to be clean in *dunya* so that you can bring out the reality of your soul.

## What You Eat and Drink Affects Your Blood

*Ahle haqqa'iq* (people of reality) come and begin to teach, elevate beyond the kindergarten understanding; that when you're washing, know the reality of that washing, also begin your internal washing. Begin to understand that your blood has to be cleansed. That when you begin to make *du'a* on your food and eating *halal*, your blood is now being washed. When you begin to be conscious of your breath and your breathing, don't put anything into your mouth that is going to contaminate

your blood. Because as you're washing for the body you wouldn't take a feces and put it on your head. So imagine whatever you put in your mouth and put in as a drink or food is going to affect the blood. Then that blood going to go and hit the heart, what they call 'heart attack'. It's attacking the heart.

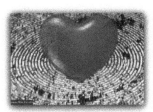

*Qalb al mu'min baytullah* (the heart of the believer is the house of God). So *Shaytan* is attacking the house of Allah ﷻ.

قَلْبَ الْمُؤْمِنْ بَيْتُ الرَّبْ

*"Qalb al mu'min baytur rabb."*

*"The heart of the believer is the House of the Lord."* (Hadith Qudsi)

*Shaytan* (Satan) knows the system and knows that Allah ﷻ is not going to be occupying the mind, Allah ﷻ is going to occupy the heart. And he says, 'This *bani Adam* (descendant of Adam), if he becomes powerful, he will be like a thousand men. It's enough for me to begin to attack him. I'll influence what he eats, I'll influence what he drinks, I'll influence what he breathes and I'll bring him down by contaminating and poisoning his blood.' And then he moves within that blood.

## Your Life Depends on the Breath of Mercy – *Nafas ar Rahmah*

It means they begin to teach in our lives, it's far greater than just washing, and somebody describing how to put their fingers and their hands. That's only washing of the outside. The reality of that water, the reality of the water within, the reality of purifying all the organs, is important. That when that blood is moving through the body, how the *zikr* (chanting) and the breath is going to purify that blood. Because then you look at the physiology of breathing. Why is *zikr* so powerful? When they say the *nafas ar Rahmah* (breath of Mercy), why it's *nafas ar rahmah*? Because everything is based on that breath.

All *masha'ikh* (spiritual masters) came and said that you have 24,000 secrets in one day, 24,000 pockets of life in one day. The quality of your life is from breath to breath; if Allah ﷻ doesn't grant a breath, the person dies.

## The *Wudu* of Inner Reality and Purification of Breath

So each one is a secret of life, so they make that breath in *zikrullah*, in remembrance, in a consciousness of Allah ﷻ, that, '*Ya Rabbi*, before I ask for everything else in this *dunya* (material world) that I want, I have to be grateful for this breath that You gave me, this reality that you gave me.' Then you begin to see the breath that we're breathing is going to the lungs, the lungs are oxygenating the blood, and that oxygenated blood is shooting into the heart which is the house of Allah ﷻ.

So if you want the house of Allah ﷻ within the heart, you have to sanctify and purify the breath. What you eat through the mouth is going to affect the stomach and the belly, and that again is going to affect the blood that is going to enter the heart. So then there is a *wudu* inside the being, inside the body that's going to affect the heart. That is the *wudu* of the inner reality.

232

## The *Zikr* of *Hu* Within Each Element is Its Power

Now that begins to affect the soul. And from the *azemat* they begin to teach that, that breath and that air that you're breathing, it contains the elements of *mai* (water). Everything around us has from the secret of water, and within the secret of water is the *zikr* of *Hu*. And through the *zikr* of *Hu*, they are able to pull out the force of energy within everything. Every molecule that exists with its *hamd* (praise), *yusabbihu bi hamdi* (exalts by His praise).

$$ تُسَبِّحُ لَهُ السَّمَاوَاتُ السَّبْعُ وَالْأَرْضُ وَمَن فِيهِنَّ ۚ وَإِن مِّن شَيْءٍ إِلَّا يُسَبِّحُ بِحَمْدِهِ وَلَٰكِن لَّا تَفْقَهُونَ تَسْبِيحَهُمْ ۗ إِنَّهُ كَانَ حَلِيمًا غَفُورًا ( ٤٤ ) $$

*17:44 – "Tusabbihu lahus samawatus sab'u wal ardu wa man fee hinna wa in min shayin illa yusabbihu bihamdihi wa lakin la tafqahoona tasbeehahum ..." (Surat Al-Isra)*

*"The seven heavens and the earth and whatever is in them exalt [praises] Him. And there is not a thing except that it exalts [Allah] by His praise, but you do not understand their [way of] exalting..." (The Night Journey, 17:44)*

*Yusabbihu bi hamdi* (exalts by His praise). With the *hamd* (praise) that Allah ﷻ gave that being like you, whether it's yourself, your physicality or your atom and molecules, the inner power within it, who is the *bi hamdi*? It's the *Hu*, it's the *zikr* of the *Hu* within that element which is its power.

## The *Wudu* of the Soul is the *Zikr Hu* هو

Then the guides begin to teach that the *wudu* of the soul is *zikr Hu*. And all *mashayikh*, their *zikr* is "*AllahHu, AllahHu*, هو الله" to bring the purity of the soul. That as you are beginning to breathe, that you wash the outside. You understood the power of water, the importance of how this water is an angelic fire that burns all badness, "*Qul jal al haqqu wa zahaqal baatil*" (Truth has come and falsehood has perished, Holy Qur'an, 17:81).

وَ قُلْ جَاءَالْحَقُّ وَزَهَقَ الْبَطِلُ، إِنَّ الْبَطِلَ كَانَ زَهُوقًا (٨١)

*17:81 – "Wa qul jaa alhaqqu zahaqal baatil, innal batila kana zahooqa." (Surat Al-Isra)*

*"And say, "Truth has come, and falsehood has perished. Indeed falsehood, [by its nature], is ever perishing/ bound to perish." (The Night Journey, 17:81)*

The *haqq* (truth) comes, the *Shaytans* (devils) move. But they go inside; you didn't scare them, they went inside to hide.

### Defeat *Shaytan* Within With *Zikr Hu*

Then Prophet ﷺ came and taught all the realities of the eating, that make the *wudu* inside because now they are hiding inside. So then is your consciousness of your breath and what you eat and what you drink and what you put into your mouth. Now the *wudu* is inside. That you're fiercely fighting all the energies inside, where they can find no safety. They're burning inside and they're burning outside with your *wudu* and they begin to leave.

### *Qul Hu* (Say *Hu*) – It is the Force of Energy for the Soul

Then they begin to teach that as you begin to breathe and make your *zikr*, that is now the force of energy upon the soul. And be *zikr Hu*, you can pull from that energy all around us. And that *zikr Hu* is from *ikhlas* and sincerity. It's the only *surah* (verse) where Allah ﷻ says, "*Qul* (say) *Hu*," forget the rest.

قُلْ هُوَ اللَّـهُ أَحَدٌ (١)

112:1 – *"Qul Huw Allahu Ahad."* (Surat Al-Ikhlas)

*"Say, He is Allah, [who is] One."* (The Sincerity, 112:1)

*"Qul Hu"* قل هو. Allah's ﷻ *qaaf* ق *"Qaf wal Qur'anul majeed"* to the *laam*, the 'lisan ul-haqq' (tongue of truth); that Allah's ﷻ *azemat* and order is upon that *Hu*.

ق ۚ وَالْقُرْآنِ الْمَجِيدِ (١)

50:1– *"Qaf, wal Quranil Majeed."* (Surat Qaf)

*"Qaf. By the honoured Qur'an."* (Qaf, 50:1)

By imitating that *Hu*, you would be dressed from that reality, blessed from that reality, and granted a dress of *ikhlas* and sincerity. It means that is the reality of *wudu* (ablution). Not just how to wash your hands. And they make many different YouTube videos on how to wash your fingers, your hands and your toes. But what's the reality of *wudu*, what's the reality within us, what's the reality of the blood within us which is our water. How to combat the inside, the outside. And then the breath and how to take all the energy that is all around us and bring it into the breath and purify and sanctify the soul.

*Subhana rabbika rabbal 'izzati 'amma yasifoon, wa salaamun 'alal mursaleen, walhamdulillahi rabbil 'aalameen. Bi hurmati Muhammad al-Mustafa wa bi siri Surat al-Fatiha.*

235

# Sickness and Bad Energy
# Affects the Children

يَا أَيُّهَا الَّذِينَ آمَنُوا اتَّقُوا اللَّهَ وَكُونُوا مَعَ الصَّادِقِينَ ( ١١٩ )

*9:119 – "Ya ayyuhal ladheena amano ittaqollaha wa kono ma'as sadiqeen."*
*(Surat At-Tawba)*

*"O you who have believed, have consciousness of Allah and be with those who are*
*truthful/pious (in words and deed)." (The Repentance, 9:119)*

Allah ﷻ is saying, *"Ittaqullah wa kunu ma'as sadiqeen,"* that be conscious of the Divine Presence, to build a consciousness of Divine Presence and to be with truthful servants. It means in relationship to energy it is very important. Mawlana Shaykh begins to describe in very simple, not complicated sort of Islamic terms, but very simple understanding of energy so that we know how to build our self and preserve our self and protect ourselves.

## The Four Categories of Pious People That Are With Allah ﷻ

It means that as we accompany truthful servants and their truthfulness means that Allah ﷻ says, 'If you want to be with Me, you have to be with *Nabiyeen, Siddiqeen, Shuhadahi wa Saliheen*' (Prophets, Truthful Servants, The Witnesses of Truth, and Righteous). These four categories are always with Allah ﷻ.

وَمَن يُطِعِ اللَّهَ وَالرَّسُولَ فَأُوْلَـئِكَ مَعَ الَّذِينَ أَنْعَمَ اللَّهُ عَلَيْهِم مِّنَ النَّبِيِّينَ وَالصِّدِّيقِينَ
وَالشُّهَدَاءِ وَالصَّالِحِينَ وَحَسُنَ أُولَـئِكَ رَفِيقًا ( ٦٩ )

*4:69 – "Wa man yuti' Allaha war Rasola faolayeka ma'al ladheena an'ama
Allahu 'alayhim minan Nabiyeena, was Siddiqeena, wash Shuhadai, was
Saliheena wa hasuna olayeka rafeeqan." (Surat An-Nisa)*

*"And whoever obeys Allah and the messenger, then those are with the ones on
whom Allah bestowed his softness amongst the prophets, the highly Righteous
[Truthful], the Witnesses to the truth, and the Righteous. And excellent are those
as companions." (The Women, 4:69)*

All these four categories must always be connected. This is why the
four corners of the Holy *Ka'bah*. It means the *Saliheen* (Righteous)
they are *Saliheen* because they are connected with *Shuhadah* (Those
who witness). There has to be an unbroken chain all the way to
*Nabiyeen* (Prophets). *Nabiyeen* is always in the presence of Allah ﷻ by
virtue of being a *Nabi* (Prophet) ﷺ.

It means then Allah ﷻ is teaching
the reality of Holy *Ka'bah* which
means the reality of moving
towards the Divine Presence. It is
not a block of stones that you are
bowing down to. You are moving
there for the reality that Allah ﷻ
is teaching, 'Submit to Me.
Submit to My Light, submit to My Majesty, submit to My Energies and
My Powers'.

The guides begin to teach us that who has the power is keep the
company of *Saliheen*, pious people who are trying to improve
themselves. And Allah ﷻ describes then, 'Don't separate. Hold tight
to the rope of Allah and do not separate.'

$$وَاعْتَصِمُوا بِحَبْلِ اللَّـهِ جَمِيعًا وَلَا تَفَرَّقُوا ۚ (١٠٣)$$

*3:103 – "Wa'tasimo bihab lillahi jamee'an wa la tafarraqo." (Surat Al-Imran)*

*"And hold firmly to the rope of Allah all together and do not separate."*
*(Family of Imran, 3:103)*

It means the *Saliheen* are always in a *jamah*, they are always gathered in

a group remembering their Lord, praying to Allah ﷻ, fasting for Divine Presence, being of service to the Divine Presence. Then what makes them to be *Saliheen* means the real *Saliheen*, they must have from within themselves from the *Shuhada*. The *jamah* of *Saliheen*, to be real *Saliheen*, to be real pious servants, one from amongst them must be from *Shuhada*. *Shuhada*

means Allah ﷻ said, and Prophet ﷺ described, that don't view them to be dead, they are very much alive in their grave.

وَلَا تَحْسَبَنَّ الَّذِينَ قُتِلُوا فِي سَبِيلِ اللَّـهِ أَمْوَاتًا ۚ بَلْ أَحْيَاءٌ عِندَ رَبِّهِمْ يُرْزَقُونَ (١٦٩)

*3:169 – "Wa la tahsabanna alladheena qutilo fee sabilillahi amwatun, bal ahyaon 'inda rabbihim yurzaqoon." (Surat Al-Imran)*

*"And never think of those who have been killed in the cause of Allah as dead. Rather, they are alive with their Lord, receiving provision."*
*(Family of Imran, 3:169)*

## Real Associations Must Have a *Shuhada* (Those Who Witness)

*Shuhada* (those who witness) means there must be people in that group that can see. Their hearts are open; they have completed the first pillar of Islam [Testimony of Faith].

أَشْهَدُ أَنْ لَا إِلَهَ إِلَّا الله وَأَشْهَدُ أَنَّ مُحَمَّداً عَبْدُهُ وَحَبِيبُ هُوْ وَ رَسُولُ هُوْ

*"Ash hadu an lah ilaha illallah,wa ash hadu anna Muhammadan abduhu wa habibuhu wa Rasuluhu ﷺ ."*

*"I bear witness that there is no diety but Allah, and I bear witness that Muhammad ﷺ is His Servant, and His Beloved, and His Messenger."*

Most *jamahs*, most groups, they don't have a *Shuhada*. They don't have somebody who is witnessing what he is saying. So it's not a real association. It's an imitated association. That, we leave alone. Whole bunch of people coming together and they are not improving themselves, nor is there anyone amongst them who is improved and is now *shuhud*. *Shuhud* means he died before his death, his desires have gone and he is now witnessing and completing at least the first pillar of Islam. That I'm witnessing there is nothing but Allah and I'm witnessing Sayyidina Muhammad ﷺ, witnessing with the eye of my heart, at least completing the first step towards that reality.

## *Shuhada* Must Witness a *Siddiq* (Truthful) Holy Companion

So then the real group of *Saliheen* must have amongst them a *Shuhada*, a *shuhud*, somebody who is witnessing. What he is witnessing, he is witnessing the next corner, must have witnessed a *siddiq*. It means the *tariqas* (Islamic spiritual paths), they are taking from the *siddiqs* because they witnessed, lived, ate and drank in the presence of Sayyidina Muhammad ﷺ. So

Prophet ﷺ gave from his Companions that you are the big *siddiqs*, that nobody can match your rank, no *awliya* can match their rank.

So then every *wali*, every pious servant whose heart is open must be witnessing one of these big *siddiqs* and taking his secret, taking his connection from that *siddiq*, from that truthful servant that served with Prophet ﷺ. And that *siddiq* must be connected to a *Rasul*, must be connected to a Prophet ﷺ, witnessing, living, witnessing, living, eating, breathing, drinking in the presence of that Prophet ﷺ,

taking from that reality, that unbroken chain. Allah ﷻ describes, 'Hold tight, *bi hablillah*, and don't separate'. This is the real rope of Allah ﷻ because *hajar al-aswad*, the black stone in *Ka'bah* is not from *dunya*. That stone is from paradise.

$$\text{وَاعْتَصِمُوا بِحَبْلِ اللَّـهِ جَمِيعًا وَلَا تَفَرَّقُوا ۚ (١٠٣)}$$

3:103 – *"Wa'tasimo bihab lillahi jamee'an wa la tafarraqo." (Surat Al-Imran)*

*"And hold firmly to the rope of Allah all together and do not separate."*
*(Family of Imran, 3:103)*

It means that *siddiq* must be able to pull you towards the presence of Prophet ﷺ and that reality no longer is from *dunya*. It means that they are supporting with heavenly support. That heavenly emanation must be coming, moving through the heart of Prophet ﷺ to the heart of the *siddiq*; from the *siddiq* to *shuhada*, which are all the *Awliyaullah*, all their dark desires have died. The king of them is taking all of that light and then filtering it out to all those who he needs to filter. And from them they are making the *Saliheen*.

وَمَن يُطِعِ اللّهَ وَالرَّسُولَ فَأُوْلَـئِكَ مَعَ الَّذِينَ أَنْعَمَ اللّهُ عَلَيْهِم مِّنَ النَّبِيِّينَ وَالصِّدِّيقِينَ وَالشُّهَدَاء وَالصَّالِحِينَ وَحَسُنَ أُولَـئِكَ رَفِيقًا (٦٩)

*4:69 – "Wa man yuti' Allaha war Rasola faolayeka ma'al ladheena an'ama Allahu 'alayhim minan Nabiyeena, was Siddiqeena, wash Shuhadai, was Saliheena wa hasuna olayeka rafeeqan." (Surah An-Nisa)*

*"And whoever obeys Allah and the messenger, then those are with the ones on whom Allah bestowed his softness amongst the prophets, the highly Righteous [Truthful], the Witnesses to the truth, and the Righteous. And excellent are those as companions." (The Women, 4:69)*

## *Husna o Rafiqan* (Those Who Accompany *Saliheen*) Receive Tremendous Energy

So then the Companions of the *Saliheen*, the *Husna o Rafiqan* and those who are like them, means they are receiving within their hearts tremendous amounts of energy. And this energy begins to dress the heart with the lights and the adornments that Allah ﷻ wants them to have, begins to perfect the submission of their religion. From the submission, what they call Islam, and bringing down worldly desires and bringing in the desire to achieve more towards Divine Presence.

That light, as it comes, as it comes, as it comes, it must be hitting the light of faith. Mawlana Shaykh is describing the light of faith which means it must be increasing the love of Prophet ﷺ, the love of all the prophets, love of the Divine Presence, love of all the holy books – that is the light of faith. Then with

submission and love becomes the station of perfection and then that servant must be reaching a state of perfection.

## Be Vigilant of Your Heart and Energy

But as far as energy is concerned, they are describing that in these real associations, they begin to send a tremendous energy. This energy begins to dress our hearts, dress our souls, dress our entire being. And then *tariqa* comes and teaches us to be vigilant, vigilant of your heart and vigilant of yourself. It means we can build energy and we can waste or lose all our energy. The most difficult is the building and the easiest is to waste and to lose all the energy.

So then they begin to teach us as you waste and lose your energy, you will begin to become depleted, your energy goes. So simple law of energy is that whoever has the most positive energy, wherever that person goes will pull all negative energy. It is the law of energy. That as soon as you put a positive charge within the heart, within the soul, just walk around with a positive charge; as soon as you put out that positive charge, by its nature, it will begin to pull all the negative charge.

So then the guides are teaching us a reality of the path, *"wa kunu ma'a saadiqeen."*

يَا أَيُّهَا الَّذِينَ آمَنُوا اتَّقُوا اللَّهَ وَكُونُوا مَعَ الصَّادِقِينَ ( ١١٩ )

9:119 – *"Ya ayyuhal ladheena amano ittaqollaha wa kono ma'as sadiqeen."* *(Surat At-Tawba)*

*"O you who have believed, have consciousness of Allah and be with those who are truthful/pious (in words and deed)." (The Repentance, 9:119)*

Why Divine Presence is saying, 'keep the presence of *saadiqeen?'* Because they emit a tremendous positive energy. It's a grant; what Allah ﷻ grants, He grants; nobody can say He cannot do it. That grant, when it begins to flow, that energy begins to flow, which means they begin to dress us with a tremendous positive charge. As they are dressing us with a positive charge, wherever we go we are pulling a negative charge. Because everybody has to be of service to Divine Presence.

## Attend Association of *Zikr* to Unload Negative Energy

The highest form of *amal* (deed) is to be of service, whether you signed up for it or you didn't, it doesn't matter. The Divine is teaching us, 'If I'm sending you that energy and dressing you from that light, you may know it, you may not know it,' but they begin to explain our reality to us. 'As I'm dressing you with that light, you must know that

wherever you go with that light, you will pull negative energy'. If you keep the company of Pious People, because they have again more positive energy than you, then anywhere you go, at least once a week you come for the *zikr*. That's why the rules of the *zikr* is if you don't come at least once a week, you're going to have difficulty. Because as that negative energy is dressing you, dressing you, dressing you, you need somewhere to go to unload that energy.

If you think you are the positive one and that you have the ability to connect to them and you are witnessing them. Because you can't say, 'I'm the positive one, I don't need you.' The only way you can say you don't need a *Shuhada* is that you have to be from the *shuhud*. If you are saying, 'I don't need to be connected to you, I can connect directly to the *siddiq*', then you must be able to witness them. By witnessing them, then they are giving you authority. That you are hearing them, you are seeing them, you are feeling them, you are connected to them, they are pulling from you difficulty.

They begin to teach us some realities of our life, that, 'I'm asking, oh, for this knowledge. I'm asking for these lights, I'm asking for these blessings.' But there is an accountability with all of

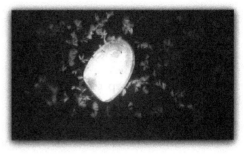

that. As they begin to load the heart with light and energies, everywhere you walk, like a light bulb on a dark night: it attracts all sorts of negative energies. As soon as you come into the association, their *madad*, their support for the association, they begin to emanate a more positive energy. 'Above every knower there is a knower.' (Holy Qur'an, 12:76)

نَرْفَعُ دَرَجَاتٍ مَّن نَّشَاءُ ۗ وَفَوْقَ كُلِّ ذِي عِلْمٍ عَلِيمٌ (٧٦)

*12:76 – "...Narfa'u darajatin man nashao, Wa fawqa kulli dhee 'ilmin 'aleem."*
*(Surat Yusuf)*

*"... We raise in degrees whom We will, and Above every knower there is a greater knower." (Prophet Joseph, 12:76)*

*"Wa kunu ma'as saadiqeen"* (Holy Qur'an, 9:119). Allah ﷻ is saying

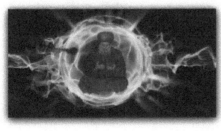

then, keep their company because an emanation of light is going to come from their hearts, from their *madad* and support, and begin to force out the positive charge. With that

positive charge, they are able to pull all the negative charge. They have been trained on how to pull that charge so that they don't die from it. It means they pull that charge through the *madad* and the connection of their Shaykhs; they must pull that energy away from us.

## If We Stay Away From *Zikr,* Our Negative Energy Overtakes Us

If we don't have that training and we don't have that understanding and we begin to keep ourselves away, our negative energy begins to overtake us. Our negative energy begins to overflow, developing bad character, bad energies, and bad sicknesses. When the negative energy begins to overflow so much, then they begin to teach us to be careful because within the association, within our homes, you bring that negativity.

If I don't dump that energy in the *zikr,* if I don't come to the association and the association pulled that charge from me, I become overloaded with a negative charge. If I go home and visualize I'm filled with a negative charge, first it's going to make me negative. All of the bad characteristics will begin to come through my heart, all bad speakings, everything bad will manifest. Then I become sick from that energy.

## Negative Energy Affects Innocent Children

If you produce so much negative charge, then the most innocent within the home will become sick. The guides teach us that within the home, the more innocent, the more their positive charge. They are *mazlum* (innocent); they have done nothing wrong for them to have a negative charge. So it means then the loved ones are in danger from our negative charge.

If we sit amongst ourselves and isolate ourselves and don't have that connection, but a light was deposited within the heart. That we came and went, came and went, came and went from the association; it means the guides deposited a light. They said that if you sit within the association a minimum of five minutes, GrandShaykh Abdullah Daghestani ق, already deposited the light into your heart. If that light enters into the heart, then they begin to teach us that you are accountable. You can't just take that light and run. That wherever you go, you are now going to be a beacon.

If you run out of charge, it means all the negativity just overtakes you, and you become sick. And if it's overflowing with negativity, your families become sick. The children are most innocent because their energy is positive and they are *mazlum*, they have done nothing wrong. So they are constantly emitting a positive charge and all the negativity begins to flow to them and they become sick.

So, in the last days and days of difficulty you find so much sickness amongst families. Because they come to *zikr*, then they go; then they go thinking they got it. But then they are filled with all sorts of difficult energies, all sorts of negativities. The *tariqa* (spiritual path) is based on keeping the association. As soon as we come back into the associations and the association pulls the energy, pulls all the negative charge and deposits with it a positive charge.

## We Don't Know the Value of the Spiritual Path

The biggest sickness is when we feel that the energy is enough for us, thank you very much, and we are on our way. It means you have taken now an *amanat*, you've taken a trust, you've taken a light and you don't have yet the tools and the ability to purify, perfect and safeguard. It means *wuquf al-qalb*, vigilance of the heart, Mawlana Shaykh describes it's like a shack. The house is a shack and the Divine Presence is granting you a gift of *tariqa*. But that gift, it's like a gold mine that you are about to put into a shack. You put a precious jewel in a shack.

## *Tariqa* is Like a Diamond in a Shack of Our Unfortified Heart

We don't know the value of *tariqa;* we don't know the value of spiritual masters and spiritual paths. But they know the value. So they are describing for us in a *dunya* term to understand. That as soon as you have been inspired to come on a spiritual path, it means these masters are depositing a tremendous diamond in your heart but your heart is like a shack. It's all broken, it has not been fortified, it has not been purified yet. You have not been perfected. We have not been perfected. They are taking us on a path of perfection.

So if that diamond is deposited within your heart, don't you think that *Shaytans* (devils) are seeing that. That they see now within the shack there is something emanating from there? And all sorts of attacks begin to come because they want that light. They want that stone. We described before that it's as if you take a whole bunch of gold and put it in your children's pockets and drop them off on Hastings and Main Street, which is a very bad neighbourhood, a rough neighbourhood. You put your kid there with whole bunch of gold in his pocket. I don't think he can survive more than five minutes.

Divine is teaching that, 'I'm depositing these lights into your heart, these blessings.' You know you have that light when you have a yearning for Divine Presence, when you want to purify yourself, when you want to perfect yourself, you want to attain a spiritual reality, and you want to elevate yourself. That's a love that you don't have, but was given to you. Most people don't have that love. When we have that love the Divine is teaching, 'I deposited that love of My Divine Presence in your heart so that you would

yearn to find Me, that you would seek Me out'.

## Spiritual Masters Take Away the Negative Energy

But that diamond that comes into your house, Mawlana describes, is like putting it in a shack. All of your spiritual practices and understandings are to fortify that shack. So then they begin to teach us over the years how to build the defense, how to fortify this so that it doesn't come under attack. But as soon as it comes under attack, then we find all our energy is dropping and all these sicknesses are coming.

Then they begin to teach us to then come back into the associations. The associations have a tremendous amount of power, that they are able to send a positive charge out and pull the negative

charge off of people. Then they send that charge up the chain, the *madad* (support), and those Shaykhs take that negativity and they do with it what they have to. It means there has to be a heavenly connection, there has to be a connection towards Divine Presence that takes this negativity away.

We pray that we begin to understand these laws of energy, and understand these realities, before they manifest in ways that are very sad and very unfortunate. They manifest themselves upon people who are innocent. Because they don't know the trust that we have entered into and they don't know that the commitment of what the soul has made. The commitment that the soul has made to Divine Presence, that when I came into this material world I would perfect myself, I would reach the *amanat* (trust) that the Divine wants us to receive, and the station that the Divine wants us to achieve.

And as soon as we fall short and distance ourself from that energy, distance ourself from what the Divine has granted. He has granted an association which is real and that association is able to transmit

249

tremendous amounts of energy. If we don't receive those energies, one – we don't get purified and two – we don't achieve the stations that the Divine wants for us.

We pray that we always keep ourselves within the association within their understanding, and within their *madad*, and that we keep ourself to be vigilant; watch out where we go, watch out in whose company we are always with and where we are going. Because that energy is going to be depleted very quickly and you will feel yourself drop, you will feel your energy drop.

*Subhana rabbika rabbal 'izzati 'amma yasifoon, wa salaamun 'alal mursaleen, walhamdulillahi rabbil 'aalameen. Bi hurmati Muhammad al-Mustafa wa bi siri Surat al-Fatiha.*

# Chapter Six

## How to Repel Negative Energy

وَ قُلْ جَاءَالْحَقُّ وَزَهَقَ الْبَطِلُ، إِنَّ الْبَطِلَ كَانَ زَهُوقًا (٨١)

17:81 – *"Wa qul jaa alhaqqu wa zahaqal baatil, innal batila kana zahooqa."* (Surat Al-Isra)

*"And say, Truth has come, and falsehood has perished. Indeed falsehood, [by its nature], is ever perishing/ bound to perish."*
(The Night Journey, 17:81)

إِنَّ اللَّهَ لَا يُغَيِّرُ مَا بِقَوْمٍ حَتَّىٰ يُغَيِّرُوا مَا بِأَنفُسِهِمْ (١١)

13:11 – *"...Inna Allaha la yughayyiru ma bi qawmin hatta yughayyiro ma bi anfusihim ..."* (Surah Ar-Ra'd)

*"Indeed Allah will not change the condition of a people until they change what is in themselves."* (The Thunder, 13:11)

251

# Build Your Spiritual Energy
# To Defend Against Extreme Negativity

*Alhamdulillah,* that by Allah's ﷻ *Rahmah* (mercy), we are still in existence and Allah's ﷻ *Rahmah* is dressing us, blessing us, and forgiving us, *InshaAllah.*

### *Turooqs* (Spiritual Paths) Are a Mercy From Allah ﷻ

That, with oceans of difficulty everywhere, the *turooqs* (spiritual paths) and the people of *haqqa'iq* are a mercy from Allah ﷻ. They are a ship of safety and protection from Allah ﷻ, from Prophet ﷺ and *Awliyaullah* (saints). The guides describe a system, that if you follow that system, it will work. It's a school; it has a curriculum. Their *majlis* and their circles are based on energy and based on teachings. The teachings are dressing the soul, the energies means coming from what Allah ﷻ wants to send. He sends to the heart of Prophet ﷺ, from Prophet ﷺ, to the *Ulul amr* and those whom Allah ﷻ granted them an authority.

### Take a Path to Follow Your Heart, Not the Head

The guides come and they teach us always as a reminder that take a path from your heart. It means take a path in which you follow your heart and not your head; and by listening to their guidance, they teach us. They teach us the tricks of *shayateen* (devils)

253

and the *nafs* (ego), because the *nafs* partners with *Shaytan* (Satan) and *shayateen*. They are very clever on how to trick the believer into using their head and not their heart. And the *turooqs* come to teach that use your heart and reach to where Allah ﷻ wants us to reach.

A reminder of the power of the heart is how we are going to protect ourselves. That everything the *nafs* is doing is through the head and then begins to fool us to make us to be busy through our head and to corrupt the heart. So it means the whole way is based on understanding, that these thoughts that come to my head, and I should be taking a path that is based upon my heart. It's not so simple as the *nafs* comes and tricks the believer openly but will in many times trick the believer that they are doing a noble cause, a noble cause. That they will do something noble and say, 'This is in the way of Allah ﷻ' and enter into that.

If that one is from the people of contemplation, they contemplate and contemplate that, 'Is this something from my heart and a benefit for my heart or is this something coming through my head and I'm going to follow that which my head is commanding me?' So as a reminder for our path is based upon the heart. That, 'I'm going to listen to my heart, I'm going to do my practices from my heart and continuously battle that which comes to my mind and try to take my path from my mind', that we are a people of contemplation and *tafakkur*.

## The First Step to Safety is to Admit to Your Nothingness

In days of difficulty, many people begin to email and begin to try to communicate with the Centre that, 'I'm feeling a tremendous amount of negative energy. That I feel like I'm coming under attack and I feel that I'm becoming sick'. And that is correct, that there is a tremendous amount of negative energy everywhere and there is a specific way in which to combat that negativity.

When we say we took a path in which we are nothing, it means that, that nothingness is a means in which to reach towards Allah's ﷻ

Support. If the servant believes in their somethingness, that they have an ability to defend against negativity, Allah ﷻ will test them. Many negative things can begin to open and that servant will quickly understand that you are nothing in the face of what Allah ﷻ has created of the unseen. The unseen that can make themselves seen or unseen that, just like an energy, begins to attack you from every means possible.

So the first step in that reality is that, 'I'm nothing, *ya Rabbi*, I'm nothing, I'm *faqir* (poor). That only by Your Grace and by Your Mercy, I'm in existence and that send Your Support'. And they begin to train, in that training, that you take a path within your heart; you have to build an energy. That energy is not your energy but that is an energy in which Allah ﷻ sends upon the heart of the believer.

## Love and Follow Sayyidina Muhammad ﷺ To Receive Allah's ﷻ Love

It means this is a very quick understanding that for me to reach towards that light and to reach towards that reality, I took a path in which to negate myself. When I begin to negate myself that I'm nothing, then Allah ﷻ begins to guide; then you connect your heart. You keep the love of Sayyidina Muhammad ﷺ because Prophet ﷺ is Allah's ﷻ Power that moves throughout creation. *"Fattabi'ooni, Qul inni kuntum tuhibbunallah fattabi'ooni."*

قُلْ إِنْ كُنْتُمْ تُحِبُّونَ اللَّهَ فَاتَّبِعُونِيْ يُحْبِبْكُمُ اللَّهُ وَيَغْفِرْ لَكُمْ ذُنُوبَكُمْ ۗ وَاللَّـهُ غَفُورٌ رَّحِيمٌ (٣١)

*3:31 – "Qul in kuntum tuhibbon Allaha fattabi'oni, yuhbibkumUllahu wa yaghfir lakum dhunobakum wallahu Ghaforur Raheem." (Surat Al-Imran)*

*"Say, [O Muhammad], If you should love Allah, then follow me, [so] Allah will love you and forgive you your sins. And Allah is Forgiving and Merciful."*
*(Family of Imran, 3:31)*

Everything and every reality is flowing from this *ayat al Kareem* (blessed verse). Our way is based on, '*Ya Rabbi*, I'm searching for Your Love, I'm searching for Your Protection'. And Allah's Command to those whom He Loves, is *"fattabi'ooni"*, follow the way of Sayyidina Muhammad صلى الله عليه وسلم.

## Prophet صلى الله عليه وسلم Transforms Allah Almighty's Power to a Degree That Creation Can Receive

Later they begin to teach through all the other teachings, that Prophet صلى الله عليه وسلم is holding the Power of Allah. Allah's *Qudra*, if it begins to move onto this *dunya* (material world), everything will be crushed. It has to go through a transformer; it has to become cool and peaceful as it's descending.

قُلْنَا يَا نَارُ كُونِي بَرْدًا وَسَلَامًا ... (٦٩)

*21:69 – "Qulna ya Naaru, kuni Bardan wa Salaman ..." (Surat Al-Anbiya)*

*"We said, "O fire, be cool and Peaceful upon Abraham." (The Prophets, 21:69)*

*"Wa ma arsalnaka rahmatan lil-'aalameen";* Allah says, 'I would not have sent the reality of Prophet صلى الله عليه وسلم except that it is a mercy towards all creation, all existence, all worlds, everything Allah has created.'

وَمَا أَرْسَلْنَاكَ إِلَّا رَحْمَةً لِّلْعَالَمِينَ (١٠٧)

*21:107 – "Wa maa arsalnaka illa Rahmatan lil'alameen." (Surat Al-Anbiya)*

*"And We have not sent you, [O Muhammad], except as a mercy to the worlds."*
*(The Prophets, 21:107)*

Its mercy is in the way that Prophet's ﷺ existence can bring the power of Allah ﷻ in an energy that is acceptable for us to receive. Allah's ﷻ *Qudra*, directly, it will burn everything. But when this *Qudra* hits to Prophet's ﷺ soul, it becomes cool and peaceful and a means in which people can reach towards that energy. That's why Prophet ﷺ described to them, 'Remember me at least one time, make *Durood e-Shareef* upon me at least one time, Allah ﷻ will allow my soul to come and make 10 *salawat* (praising)'.

عَنْ أَنَسِ بْنِ مَالِكٍ رَضِيَ اللهُ عَنْهُ، قَالَ: قَالَ رَسُولُ اللهِ – صلى الله عليه وسلم -: "مَنْ صَلَّى عَلَيَّ صَلَاةً وَاحِدَةً، صَلَّى اللَّهُ عَلَيْهِ عَشْرَ صَلَوَاتٍ، وَحُطَّتْ عَنْهُ عَشْرُ خَطِيئَاتٍ، وَرُفِعَتْ لَهُ عَشْرُ دَرَجَاتٍ "

*Qala RasulAllah (ﷺ): "Man Salla `alaiya Salatan wahidatan, Sallallahu `alayhi `ashra Salawatin, wa Huttat `anhu `ashru khaTeatin, wa ruf`at lahu `ashru darajatin."*

*Prophet Muhammad (pbuh) said: "Whoever sends blessings [Praises] upon me, God will shower His blessings upon him ten times, and will erase ten of his sins, and elevate [raise] his [spiritual] station ten times." (Hadith, recorded by Nasa'i)*

Allah ﷻ, through Prophet ﷺ, is giving to us a formula from Allah ﷻ, that this *Durood e-Shareef* means the light of Prophet ﷺ begins to dress our soul, bless our soul. That is a *qudra* (power) that is an energy that dresses the reality.

## 99% of People Use Their Head Not Their Heart

It means then the spiritual guides take a way of *tafakkur* and contemplation, that we must accompany those people who are the people of *tafakkur*. That's why we started the talk with the people of the brain [head] and people of *tafakkur* [heart]. 99.9% of people are people of the brain, whether they are an *imam*, whether they are an *aalim* (scholar), whether they think they are *Sufiya* or they are *ahl al-haqqa'iq* (people of reality); they are using their brain. Most have not trained to use their heart.

## People of the Heart Continuously Test You, Until You Negate the Head

The way of the heart has a very specific training in which they took a *bayah* (allegiance) and they accompanied a Shaykh. They accompanied a Shaykh for many years of their life in which that Shaykh continuously tested and continuously crushed them, and crushed them and crushed them. So that of their mind and of the path of which they use their head, was destroyed. And they

became the people in which they use their heart. They had continuous testing.

Those who inherit from that, they are also authorized in that form of testing. As much as you accompany them and you are with them, whether through form or through the Internet, it means they continuously test you not to use your head, not to use your head, use your heart. So that everything that's coming to your head, battle that thought that comes to your head and begin to use the tools that were given to you for your heart.

So it means these people are different. These realities are different. The people of the heart and the opening of the way of the heart, through all their training, they teach you that when you sit for *tafakkur* (contemplation), negate yourself, negate yourself.

## You Don't Have the Energy to Protect Yourself

Those who are watching and concerned with energies, you don't have an energy in which to protect yourself against negativity because it's not about my energy to protect myself. It's about me negating myself to be nothing. If I can reach a state in which I'm nothing, then Allah ﷻ dresses from *"ateeullah wa atee ar-rasul wa Ulul amrin minkum"*. It means those lights are the lights in which the believer needs within their being.

يَاأَيُّهَا الَّذِينَ آمَنُوا أَطِيعُواللَّه وَأَطِيعُواْالرَّسُولَ وَأُوْلِي الْأَمْرِ مِنْكُمْ...(٥٩)

4:59 – *"Ya ayyu hal latheena amano oAtiullaha, wa atiur Rasola, wa Ulil amre minkum..." (Surat An-Nisa)*

*"O You who have believed, Obey Allah, Obey the Messenger, and those in authority among you..." (The Women, 4:59)*

It means Allah ﷻ says, *"Ittaqullah wa kunu ma as saadiqeen"*, that have a consciousness and keep the company of the *saadiqeen*, keep the company of truthful servants.

يَا أَيُّهَا الَّذِينَ آمَنُوا اتَّقُوا اللَّه وَكُونُوا مَعَ الصَّادِقِينَ (١١٩)

9:119 – *"Ya ayyuhal ladheena amano ittaqollaha wa kono ma'as sadiqeen." (Surat At-Tawba)*

*"O you who have believed, have consciousness of Allah and be with those who are truthful/pious (in words and deed)." (The Repentance, 9:119)*

We said before, Allah's ﷻ Words of Holy Qur'an, is for all time; that we must keep their company physically and spiritually. As you are keeping the company physically, they train you on how to keep their company spiritually. How to enter your *tafakkur* and contemplation, how to negate the self. That, 'Ya Rabbi, I'm not here to listen to myself. I'm asking to be with Your truthful servants, whom are truthful in their word and in their deed'.

## Lights and Souls of *Awliya* (Saints) Are Everywhere

It means their lights and their *arwah* are everywhere and the light of their soul is free. How to connect with that light, how to connect with the energy of that reality, to be dressed from that? Before you can reach to *"ateeullah"*, before you can reach to *"atee ar-Rasul"*, it means that we must be accompanying and keeping the energy of *"Ulul amrin minkum"*.

$$ يَاأَيُّهَا الَّذِينَ آمَنُوا أَطِيعُواللَّه وَأَطِيعُوٱلرَّسُولَ وَأُولِي الأَمْرِ مِنْكُمْ...(٥٩) $$

*4:59 – "Ya ayyu hal latheena amano oAtiullaha, wa atiur Rasola, wa Ulil amre minkum..." (Surat An-Nisa)*

*"O You who have believed, Obey Allah, Obey the Messenger, and those in authority among you..." (The Women, 4:59)*

By negating myself and taking a path in which I negate myself is to reach the energies of these *Ulul amr*, that wherever they are, how to reach to them, how to be dressed by them, how to be dressed by that energy. Asking that, send your *madad*, send your support.

This is not worshipness. When people come back and make comments, 'Is this like a *shirk*, is this like a worship?' Worship is only for Allah ﷻ. This is for support in which Allah ﷻ is continuously telling us, that only people of *tafakkur* understand these realities. And keep the  company of truthful servants, not only physically but in spirituality, by being nothing, by being nothing and asking for their *madad*.

## How to Spiritually Connect and Make *Tafakkur* (Contemplation)

The guides begin to teach you a specific way in which to train yourself.

 That to lock off your senses, close off your eyes, close off your ears. Enter into a station like the *qabr* (grave) in which you enter into a room with just a candlelight and be nothing. In that nothingness, how to be dressed by that light, call upon these *Ulul amr* and have a dialogue and a relationship with

the Shaykhs in their spirituality. Say, 'I'm nothing *Sayyidi*, that you be with me, it's not necessary for me to see you, but I know that you are there with me. Dress me from your light, bless me from your light'. With all your belief, that in every *salah* (daily prayer), [know] that 'my Shaykh is my *imam*. He must be there to be present with me, I'm not worthy of seeing'. Don't busy your mind and keep saying, 'I want to see you, I want to see you,' and then you get upset when you don't see. You are not worthy of seeing them. Don't give your *nafs* (ego) in anything that you do, any type of happiness.

## Don't Take Credit for the Spiritual Experiences

They said that Imam Ali ؑ described that, 'Even in my annihilation, there is an annihilation'. It means that, if in your *tafakkur*, you contemplate and somebody sends a *khashf*, like a vision comes and *awliya* (saints) show something. You are sitting and meditating and all of a sudden, oh, they come with a *jubba* (robe) from paradise, they come with the swords of paradise, they come with water from paradise. And you want to come to the Shaykh and talk about it, why? Why would you give your *nafs* (ego) any credibility? Why would you give your *nafs* any ability to understand what's taking place and give it any type of credit?

Even in your annihilation is to annihilate. 'I'm nothing, that what I'm seeing, *ya Rabbi*, is not for me, I'm not worthy of that, I'm no one. My *nafs* is even playing with me on these subjects'. And if it's real, *alhamdulillah*, Allah ﷻ knows what's real; it's only for Allah ﷻ to know. And if it's not real, at least you negated your *nafs* playing with you.

## Spiritual Connection Requires Good Character

There are so many different trainings. As they are training you to be nothing, to be nothing, then Allah ﷻ is reminding us, keep their company. The physical company but the spiritual is much harder. How to continuously keep them under that *nazar* (gaze) that, 'Be with me, dress me from your light'. The guides begin to remind you that, 'We can't be with you if your character is bad'. *"Qul jaa al-haqq wa zahaq al-baatil".* The truth and the false, we don't go together.

وَ قُلْ جَاءَالْحَقُّ وَزَهَقَ الْبَطِلُ، إِنَّ الْبَطِلَ كَانَ زَهُوقًا (٨١)

*17:81 – "Wa qul jaa alhaqqu wa zahaqal baatil, innal batila kana zahooqa."*
*(Surat Al-Isra)*

*"And say, Truth has come, and falsehood has perished. Indeed falsehood, [by its nature], is ever perishing/ bound to perish." (The Night Journey, 17:81)*

Then they motivate, that keep your character to be correct, keep your character to be clean. Keep your reality to be a truthful light because then their truthful light can accompany. But their truthful light doesn't accompany anything false. It means the whole science of this reality on how to negate myself, how to keep their company, how to with all my faith like a mountain, but he's present with me. *Shaytan* is present with you. And what power *Shaytan* is taking? *Shaytan* takes from *'Izzatullah, 'izzat ar-Rasul wa 'izzat al-mu'mineen;* he's taking from the power of the *mu'mineen.*

وَلِلَّهِ الْعِزَّةُ وَلِرَسُولِهِ وَلِلْمُؤْمِنِينَ وَلَكِنَّ الْمُنَافِقِينَ لَا يَعْلَمُونَ (٨)

262

63:8 – *"…Wa Lillahil 'izzatu wa li Rasooli hi wa lil Mumineena wa lakinnal munafiqeena la y'alamoon…" (Surat Al-Munafiqoon)*

*"…And to Allah belongs [all] honor, and to His messenger, and to the believers, but the hypocrites do not know." (The Hypocrites, 63:8)*

## *Ulul Amr* (Saints) Carry Muhammadan Light and Power

So it means these *Ulul amr* are much more powerful than *Shaytan*. So they are there, they are right in front of us, but we can't see them. Why can't we see? Because of the bad character, because of the trick that *Shaytan* and the *nafs* is putting upon the mind and blocking the mind and distracting the heart. But with all my faith that they are, and with all my faith asking, dress me from your light, bless me from your light. As you negate yourself, their light is dressing, their light is dressing. If they begin to dress on the soul, you be dressed now with a *qudra* (power) because *"La hawla wa la quwwata illa billahil'aaleeyil 'Azheem."*

لَا حَوْلَ وَ لَا قُوَّةَ إِلَّا بِاللهِ الْعَلِيِّ الْعَظِيمِ

*"La hawla wa la quwwata illa billahil 'Aliyil 'Azheem."*

*"There is no Support and No Power except in Allah."*

It means these *Ulul amr*, they carry the lights of Prophet ﷺ. Prophet

ﷺ is the ocean of Allah's ﷻ *Qudra* (power). It means the *hawla* and support is coming by these *Ulul amr*, the ones we see and the ones we don't see. Their power is everywhere. So for the believer, Allah ﷻ is challenging us, connect to that unseen power. As soon as you negate yourself and you make a path of *tafakkur*, it's like you are searching

on how to plug in.

Then all of their teaching will be on how to bring everything down and how to connect to their energy. By connecting to their energy, you begin to feel a *fa'iz* (blessing) and a dress upon the soul.

## Reality of Attraction and Magnetism *(Haqiqat al-Juzba)*

*Haqiqat al-Juzba* (Reality of Attraction), from the powers of the heart, there are six powers of the heart that *Awliyaullah* (saints) will open

upon the heart of those whom following. The heart, the power that we are talking about now as a defense against difficulty, is *haqiqat al-juzba* – how to bring an energy upon myself greater than my own energy. The way of *tafakkur* is that when you begin to train on how to contemplate, how to contemplate, they begin to teach you to purify your inside, correct all of your inside. And that this iron within the body that Allah ﷻ gave to you, perfect and cleanse your iron so that the iron within your being is perfected and clean. What you eat and what you drink is going to affect that.

Once you begin to take a path in which you clean this iron and now you want to connect with that energy, they begin to teach, negate yourself and ask to be with these *Ulul amr*. 'Ya Rabbi, the *Awliyaullah* that are always present, I'm asking for their support, asking for their *madad*; let my heart to be connected with them and with all my belief, I believe that they are present with me'. And begin to ask that, 'Dress me from your light, bless me from your light'. Our way is based on how much of that light we can take. How much of that good character that we can develop, so more and more light comes, more and more *fa'iz* comes.

## Light and Energy of *Ulul Amr* Purifies and Perfects You

When they begin to dress that being, all of their energy is now charged. It becomes supercharged. The more energy that you can bring upon yourself, from *"Ateeullah, wa atee ar-rasul wa Ulul amrin minkum"*, because we are going up this way, upwards.

يَاأَيُّهَا الَّذِينَ آمَنُوا أَطِيعُوا اللَّه وَأَطِيعُوا الرَّسُولَ وَأُوْلِي الْأَمْرِ مِنْكُمْ (٥٩)

*4:59 – "Ya ayyu hal latheena amano oAtiullaha, wa atiur Rasola, wa Ulil amre minkum..." (Surat an-Nisa)*

*"O You who have believed, Obey Allah, Obey the Messenger, and those in authority among you..." (The Women, 4:59)*

As much as we keep the presence of the *Ulul amr* and the dress of the *Ulul amr* (saints), they are perfecting our lights. In your *tafakkur* and contemplation, you visualize that the *Ulul amr* are there and you begin to be able to feel their energy and ask to be dressed by their energy. The *Ulul Amr* are cleaning, perfecting, cleaning, and perfecting, to take us to the presence of Prophet ﷺ. So when that energy is perfected, they take you to the presence of Sayyidina Muhammad ﷺ.

*Ruhaniyat Nabi* (Prophet's spirituality) ﷺ must be present, in that *ruhaniyat*, that Prophet's ﷺ *fa'iz* (downpouring blessings) begin to dress the believer, Prophet's ﷺ lights begin to dress; and they begin to change even the colour of the light that's being dressed upon them. Those are the lights of protection.

## All the Training is to Prepare People for the Upcoming Difficulties

As much as we can negate ourself and bring these lights that this being becomes charged with an energy that pushes away many *shayateen* (devils), pushes away many different beings that have a bad intention. If the energy within the person is not strong enough, everything can begin to attack it, and now many people are feeling an attack. They feel the negativity is coming everywhere and they feel they don't have the ability to push the negativity away. And all of these practices and all of these trainings were not for entertainment, but to prepare people for difficulty that's coming upon this earth.

What they want us to understand is that you have to negate yourself. As much as your self is there, that energy is not. When we negate that, '*Ya Rabbi*, I'm nothing. *Ya Rabbi* dress me from their power.' As soon as you ask for the *madad*, these *Awliyaullah* (saints) must be present. They are here to serve Allah 'جل جلاله and serve Sayyidina Muhammad صلى الله عليه وسلم. We are not seeing them, it doesn't matter, but we are asking to be dressed by them, blessed by them, that, 'Dress that light upon me. Let me to begin to feel myself in these oceans of light'. Every association is under their dress; every *salah* (daily prayer) is under their dress.

## These are Special Associations, They Dress You With Light and Energy

It means then we begin to understand that the importance of these associations and the importance of these teachings, they are not everywhere. These associations and the light that these associations have, they are an authorized association. Every time you step in that association, they are going to dress you. And every time you miss the association, the dress is very light upon you. If they can't send enough in the time that's been given to them, you don't have the ability to carry it. That's why when you think you can miss and do whatever you want, you are not taking the dress that Allah ﷻ has destined for you. It's a dress. If they send too much, you'll be sick, you'll have a flu, you'll enter into a state like death; it's too much for the physicality to take at any one time.

So every association has a dress from that reality. Every association has a preparation for what is coming because we are *jahl* (ignorant) and we don't understand and we don't see. We think everything is just blue, everything is just great. But something is coming. Difficulty is coming. If *insaan* (mankind) doesn't build themself and their soul, they have no way of surviving what's coming, which is okay too because if they take you and get rid of your body, they'll bring your soul to witness that reality. But we would prefer to witness it with body and with soul.

## The Importance of *Barakah* (Blessings) of Holy Places

### Story of Prophet Zakariyah ﷻ and Sayyidatina Maryam ﷻ

Then the training is important; the lights are important; these realities are important. Not every place is the same. One example of that, and I've told before, is with Sayyidina Zakariyah ﷻ.

ذِكُرُ رَحْمَتِ رَبِّكَ عَبْدَهُ زَكَرِيَّا (٢) إِذْ نَادَىٰ رَبَّهُ نِدَاءً خَفِيًّا (٣) وَإِنِّي خِفْتُ الْمَوَالِيَ مِن وَرَائِي وَكَانَتِ امْرَأَتِي عَاقِرًا فَهَبْ لِي مِن لَّدُنكَ وَلِيًّا (٥)

*19:2-3,5 – "Zikru rahmati Rabbika 'abda hu Zakariyah. (2) Iz naadaa Rabba hu nidaa an khafiya. (3) Wa innee khiftul mawa liya min waraa'ee wa kaanatim ra atee 'aaqiran fahab lee mil ladunka waliyya. (5) (Surat Maryam)*

*(This is) a mention, Remembrance of the mercy of your Lord to His servant Zakariya (Zachariah). (2) When he called to his Lord a private (secret) supplication. (3) And indeed, I fear (what) my relatives (will do) after me, and my wife has been barren, so give me from Yourself an heir (5)." (Mary, 19:2-3, 5)*

267

Sayyidina Zakariyah عليه السلام is a prophet of Allah ﷻ and all his life making a *du'a* (supplication), a specific *du'a* that was not answered. So it means that however pious you think you are there is something specific that Allah ﷻ wants you to learn. Sayyidina Zakariyah عليه السلام, 99 years, how old was Sayyidina Zakariyah عليه السلام? Not getting the *du'a*, not getting the *du'a* (supplication), until he walked into the niche of Sayyidatina Maryam عليها السلام. When he walked into the niche of Sayyidatina Maryam عليها السلام, he's witnessing now that there are many things happening in this niche.

Although his whole life is in his temple. His whole life is in his temple; the niche is inside the temple. The niche is inside the temple. So it's not a matter of just you are anywhere, you're in the vicinity. No, no, Allah ﷻ is very specific. His whole life he is in the temple making a *du'a* and it's not being granted, because Allah ﷻ wants a whole package. His *du'a* is not granted until he walked into this room, which requires humility because he's a prophet of God and she is a *waliya* (saint). And he recognizes that as a prophet of God, because you have to be humble, my *du'a* is not coming, but this person seems like all their *du'as* are coming. Every *ni'mat* is flowing, every food is in abundance that even he's astonished and asked, 'Where is this food coming from?' And she is surprised, 'What do you mean where is this food coming from? You don't know? You are a prophet of God!' At that moment he made *du'a*, and at that moment Sayyidina Jibra'il عليه السلام appeared to him and said, 'Your *du'a* was accepted'.

فَتَقَبَّلَهَا رَبُّهَا بِقَبُولٍ حَسَنٍ وَأَنبَتَهَا نَبَاتًا حَسَنًا وَكَفَّلَهَا زَكَرِيَّا ۖ كُلَّمَا دَخَلَ عَلَيْهَا زَكَرِيَّا الْمِحْرَابَ وَجَدَ عِندَهَا رِزْقًا ۖ قَالَ يَا مَرْيَمُ أَنَّىٰ لَكِ هَٰذَا ۖ قَالَتْ هُوَ مِنْ عِندِ اللَّـهِ ۖ إِنَّ اللَّـهَ يَرْزُقُ مَن يَشَاءُ بِغَيْرِ حِسَابٍ (٣٧) هُنَالِكَ دَعَا زَكَرِيَّا رَبَّهُ ۖ قَالَ رَبِّ هَبْ لِي مِن لَّدُنكَ ذُرِّيَّةً طَيِّبَةً ۖ إِنَّكَ سَمِيعُ الدُّعَاءِ (٣٨) فَنَادَتْهُ الْمَلَائِكَةُ وَهُوَ

قَائِمٌ يُصَلِّي فِي الْمِحْرَابِ أَنَّ اللَّهَ يُبَشِّرُكَ بِيَحْيَىٰ مُصَدِّقًا بِكَلِمَةٍ مِّنَ اللَّهِ وَسَيِّدًا
وَحَصُورًا وَنَبِيًّا مِّنَ الصَّالِحِينَ (٣٩)

*3:37-39 – "…kullama dakhala 'alayha Zakariyya almihraba wajada 'indaha rizqan, qala ya Maryamu anna laki hadha? qalat huwa min 'indi Allahi innAllaha yarzuqu man yashao bighayri hisab." (37) 'Hunalika da'a zakariyya Rabbahu, qala rabbi hab lee min ladunka dhurriyyatan tayyibatan, innaka samee'ud du'a (38) 'Fanadat hu almalaikatu wa huwa qaaimun yusallee fil mihrabi annAllaha yubashshiruka bi Yahya …(39)" (Surat Al-Imran)*

*"Every time Zechariah entered upon her in the prayer chamber, he found with her provision. He said, "O Mary, from where is this [coming] to you?" She said, "It is from Allah . Indeed, Allah provides for whom He wills without account. (37) At that, Zechariah called upon his Lord, saying, "My Lord, grant me from Yourself a good offspring. Indeed, You are the Hearer of supplication. (38) "While he was standing in prayer in the chamber, the angels called unto him: 'Indeed, Allah gives you good tidings of Yahya (John), …(39)" (Family of Imran, 3:37-39)*

## People of the Heart Carry a Secret from Allah ﷻ and Prophet ﷺ

So why you go anywhere, you make *du'a*? That doesn't make, it's not correct. Not anywhere you go Allah's ﷻ Secret would be there, that Allah ﷻ has Secrets. When you use your heart and not your brain, your brain says, 'Go everywhere, you are holy; wherever you step, everything will happen' – no! When you use your heart and think that maybe Allah ﷻ has placed a secret; based on that secret I'll go there and make my *du'a*. Based on that secret, maybe their teaching is something that my soul is in need of. Because everywhere else I go I'm hearing the same thing through my head; for 30 years I heard the same thing, and they keep repeating it through their head for 30 years.

But there is a reality from the heart; and the people of the heart, they carry a signal in which Allah ﷻ, Prophet ﷺ and *Ulul amr* are now transmitting that signal. That signal, when you pick up their teaching, it's a dress upon the soul. It's a blessing upon the soul. It's a preparation for the soul. And their associations are not like regular associations. Their associations have a secret and that if they enter into that secret, they will be dressed by whatever they eat in that niche, whatever they drink in that niche, whatever *du'a* they make in that niche, maybe Allah ﷻ will accept it there.

*Subhana rabbika rabbal 'izzati 'amma yasifoon, wa salaamun 'alal mursaleen, walhamdulillahi rabbil 'aalameen. Bi hurmati Muhammad al-Mustafa wa bi siri Surat al-Fatiha.*

# Energy Attacking the Body and its Defense Mechanism and Realities of Enneagram

Everything is a testing and a lesson in our lives. Divine says if I don't beat you now, you will get a beating in the grave. I don't want to beat you in the grave. Take your beatings, take your lessons, and take your examples. It's bringing your physicality down. I'm trying to dress your soul, not dress your physicality, not to make your physicality to be important and to be crowned. I'm

trying to crush your physicality and bring the reality of the soul out. I want your soul in my presence.

Then everything we start to contemplate that, 'Why did it happen?' Then the Divine says that, 'Why are you better than any of the prophets? Didn't they have difficulty? Weren't they whipped and beaten, or didn't people throw rocks at them? Didn't people yell at them, accuse them and all sorts of physical torment to them?' So what's wrong with a little bit of difficulty because none of us are receiving the difficulty that the prophets received.

So constantly turning it over to God and to the Divine. Inspiration comes back that it's not that bad. Wasn't it a little bit of cleansing that, it sort of brings out different issues that we weren't aware of. Then the

Shaykh is teaching that that brings out the perfection of character. So when something happens, contemplate about it. Find an issue in yourself and why it happened and that resolves a character defect.

## The Enneagram is Not a Self-Help Program

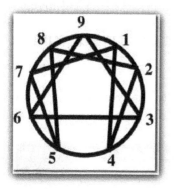

This, by the way, is the study of the enneagram. This is all the Naqshbandi realities of the enneagram. For anyone who is interested in the enneagram, they have to realize that enneagram today of psychology is a self-help program. They took out the mentor and they made it a self-help program, which no self-help ever works. That's like a surgery by book, where you sort of lie down and cut and pull your own organ out and stitch it up. Self-help, by the virtue, self-help you have to be true to yourself. Most people are not true to themselves and what their character defect is.

## The Real Enneagram Are the Spiritual Guides

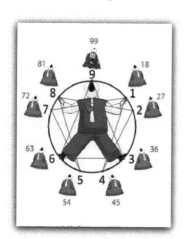

So the understanding of enneagram today where they say, okay you have to recognize you are an angry person and then use these chants to fix that. That enneagram is an innovation of a reality. The real enneagram are the spiritual mentors. They have the knowledge of our self. Once you are in their association, their prayer for you is that the testing starts and that cleansing starts. That, 'My Lord, that person is asking to ascend, let their testing begin.'

## The Guides Pray for the Students' Character Defects to be Resolved

Then Divine will say, 'I know what's inside of them and that which they don't know about themselves, bring it out.' If you don't bring it out, that sickness stays and you are buried with it. At that time you will have to deal with it. At that time, they say it's 70,000 times more difficult than dealing with it now because you can deal with being angry now. The postman is yelling at you, you don't know why he yelled at you and threw a package versus dealing with issues of the grave and having cleansing in the grave.

So the Shaykhs make their prayers that, 'Bring out the defects in the character of my followers. What's hidden inside them, because they think of themselves nicely but bring out what is bothering You in their character so that You will be pleased with them.' Then all the testing starts, all the testing starts. Most of the testing is by our own associations because the most painful tests are from the people you love. A stranger tests you and says, 'Oh that guy was crazy, you should keep driving.' But ourselves, our communities, our fellow students, our homes, our loved ones; they have all the buttons. So they are inspired by the Divine; press 1, 2, 3 – boom! Everything changes.

With that realization, we have to be happy. The Shaykh's prayers are moving. The Divine says, 'I'm going to bring out all of the sickness because of their prayers.' So the real enneagram are the mentors, praying for the real character defect to come out. Not the one that you think you have, but the one that you weren't aware of having, and how much difficulty it's causing onto your soul. That becomes the cleansing process. That brings out all of these character defects.

## The Divine Presence is in the Heart, at the Center of the Star

That is that reality of that energy moving up the legs and the heavenly

energy trying to dress the heart and to empower the soul. At this point, [Shaykh points at top of the upper triangle] if this is the head, right here [draws in center of the upper triangle, in star diagram], is the heart. So when this comes together as the Star of David, you'll see the center of that whole star is the Divine Presence because Allah ﷻ, the Divine, is telling us, 'I cannot be found in the heavens or on earth, except in the heart of my believer.'

مَا وَسِعَنِيْ لَا سَمَائِيْ وَلَا اَرْضِيْ وَلَكِنْ وَسِعَنِيْ قَلْبِ عَبْدِيْ اَلْمُؤْمِنْ

*"Maa wasi`anee laa Samayee, wa la ardee, laakin wasi'anee qalbi 'Abdee al Mu'min."*

*"Neither My Heavens nor My Earth can contain Me, but the heart of my Believing Servant." (Hadith Qudsi conveyed by Prophet Muhammad (pbuh))*

Because if we are going to a place where God is sitting somewhere on a chair, it's not possible. The Creator is outside the circle of creation. There are prophets, there are angels, there are many heavenly beings; but the Divine is showing us, 'The only place you can truly find My Power is in the heart of believer. If I'm on that heart, then you're going to find all the secrets of that Divine enlightenment opening on that servant.'

### The Battle of Positive and Negative Energies For the Throne of the Heart

So then showing us here that that Divine heart has to be empowered. All of that emanation is going towards that essence. All of the material desire is also trying to attack that Divine Throne. Its interest is in toppling the throne. So like an old movie of kings and it's exactly like a battle for a kingdom; that negative desires wants to topple the throne. So the negativity starts to move up into the body, starts to energize. Again this is from the prophetic teaching that Prophet Muhammad ﷺ taught, 'If you guarantee for me your mouth and your genital, I will guarantee for you

paradise,' because these are the two openings that are going to control these realities.

So along this, that evilness is going to attack that point. Then as he's attacking and moving up towards our being, because it's a battle of one on one. It's a battle of one individual against all of the energies of negativity. So what does he do before he comes? He starts to move into the blood; and his movement, that energy, that negativity is moving in the blood system, attaching itself to the iron.

### Energy Moves Through the Iron in the Blood

How does energy attach to our physicality? It moves through the water but it needs something to attach to, energy, and it attaches to iron. And our medical people, they are going to find more and more an understanding that all infection has to have a root in iron. It means if no trace of iron, it can't attach itself to something. Infection or infestation of negative energy. That the negative energy's going to move and attach itself to iron, and starts to move up like a battle, marching, marching, upward.

## The Negative Energy First Attacks the Liver and Kidneys

The first line, because it cannot hit the heart directly; the heart is, by our nature, too much power. So it doesn't attack straight towards the castle, like old time castles, you can't. So where is it going to go? To your liver and to your kidneys. Its first line because it's moving in the blood like soldiers marching, marching, hit to where – the liver and kidneys. Because these are the big filters. These are the big barrier for the heart. It filters and cleanses.

So then that negativity's influence is to destroy the liver and destroy the kidneys. And the biggest sicknesses we have nowadays are liver disease, kidney disease, and hypertension. It is hitting, hitting, hitting, hitting; then 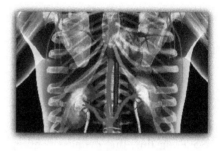 when added hitting is encouraged, he says, drink something. Don't drink water because water purifies the system, but drink spirits because it's fire, it's gasoline onto a fire. So pour that gasoline in and it starts to move. And with that, their armies are moving faster and as a fact, it collapses the liver, collapses the kidneys. And like the movie, 'Lord of the Rings', the barrier is crushed. They have breached the kingdom, hit it down and it's a free for all at that point. They are running like crazy, moving up the system.

## The Next Point of Attack is the Lungs – Tree of Life

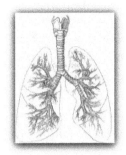

Where is the next system that they're going to collapse very fast once they have breached the kidneys and the liver is the lungs; it's the tree of life. So on 'Lord of the Rings', they had one who burnt that tree. There was one tree in front of the palace because they're dead and he kept seeing a vision of it always on fire. It's because evilness is going to take out the lungs. The lungs are the breath of life. It's the breath and the gift from God for your existence.

So they turn breath on fire with smoking, because smoking and drinking go nicely together. It's not a coincidence, it's because they're encouraging you. We hit the liver and the kidneys; now start to smoke, smoke, smoke, as if to throw a fire onto the lungs. Because that is the blood force, that the blood is going into the lungs to be purified, releasing its gases. It's like a tree outside, it has 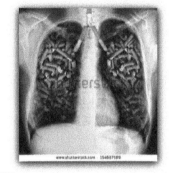 all of its contaminants and saying that, 'We are coming to the lungs, giving you our waste. Give us back what God has given to us.' Then we throw back into it more fire.

## Then There is a Heart Attack and the Kingdom Collapses

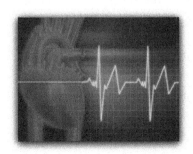

So the blood was trying to get rid of the fire and we threw back in more fire. It means, boom, at that time, it hit the lungs, collapsed the kingdom and went straight for the heart and toppled the throne. At that time, it's a heart attack; the heart has been attacked. It means the Divine Throne has been flipped and that individual has been attacked and the kingdom has been taken over.

To understand a heavenly reality, it's easier to see how much of an influence it has in the negative world. You see this happening on a daily basis. You may not see the angelic version and say, 'Oh I've never seen an angelic person walking around,' but we see all of this happening in all our lives. And we see how that influence is moving in and trying to get us to do all of these things and attack all of our faculties and flip the heart.

## Conquer This Battle by Purifying Your Breath With *Zikr* of *Hu*

So then the spiritual crisis that we are trying to open and trying to realize is how to conquer that. It means then, how are you going to conquer this whole attack and energize the soul? The breathing. That's why meditation is body, mind, and soul.

First thing on the body, when heavenly protection is coming, the heavenly advice to the physicality is saying, 'Okay, doesn't matter if you lost the fight, there is always hope.' Because at the last minute Gandalf came down and rode down and annihilates all of the attack, in the 'Lord of the Rings'. So the Divine is showing us that even if you have been attacked and everything has been taken over, there is still hope. The hope is in the breathing.

As soon as we start spiritual breathing, understanding the power of that Divine breath, and breathing with Divine recitation, "*Huuuu*", the blood starts to move. The iron on that blood becomes angelic energy fighting off negative energy. So the first force of energy that starts to come because it's a far superior power. It means if you call upon Him, God says, 'If you call upon Me one step, I come

99 steps.' It means His Power is far more superior than any type. As soon as you call upon Him by the breath, it means that energy comes onto the iron, onto the blood, onto our being, and pushes away the negative influence.

So then the power of breathing and then re-establishing that tree of life. That's why the holy tree, the tree of life, the tree of certainty, in all religions, in all spiritual paths; it's the tree of life. So success of our life is based on how are we going to treat that tree? We have to guard it. So immediately everything pertaining to that tree is our importance. How are we going to take care of it, how are we going to nourish it, how are we going to breathe and bring that energy into the tree.

## Re-establish the Kingdom and Guard the Throne of the Heart

So then the Divine is showing us that's why it's called the '*Nafas Rahmah*', the 'breath of mercy' because that breath is going to come in and energize that blood, energize that iron. And what does it do, that blood immediately flows into the heart and energizes the heart. That's the first part of our castle that has to be re-established. You have to put back the throne. We have to energize and put all your guards around the throne that nothing now can come to the king.

The first object of the battle is to protect the king. So protection of the throne; the first line of protection is breathing. As soon as you breathe and bring that energy and bring all of that *qudra* (power), it starts to empower. The heart now becomes alive. The breath that's coming in, the energy that's coming on is moving into the heart, energized with *zikr*, with recitation. The heart is then stamping that blood, putting its Divine seal, and sending that blood now towards all the organs.

It means they came now to the Divine king; they took their initiation, they received their stamp. Each cell like a little soldier, each piece of blood, each atom of blood, like a soldier, coming before the king of the heart. Each one is being stamped by the beat of the heart which is from the Divine Essence, stamped, empowered and told, 'Go, go my son towards all your organs and purify them. And bring us back towards the heavenly kingdom'. That's what sends that energy back to the kidneys, back to the liver, which means it nourishes all of the essential organs from the heart.

So then the first level of our taking this serious is the breathing. So it's not something small. It's not something we can try to do here and there; but if we are serious about trying to open that reality, then deep understanding of the power of the breath. That has to do with the body. This has to do with the understanding of the body.

## Reality of Divine Heart That is Beating in the Prophetic Heart

Bringing the energy to the heart, establishing that order, establishing that power is that first process and the importance of the process. It's the first step in understanding our physiology and who knows himself will know his Lord. This will be used in our understanding of, with all that majesty that's described, *"Wa laqad karramna bani adama…"* (We have honoured the creation of Adam, Holy Qur'an, 17:70)

وَلَقَدْ كَرَّمْنَا بَنِي آدَمَ...

*17:70 – "Wa laqad karramna bani adama…" (Surat Al-Isra)*

*"And We have certainly honoured the children of Adam…"*
*(The Night Journey, 17:70)*

## 1. First Heart: The Divinely Heart

This is the only creation; we won't go into that but just to say this before we start the levels of the heart that inside that heart is a divine essence that beats. We call that the divine heart. That divine heart cannot be seen but it is beating in the prophetic heart because the

prophets are the pillars of creation. So you cannot find that divine power, you cannot reach to it but it's an energy; it's a power that is beating on the prophetic heart. From the prophetic heart is the Adamic heart – Adam.

## 2. Second Heart: The Prophetic Heart

This is the importance of *tariqa* (spiritual path). The divine essence that beats, beats to where first, because you have to know the bulls eye. Its beat, divine beat, is to His messengers because His Gaze is on them. Because His Gaze is on them they were able to deliver a message. So we say then a second part is the prophetic heart. Divine Heart is the Divine Essence that is radiating out as a power that can't be reached. But where is your *qibla* (direction), where is it going to be, where are you going to focus yourself to find that energy? You are going to find it at the prophetic heart because the prophets, their heart was in complete submission, beating divine.

As their heart was beating, again is the symbol [gestures towards symbol], they were created for that perfection and it's not a random choice. They have been created to what, to be in complete submission. So their heart is complete Divine Presence and that heart – that's why the heart is on the outside; it speaks towards creation from the love of the Divine. It is on earth in Divine love, not from Divine fire or anger or fighting; its whole existence is to speak to the Divine.

## Prophets Were in Total Submission – *WajhaAllah* (The Holy Face)

So in the enneagram, *WajhaAllah,* we call the Face of God. Why? Because these prophets, their ears, their eyes, their nostrils and then the tongue is the whole heart.

$$...كُلُّ شَيْءٍ هَالِكٌ إِلَّا وَجْهَهُ لَهُ الْحُكْمُ وَإِلَيْهِ تُرْجَعُونَ (٨٨)$$

*28:88 – "...Kullu shayin halikun illa wajha hu lahul hukmu wa ilayhi turja'oon." (Surat Al-Qasas)*

281

*"... Everything (that exists) will perish except His Face. To Him belongs the Command, and to Him will you (all) be brought back." (The Stories, 28:88)*

It means their whole existence is just to speak the Word of God. Their ears are in complete submission. You see how this is a face? [pointing at the Heart of *Hu wa Hu* diagram] And it's next two ears here, this, two eyes, two nostrils and the tongue is the whole heart because their whole existence is just to speak from God. Their hearing is not to hear from people. They don't take the opinions of people but their hearing was in complete submission to the Divine.

Their eyes were watching creation. So any time we were calling upon a prophet or asking for a prophet's intervention or a saint's intervention, is 'Please gaze upon me with your spiritual vision, because their ears are in submission.'

يَا أَيُّهَا الَّذِينَ آمَنُوا لَا تَقُولُوا رَاعِنَا وَقُولُوا انظُرْنَا وَاسْمَعُوا... (١٠٤)

*2:104 – "Yaa ayyuhal ladheena aamano, laa taqolo ra'yina wa qolu unzurna wasma'o; ..." (Surat Al-Baqarah)*

*"O you who believe! Do not say (to Prophet Muhammad (saws)) Raina, listen to us, and say Unzurna (gaze upon us) and you listen (to him (saws), ..."*
*(The Cow, 2:104)*

So they are taking constant command but what they can give you is their vision. So their eyes gaze upon creation; their eyes have light and power. So if their eyes are upon us then we reach that satisfaction. Their breath is completely for Divine. It means they are able to bring all that Divine energy and realize that essence. And, as a result, the one and most powerful is the tongue. And that whole existence is just to speak, speak and raise us. This is the second heart.

## 3. Third Heart – The Adamic Heart

The third heart which we created creation in our image is Adamic heart – the heart of the Prophet Adam that was created by two hands. So Adam آدم

– *Alif* ا, *Dal* د, *Meem* م means the *Alif* ا is at the Essence of Allah ﷲ and the *Dal* د and the *Meem* م. So then showing you these three of Adam, that Adam is a result of the *Alif* ا of Allah ﷻ, the Essence of Allah ﷻ, the *Meem* م

of Muhammad ﷺ محمد which represents the prophetic kingdom and the *Dal*, the 'D' د of the *dunya* دنيا.

آدم = ا    د    م

الله    دنيا    محمد

Adam = Alif, Dal, Meem

Allah, Dunya, Muhammad ﷺ

It means that these are the three lights that Mawlana Shaykh teaches us; the light of God, the light of Prophet ﷺ, from Prophet's ﷺ light is the light of creation coming out.

This teaches us about our greatness. Why? Because God is now showing us, 'You are the only creation that can reach towards those realities because you are from those realities.' You use your Adamic heart to move towards that ocean to the prophetic heart. And in the prophetic heart, you find yourself in the Divine Heart. So you use your vessel, you find yourself in their vessel. If we can find ourself in their vessel, that is in the Divine Vessel because the Divine is looking into their heart.

وَآيَةٌ لَّهُمْ أَنَّا حَمَلْنَا ذُرِّيَّتَهُمْ فِي الْفُلْكِ الْمَشْحُونِ (٤١)

36:41 – *"Wa ayatul lahum anna hamalna dhurriyyatahum fil fulkil mashhooni."* (Surat Yaseen)

*"And a sign for them is that we have carried their atoms/forefathers in the loaded ship."* (Yaseen, 36:41)

That becomes the understanding of why then the levels of the heart and why the first level of understanding is, 'We have honoured the creation of Adam.'

وَلَقَدْ كَرَّمْنَا بَنِي آدَمَ وَحَمَلْنَاهُمْ فِي الْبَرِّ وَالْبَحْرِ وَرَزَقْنَاهُم مِّنَ الطَّيِّبَاتِ وَفَضَّلْنَاهُمْ عَلَىٰ كَثِيرٍ مِّمَّنْ خَلَقْنَا تَفْضِيلًا (٧٠)

17:70 – *"Wa laqad karramna banee adama, wa hamalna hum filbarri wal bahri wa razaqnahum minat tayyibati wa faddalnahum 'ala katheerin mimman khalaqna tafdeela."* (Surat Al-Isra)

*"And We have certainly honoured the children of Adam and carried them on the land and sea and provided good and pure sustenance and bestow upon them favours, and preferred them over much of what We have created, with [definite] preference."* (The Night Journey, 17:70)

'We have made you from that and you're the only creation that can go into your heart to reach to the prophetic heart; the zebras can't, the bears can't. There's nothing else in creation that can go into their heart and find themselves in the prophetic heart, and the prophetic heart into the Divine Kingdom. So then you use that to go back towards that reality and open that reality; and that goes into the study of the heart.

*Subhana rabbika rabbal 'izzati 'amma yasifoon, wa salaamun 'alal mursaleen, walhamdulillahi rabbil 'aalameen. Bi hurmati Muhammad al-Mustafa wa bi siri Surat al-Fatiha.*

# Keep *Wudu* at All Times to Avoid Sickness, Sins, and Loss of Sustenance

When you travel around, it is always a reminder for ourselves that the *tariqa* (spiritual path) comes and teaches to carry the best of character. And that character has the best of discipline. One important discipline that is very important for our life and one of the most important disciplines of our life is to keep yourself always in a state of *wudu* (ablution). Because I'm always astonished when we go out, as soon as they call the *azaan* (call to prayer), everybody is running for bathrooms and washing.

## Concept of *Wudu* (Ablution) is Not Only For *Salah* (Daily Prayer)

The way of the *Rijal* (Men of God), the way of Sayyidina Muhammad ﷺ is to keep oneself always in a state of *wudu*. If you are making *wudu* upon *wudu* for the sake of *barakah* and blessings, *alhamdulillah*; that's from *azemat*. But most likely it's from a state in which people are running, that they don't keep themselves in *wudu*. The only understanding of *wudu* is that it is only for *salah* (daily prayer). It means you are in *majlis* of *zikr*, *majlis* of *mahfils*, only when they call the *azaan*, everybody is running to go and wash. This is *tark al adab* (bad manner) and for us it's completely forbidden.

The source of all difficulty, the source of all sickness, the source of the *rizq* and sustenance, everything to be cut is when the servant is unable to keep themself in the state of ritual purity. Our life is based on that understanding. Later in your life you will depend upon that if you begin to feel energy. We have to believe that this is like a light in the heart; Allah ﷻ begins to deposit these lights and every *Shaytan* and every bad energy that is surrounding is trying to attack that light.

## The Etiquette of *Ghusul* (Shower) and *Wudu* (Ablution)

So just on an energy understanding that as soon as you carry a positive charge, the negative charge is going to be moving towards you. What Prophet Muhammad ﷺ brought for us as a protection against that negativity is a state of *wudu*. Also the power of your *ghusl*, your shower, with all of  its *adabs* (etiquette). We said before in the other talks on energy, that not to urinate into the shower, the shower has to be a ritual purity. It has to be a state of *ghusl*, like you have passed away and you are going to be washed and presented to Allah ﷻ. It means you keep the *adab* of the shower.

Then throughout the day is to keep yourself in a ritual state of purity. As soon as you negate the *wudu*, you need to wash. We don't have to go into all of the ways that *wudu* is negated, those are pretty obvious. For anyone who studies a little bit on YouTube, that if you urinate, defecate, or pass things through your bodily orifices, you have to wash. And don't postpone that wash and keep yourself instantly in a state of *wudu*.

## Keep the State of *Wudu* and Ritual Purity at All Times

I don't understand the concept, where people can use the facilities and then go out throughout their day. And the concept of *wudu* for them is only at the time of *salah, azaan* goes off, and they wash. Our way is that you have to be washed at all times. As soon as you lose your *wudu* by using the facility, enter back into a state of *wudu* which means go wash, come out, make your two *rakat Salat ul-Wudu* (prayer of ablution) and you begin to seal the body. When you seal the body that is your defense against every difficulty.

Your being is like a kingdom in which Allah ﷻ wants to deposit lights and wants to deposit blessings; and *shayateen* (devils) and negative energy want to destroy that kingdom. They want to attack you, hit you, harm you, and make everything to be dropped from you. So like the movie 'Lord of the Rings', it means orcs, these demons, are always trying to break through your walls, trying to break and penetrate. So it means that by keeping yourself in a state of *wudu*, you washed, you cleansed, you now have a shield of protection around you. That shield of protection, it keeps away all that negativity.

## You Must Keep *Wudu* in Holy Associations

Then, especially for the Milad an-Nabi ﷺ, (Birthday celebration of Prophet Muhammad ﷺ), it's important to reiterate and to ask people that are coming that keep yourself in *wudu*. At any time that you lose your *wudu*, you immediately go wash, again keep yourself in that state. That is your state of protection. That is a state in which one must enter into all of these associations, because of the *ruhaniyat* and because of the heavenly lights in the association. You want to be able to receive those lights, be dressed by those lights, blessed by those lights. Those lights don't come into dirtiness. As soon as the servant enters into a state of dirtiness where they are not clean, then it creates a conflict within that energy field. So it means then the concept of ritual purity and ritual washing is very important for us. It is very important in its energy and the receiving of energy.

## Losing *Wudu* Makes You Vulnerable to Negative Energy and Sickness

Now, when the negative energy attacks, it begins to create a difficulty in everything we do in our lives. It means that if we go about our life without washing, it means you go to the restroom, you go back to work, as soon as you touch that computer, you have no protection. So everything from that device is coming, everything from the floor is coming, everything from the surrounding people, all that negativity is being dressed upon that servant. That leads to all sickness; that leads to all types of difficulties and negativity. Because now you are an energy field in which a tremendous negative charge is entering into the body and trying to create a conflict.

So it means disease, the sickness and the reality of sickness is when negative energy is able to penetrate that field and enter into the body and begin to disrupt everything in life. The excess amount of negative energy is going to again influence the *rizq* and the sustenance of the servant, because again that *barakah*, that light, is being blocked and as a result, all sorts of negativities come and they push away the *Rahmah* (mercy) of Allah ‎ﷻ.

## Follow the True Guides Who Keep the *Sunnah* (Way of Prophet ﷺ)

So it means everything that Sayyidina Muhammad ﷺ brought for us

has a tremendous reality. The *ahl al-haqqa'iq* (people of realities), and our beloved Shaykhs, they keep such an *azemat* and such a reverence and respect for Prophet ﷺ that whatever Prophet ﷺ brought for us, we try our best to adhere to that and to keep

that way in that reality to be dressed by that light, be blessed by that light. Later in our lives, we would come to understand how it protects us.

That's why the *wajib ul-taqleed* is to follow the common Shaykhs. By following them, you don't have to ask any questions. If you would have followed them, you would have understood that. You would have seen how they are always washed, how they pray, how they interact with people. As a result of living your life by copying them, not by thinking, thinking is blocking every door, it is by copying them, copy, copy until you understand. As soon as you copy them, you will be dressed by those realities. Later in life, they inspire within your heart, 'Oh, that's why I've been washing all the time because it's a protection, it keeps away sickness, keeps away difficulty; it safeguards my *rizq*,' because the *rizq* and sustenance coming to you is because of Allah's ﷻ *Rida* and Satisfaction.

When that light and these blessings are dressing the soul, Allah's ﷻ happy with that soul like an adornment, like a dress, like heavenly medallions. As a result of Allah's ﷻ *Rida* and Satisfaction, these *fa'iz* and these blessings begin to dress the soul. One is the *rizq*, the

291

sustenance for the soul, and once the soul receives its sustenance, the *rizq* for the body is following. So, first the sustenance comes upon the soul. If not written upon the soul, it doesn't matter what the body's trying to do, where it's trying to go, how it's trying to conquer the world, nothing opens. The opening comes from the soul.

So by the soul understanding, the soul practices, the *zikr*, the *wudu*, all of the *mahfil*, the *salawats* on Prophet ﷺ, all of the *fard* (obligatory), all of the prayers; all of that is bringing the sustenance upon the soul. When the soul is sustained and the *rizq* is flowing through the soul, it overflows onto the body. And everything that the body is in need from Allah ﷻ becomes attained and dressed upon that being.

It means then everything is in the secret of that *wudu*, keeping that *wudu*, keeping the *ihtiram* of the *wudu*, so that we are protected. As days of negativity increase and increase and increase, it becomes even more important for people who are working and surrounded by negative energies, even more important. Can you imagine that you lose your *wudu* and you are just interacting? How much difficulty comes to you?

## Don't Let Your Shield of Protection Drop

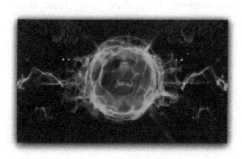

It becomes for you to understand, because we can't put everything into words, that you have a shield of protection and the *shayateen*, that when you have *wudu*, the *shaytans*, they can't approach because of that light. As soon as the shield drops, you are fair game and they are firing arrows that you can't imagine. Those can affect the person in ways that they can't imagine. It can affect their entire shield of protection which can be dropped because of that reality.

So it means later in our lives when we becomes sensitive and *latif*, you feel the energy. You feel that, oh, an attack is coming, things are moving towards you, so that you keep that *wudu* as a means of safety for your life. But until you feel that, it's important to understand that and to keep that practice.

*Subhana rabbika rabbal 'izzati 'amma yasifoon, wa salaamun 'alal mursaleen, walhamdulillahi rabbil 'aalameen. Bi hurmati Muhammad al-Mustafa wa bi siri Surat al-Fatiha.*

# Sins Open the Door to Doubt and Destroy Faith

...فَنَادَىٰ فِي الظُّلُمَاتِ أَن لَّا إِلَٰهَ إِلَّا أَنتَ سُبْحَانَكَ إِنِّي كُنتُ مِنَ الظَّالِمِينَ (٨٧)
فَاسْتَجَبْنَا لَهُ وَنَجَّيْنَاهُ مِنَ الْغَمِّ ۚ وَكَذَٰلِكَ نُنجِي الْمُؤْمِنِينَ (٨٨)

*21:88 – "...Fanada fizh zhulumati an  la ilaha illa anta Subhanaka,  innee
kuntu minazh zhalimeen.(87). Fastajabna lahu wa najjayna hu minal ghammi,
wa kadhalika nunjee almumineen." (Surat Al-Anbiya)*

*"...But he cried out through the depths of darkness, "There is no god/diety except
You; Glory to you: Indeed I have been of the wrongdoers/Oppressor to Myself!"
(87) "So We responded to him and saved him from the distress. And thus do We
save the believers. (88)" (The Prophets, 21:88)*

Yaa Rabbi, forgive us. *Fastajabna lahu wa najjainahu minal ghammi
wa kadhalika nunjil mu'mineen.*

*Alhamdulillah,* always praying that Allah's ﷻ Mercy to dress
us and bless us and that we exist and live within that Mercy. Allah ﷻ is
constantly forgiving us and dressing and blessing us. To share from
Mawlana Shaykh Hisham's teachings that, in this holy month of Rajab,
Allah ﷻ made from the realities of the *Arifeen* that everything is
multiplied by 9.

## Why Allah ﷻ Wanted 63ʳᵈ Chapter of Qur'an to be *Munafiqoon*?

That 9 multiplied by the seventh lunar month brings the reality of 63 (9×7=63). Why Allah ﷻ wanted the 63ʳᵈ *Surah* in Holy Qur'an in this holy month [Rajab] to be the *munafiqeen*? In the way of *ma'rifah thumma amanoo thumma kafaroo*.

إِنَّ الَّذِينَ آمَنُوا ثُمَّ كَفَرُوا ثُمَّ آمَنُوا ثُمَّ كَفَرُوا ثُمَّ ازْدَادُوا كُفْرًا لَمْ يَكُنِ اللَّـهُ لِيَغْفِرَ لَهُمْ وَلَا لِيَهْدِيَهُمْ سَبِيلًا (١٣٧)

*4:137 – "Innal ladheena amano thumma kafaro thumma amano thumma kafaroo thumma izdado kufran lam yakuni Allahu liyaghfira lahum wa la liyahdiyahum sabeela." (Surah An-Nisa)*

*"Indeed, those who have believed then disbelieved, then believed, then disbelieved, and then increased in disbelief – Allah won't forgive them, nor will He guide them on a path/way." (The Women, 4:137)*

That not believing, then believing, believing, and not believing, that *InshaAllah* [we] moved past that ocean. And now moving towards the oceans of faith. They describe for us a barrier before the way of Allah ﷻ is to face the hypocrisy. Not calling out other people as hypocrites but the hypocrite within myself. That for the *Arifeen* and to be Gnostic and to be understanding in Allah's ﷻ Way, and for Allah ﷻ to grant sincerity, requires a character which you analyze and took a *hisaab* (an account) for yourself before Allah ﷻ begins the *hisaab*.

With the *barakah* (blessing) of *Awliyaullah* and guidance within our lives, it is like a hand over us that constantly is recalibrating. That they say only a fool represents himself in a court of law. It means one who does not have a lawyer, a *wakeel*, and tries to represent themselves in Allah's ﷻ Divine Presence, *Shaytan* is going to be all over them. That *Shaytan* makes every *amal* (action) to seem good to the servant. *Awliyaullah* come into our life and inspire us that by keeping their company and fulfilling the way and the *Sunnah* of Sayyidina

Muhammad ﷺ. *Itibah* means to keep the company of pious people and they teach, you learn and observe and that calibrates our life.

## Our Actions Affect Our Belief (Good or Bad)

This ocean and this reality of the holy month of Rajab is a reminder for the hypocrite that lies dormant within the self. They want us to understand the concept of sin, belief and *shak* (doubt).

When everything is good and the actions and *amal* is good, Allah ﷻ says, *"Bismillahir Rahmanir Raheem, atiullah wa ati ar-Rasula wa Ulul amri minkum, wa 'izzatullah wa 'izzatur Rasul wa 'izzat al-mu'mineen."*

يَاأَيُّهَا الَّذِينَ آمَنُوا أَطِيعُوااللهَ وَأَطِيعُواالرَّسُولَ وَأُولِي الْأَمْرِ مِنْكُمْ...(٥٩)

*4:59 – "Ya ayyu hal latheena amanoo Atiu Allaha wa atiur Rasola wa Ulil amre minkum..." (Surat An-Nisa)*

*"O You who have believed, Obey Allah, Obey the Messenger, and those in authority among you." (The Women, 4:59)*

...وَلِلَّهِ الْعِزَّةُ وَلِرَسُولِهِ وَلِلْمُؤُمِنِينَ وَلَكِنَّ الْمُنَافِقِينَ لَا يَعْلَمُونَ (٨)

*63:8 – "...Wa Lillahil 'izzatu wa li Rasooli hi wa lil Mumineena wa lakinnal munafiqeena la y'alamoon." (Surat Al-Munafiqoon)*

*"...And to Allah belongs [all] honor, and to His messenger, and to the believers, but the hypocrites do not know." (The Hypocrites, 63:8)*

## Good Actions Bring *Fa'iz* and Blessings

It means this light, this guidance, this *fa'iz*, everything begins to dress the servant. Especially the servants in the *turooq*, in the Way of Prophet ﷺ inheriting the Way of Sayyidina Muhammad ﷺ, that they don't leave themselves unattended or to be by themselves. As the Companions took the hand of Prophet ﷺ for the completion of their faith, the *tabi'yeen, wa tabi at-tabi'yeen*, which was the whole way of life. They took the hand of guidance and they didn't release that hand until they took their last breath.

$$وَاعْتَصِمُوا بِحَبْلِ اللَّهِ جَمِيعًا وَلَا تَفَرَّقُوا ۚ (١٠٣)$$

*3:103 – "Wa'tasimo bihab lillahi jamee'an wa la tafarraqo." (Surat Al-Imran)*

*"And hold firmly to the rope of Allah all together and do not separate."*
*(Family of Imran, 3:103)*

That way of guidance is a teaching for us. If what you are doing from these *amals* (deeds) and it is good and Allah ﷻ finds acceptance in that *amal*, you feel the emanations from Divinely Presence. *Izzatullah* is flowing into the heart of *izzatur Rasul*, in the heart of Prophet ﷺ. *Izzatur Rasul* means the *nazar* (gaze) of Sayyidina Muhammad ﷺ is upon those *Ulul amr* (saints). If their action is correct then the *nazar* of the *Ulul amr* through their soul, not their physicality, but what Allah ﷻ is dressing on their soul. *Wa kunoo ma as-sadiqeen.*

## *Awliya* Dress Us From the Light and Emanation of RasulAllah ﷺ

$$يَا أَيُّهَا الَّذِينَ آمَنُوا اتَّقُوا اللَّـهَ وَكُونُوا مَعَ الصَّادِقِينَ (١١٩)$$

*9:119 – "Ya ayyuhal ladheena amanoo ittaqollaha wa kono ma'as sadiqeen." (Surat At-Tawba)*

*"O you who have believed, fear Allah and be with those who are true (in words and deed)." (The Repentance, 9:119)*

Allah ﷻ ordered us to keep their company. Why? because the *izzat* of Allah ﷻ is dressing the *izzat* of Sayyidina Muhammad ﷺ. Not everybody can take that power. It means that power is coming like a transformer to be cool and peaceful.

قُلْنَا يَا نَارُ كُونِي بَرْدًا وَسَلَامًا ... (٦٩)

21:69 – *"Qulna ya Naaru, kuni Bardan wa Salaman ..." (Surat Al-Anbiya)*

*"We said, "O fire, be cool and Peaceful ..." (The Prophets, 21:69)*

Nobody can take the *izzat* of Allah ﷻ except Sayyidina Muhammad ﷺ. That is why Allah ﷻ says, 'If I reveal My Qur'an on the mountain it will be like dust, but the heart of Sayyidina Muhammad ﷺ is firm.'

وَ أَنزَلْنَا هَذَا الْقُرْآنَ عَلَىٰ جَبَلٍ لَّرَأَيْتَهُ خَاشِعًا مُّتَصَدِّعًا مِّنْ خَشْيَةِ اللَّهِ... (٢١)

59:21 – *"Law anzalna hadha alQurana 'ala jabalin laraaytahu, khashi'an mutasaddi'an min khashyatillahi...." (Surat Al-Hashr)*

*"Had We sent down this Qur'an on a mountain, verily, you would have seen it obliterated to dust (from its power)..." (The Exile, 59:21)*

Nobody can come between *laa ilaha ilAllah Muhammadun RasulAllah*. The *Ulul amr* are inheriting from Prophet ﷺ. They take that *izzat*, they take that *fa'iz* and they begin to emanate out. They are like *qamarun*, like moons, from this Nation that take from the sun, and from the reality of Prophet ﷺ.

299

All of it is in the *Hadith* but you can't sit here and just keep repeating books and books of *Hadith*. Where Prophet ﷺ said, 'My Companions are like stars.'

أَصْحَابِيْ كَالنُّجُــوْمُ بِأَيِّهِمْ اَقْتَدَيْتِمْ اَهْتَدَيْتِمْ

*"Ashabi kan Nujoom, bi ayyihim aqta daytum ahta daytum."*

*"My companions are like stars. Follow any one of them and you will be guided."*
*Prophet Muhammad (pbuh)*

If his Companions are like stars, he has got to be the *sahib*, the owner of all stars! He has to be the *shams* (sun) for all the stars, but the humility is to say, 'My Companions are all stars.' If the Companions are stars then Prophet ﷺ is the sun for the entire universes of Creation.

It means if that sun is shining upon the *Ulul amr* they are like a moon reflecting light. That *fa'iz* begins to dress the student. That light begins to dress them, that *izzat* begins to dress them and they begin  to have more and more faith. And have more and more *himmah* (zeal) to complete what Allah ﷻ wants to be completed.

## Understand the Concept of Belief, Sin, and *Shak* (Doubt)

Then the reminder comes that when the ocean of *shak* (doubt) comes, why is it coming? This is in the way of knowing myself that as soon as I have a doubt they want me to analyze everything. That go back to yourself and find out what is happening because the reality is that you build with your good actions like a shield of protection all around you.

If you watched the old Star Trek movies, there is a force field. There is a force field all around the believer based on good actions. When Allah ﷻ is happy, Prophet ﷺ is happy, the *Ulul amr* (saints) are happy; your force field is working. Your heart is emanating this field of energy all around you that *Shaytan* has a very difficult time penetrating.

## Sins Create a Hole in Our Force Field of Protection

What does *Shaytan* want? He says I can't get into that force field, let me bring some *sayyi'at*, let me bring some sins and *gunnah*. As soon as

the servant enters into sins that field has a hole. As soon as the hole comes into the servant, the *Shaytans* are moving. And *Shaytan's* purpose is to move with all his minions into that hole to block the reflection of that *fa'iz*. Now the servant is receiving less *fa'iz*, less emanations, less *juzba* (attraction) and connections and they feel themselves to be detached. If their heart is alive, they understand the connection is now in difficulty.

There are *shayateen* (Satans) who are entering into the force field that Allah ﷻ is putting around the believer and that is why *Shaytan* wants sins. It means everything that *Shaytan* brings is in order to bring down that force field of the believer. As soon as they engage in sins, where it can be from eating wrong, from seeing wrong, from doing wrong and especially from acting wrong. Anything that Allah ﷻ is not pleased with in the character of that servant, it creates an opening and that is all *Shaytan* wants.

That is why we give the analogies about movies. Why? Because more people are watching movies than those who are watching this. There are twenty million people or fifty million or a billion people watching a movie and there are only fifty people watching this. So what is Allah ﷻ teaching through? The movies. There must be an understanding in everything that is coming out, there must be a *hikmah* (wisdom), unless it is fully under the hands of *shayateen*. In these movies they begin to show that the only way into the palace is when they bomb a hole in the wall. If they can bomb a hole in the wall every *Shaytan* is running through that palace.

Allah ﷻ is describing, you are like that, you have an energy field with your good actions and good *amal* (actions) and you are protecting yourself and making this force to be very strong.

$$\text{وَ قُلْ جَاءَالْحَقُّ وَزَهَقَ الْبَطِلُ، إِنَّ الْبَطِلَ كَانَ زَهُوقًا (٨١)}$$

*17:81 – "Wa qul jaa alhaqqu wa zahaqal baatil, innal batila kana zahooqa."
(Surat Al-Isra)*

*"And say, "Truth has come, and falsehood has perished. Indeed falsehood, [by its nature], is ever perishing." (The Night Journey, 17:81)*

If that force is strong and keeping away negativity, because *haqq* (truth) pushes away falsehood, then you feel the *fa'iz*, you feel the emanations. You feel the *himmah* (zeal), you feel like you want to do more and your faith is growing day by day.

## Doubt is a Sign of Doing Something Wrong

For the *Ahlal Muhasabah*, the people who take account, they say; that as soon as you feel a doubt, go back into your accounting and *muhasabah*; that you are doing something wrong. The doubt doesn't just come, it comes through a hole. What is it that you are doing incorrect in your actions and begin to take an accounting that, what did I do today, what did I do yesterday, what did I eat, what did I say, what were my actions. Go through every action that we did for that

302

day and begin to analyze, 'Was Allah ﷻ happy with what I ate, with what I drank, with what I did, with what I said? Did I pray?' Some people don't even pray. Then you are definitely detached from that light.

If you detach from that light that is all *Shaytan* wants, 'Don't pray your *Maghrib* (sunset) prayer, go to sleep, go to sleep.' Okay if you don't pray then you opened a hole through this field because you are not good with Allah ﷻ, you are not good with the angels and definitely Prophet ﷺ is ashamed.

You have to keep the way of Sayyidina Muhammad ﷺ, keep the way of what Allah ﷻ gave to Sayyidina Muhammad ﷺ. It is not because Allah ﷻ wants anything from it, you are not making Allah ﷻ richer by praying. But Allah ﷻ wants for us all this *izzat*. He says, 'I want to dress you with all these blessings. I want to give from all these emanations so that your Islam becomes real.' You taste it in your heart, you feel the energy that is emanating, your Islam becomes real, your love for Sayyidina Muhammad ﷺ becomes real, Allah ﷻ wants to give all of that.

## When You Don't Eat *Halal* (Permissible) Food, Who Benefits?

If we don't come to receive it and we don't pray the one who benefits from that is *Shaytan*. When we don't eat what is correct, the one who benefits is *Shaytan* and *Shaytan* enters the system. He is fiercely looking at the body. He says, 'Give me a bad action, give me an anger and I am going to enter in.' As soon as that opening happens, and you eat something incorrect, eat something that is not right and has not been *halal* for you, *Shaytan* is coming in through that food and *ta'am*.

## What Makes You Question the *Madad* and Intercession?

If you do an action that is incomplete in worshipness, *Shaytan* comes through that. As soon as *Shaytan* comes we find ourself having doubt; Oh yeah, where is the *madad*, what is this concept of *madad* (support), what is intercession. What is *tariqa* (spiritual path), who are these Shaykhs? You think you became clever and Einstein entered into your brain to think of something. No, *Shaytan* is playing with you now, because there is a hole in your force field.

That (strong) faith is like walking on water. Every reality Allah ﷻ wants to dress us with is exactly like walking on water. As soon as you have doubt you are already falling into the ocean. We pray that Allah ﷻ inspires within our self to take an account of ourselves to destroy the inner hypocrite.

## The Hypocrisy of Kissing *Hajarul Aswad* and Not Kissing the Holy Hair of Prophet ﷺ

That is why wherever these *Ulul amr* go they expose the hypocrisy.
And they engage with people for them to take a *hisaab* (accounting) of themselves. We said before they come and say, 'Why do you have to kiss the hair of Prophet ﷺ?' Why are you kissing the black stone? What is wrong with people!?

They don't understand the religion anymore. Why are you making *tawaf* (circumambulation) around stones and then fiercely fighting to kiss the black stone because that stone is from Paradise. But oh, Prophet ﷺ is the owner of Paradise, the owner of *dunya*, owner of everything, the revealer of Holy Qur'an. You don't think you should be kissing the hair of Sayyidina Muhammad ﷺ?

When they go around with the Holy Hair, they want to point out the hypocrisy. What is the religion that you are following? So that they can bring out this sickness. Why? Because *Shaytan*, he didn't know what sickness he had. He thought his *amal* (action) was so great and that he thought I prostrated for you, 70,000 years, *ya Rabbi*. There is nowhere from here up to Heavens that *Shaytan* did not prostrate.

But Allah ﷻ took him in one shot. I will ask one thing from you and the only thing I ever ask from you is to bow down.

وَعَلَّمَ آدَمَ الْأَسْمَاءَ كُلَّهَا... (٣١)

قَالَ يَا آدَمُ أَنبِئْهُم بِأَسْمَائِهِمْ... (٣٣)

وَإِذْ قُلْنَا لِلْمَلَائِكَةِ اسْجُدُوا لِآدَمَ فَسَجَدُوا إِلَّا إِبْلِيسَ... (٣٤)

2:31 – "*Wa 'allama Adamal Asma a kullaha,..*"

2:33 – "*Qala ya Adamu anbi hum bi asmayihim…*"

2:34 – "*Wa idh qulna lil malayikati osjudo li Adama fasajado illa ibleesa…*"
(*Surah Al-Baqarah*)

"*And He taught Adam the names – all of them…*" (31)

*"He said: "O Adam! Tell them their names ..." (33)*

*"And [mention] when We said to the angels, "Bow Down to Adam"; so they prostrated, except for Iblis..." (34) (The Cow)*

Bow down? Why? Because the knowledge that these *Bani Adam* have and what is important in Allah's Divinely Presence is *ilm*, the whole dialogue between Sayyidina Adam and the angels was based on knowledge. That as soon as they bowed down Allah said, teach them what I taught you. The angels were astonished at the light that was reflecting and the knowledges that the *Bani Adam* and Sayyidina Adam were inheriting.

Allah said the knowledge they have is superior to you and he *(Shaytan)* didn't know his own reality because he takes from *izzatullah*, *'izzat ar Rasul* and *'izzat al Mu'mineen*.

$$...وَلِلَّهِ الْعِزَّةُ وَلِرَسُولِهِ وَلِلْمُؤْمِنِينَ وَلَكِنَّ الْمُنَافِقِينَ لَا يَعْلَمُونَ (٨)$$

*63:8 – "...Wa Lillahil 'izzatu wa li Rasooli hi wa lil Mumineena wa lakinnal munafiqeena la y'alamoon..." (Surat Al-Munafiqoon)*

*"...And to Allah belongs [all] honor, and to His messenger, and to the believers, but the hypocrites do not know." (The Hypocrites, 63:8)*

He *(Shaytan)* takes from behind the *mu'mineen* (believer) his power and his understanding. What Allah gave to the *mu'mineen* and the *Ulul amr*, they are above the rank of *malaika* (angels). That is why they serve them. That is why Allah established the order by asking them to make *sujud*, bow down to them; their knowledge is superior to you, your life is to serve them because they carry Nur Muhammad ﷺ.

It means that reality is huge, that was a *sajdah* (prostration) of *ihtiraam* (respect) not for worship. Why *ihtiraam*? Because the light within their heart of what they are carrying from Prophet's ﷺ light. What is important to Allah and Allah describes, whom We give a knowledge, *ilm laduni wa hikmat bis Saliheen* (We have given them a tremendous bounty).

$$\text{فَوَجَدَا عَبْدًا مِّنْ عِبَادِنَا آتَيْنَاهُ رَحْمَةً مِّنْ عِندِنَا وَعَلَّمْنَاهُ مِن لَّدُنَّا عِلْمًا (٦٥)}$$

*18:65 – "Fawajada 'abdan min 'ibadinaa ataynahu rahmatan min 'indina wa 'allamnahu mil ladunna 'ilma." (Surat Al-Kahf)*

*"And they found a servant from among Our servants to whom we had given mercy from us and had taught him from Us a [certain] knowledge." (The Cave, 18:65)*

## The Hypocrisy and Double Standards of *Masjid* and Parties

It means this is all that Allah ﷻ wants for us. That door can't be achieved when the servant is living in hypocrisy. You make a set of rules for the *masjid* (mosque) but you live by a completely different set of rules on the street. What is that? We are all one community. With Facebook it is made so much easier. We can sit, from our phones and watch everybody's lives. They argue with me in the *masjid* I should be doing this, this, this. Eh, on their Facebook they are posing with women who are not their wives and they don't have covered clothes. What is that? Is that anything left of Islam or Islam is something now we just say by tongue? Everything we say now is by tongue but not by action and not by belief.

Every party is okay with no head covers, all mixed groups, music playing, Bollywood shows playing, that's fine, great. In the *masjid* we have different rules, in the *masjid* we don't say hello to each other, 'I don't know you, oh you be quiet.' If it's not *masjid* we are all knowing each other, everybody says, hey, how are you?

This is not Islam. This is the oceans of hypocrisy. That is why they don't enter into the oceans of being a *mukhlis* (sincere). Allah ﷻ does not open for them sincerity. Sincerity is, that, *ya Rabbi*, You are everywhere. Everywhere is Your *masjid*. I am asking for my heart to be your *masjid*, that You are with me everywhere, *ya Rabbi*. That every night to cry, *ya Rabbi*, destroy the hypocrite within me. That everything I do hypocritical that You are not pleased with, *ya Rabbi*, take it to be destroyed.

## Don't Be Extreme – Be Real and Genuine in Your Belief

*Ya Rabbi*, make me to be firm in my belief. That firmness does not mean to be extreme. It means to be real. It means to be genuine. That you know this world is hard. As you are easy with all the people in your office, be easy with the people in the *masjid*. Why are you bothering the people in the *masjid* but in your offices you are hugging, kissing and shaking hands with everyone? Take the middle ground that Prophet ﷺ wanted for us.

Take the middle path and that middle path as long as it is real, Allah ﷻ will be happy with the servant. *Ya Rabbi, anna 'abduka ajiz wa faqeer* (I am a poor and weak servant), my eyes are seeing all these *gunnahs* (sins), have mercy upon my soul, *ya Rabbi*. Take away all these bad characteristics. Take away all of this hypocrisy that destroys everything from Your Way.

Then, we begin to attack all these sins and block them so that that force field is around us. And then we begin to feel the emanation, feel the lights, feel the power of the *zikr*. And then we will be inspired to keep attending.

Every time a *waswas* (whispering) comes to you to come against the path and come against the Way, is a time for accounting. What am I doing that is allowing these *Shaytans* to come and bring doubt in my way and in reaching Allah's ﷻ *rida* and satisfaction?

We pray Allah ﷻ dresses us and blesses us in this holy month with these lights and blessings. By *Awliyaullah* talking from these realities, we pray that they lift these characteristics away. That the intercession of Sayyidina Muhammad ﷺ is just one *nazar* (gaze) upon the soul that is like a sun which burns all difficulties and that Allah ﷻ be pleased with us.

*Subhana rabbika rabbal 'izzati 'amma yasifoon, wa salaamun 'alal mursaleen, walhamdulillahi rabbil 'aalameen. Bi hurmati Muhammad al-Mustafa wa bi siri Surat al-Fatiha.*

# Chapter Seven

## Protect Your Energy by Following the Prophetic Way (Sunnah)

قُلْ إِنْ كُنْتُمْ تُحِبُّوْنَ اللَّهَ فَاتَّبِعُوْنِيْ يُحْبِبْكُمُ اللَّهُ وَيَغْفِرْ
لَكُمْ ذُنُوْبَكُمْ ۗ وَاللَّهُ غَفُوْرٌ رَّحِيْمٌ (٣١)

3:31 — *"Qul in kuntum tuhibbon Allaha fattabi'oni,
yuhbibkumUllahu wa yaghfir lakum dhunobakum wallahu
Ghaforur Raheem." (Surat Al-Imran)*

*"Say, [O Muhammad], If you should love Allah, then follow
me, [so] Allah will love you and forgive you your sins. And
Allah is Forgiving and Merciful." (Family of Imran, 3:31)*

Sayyidina Prophet Muhammad ﷺ said:

وَمَنْ أَحْيَاءٍ سُنَّتِيْ فَقَدْ أَحَبْنِيْ وَمَنْ أَحَبْنِيْ كَانَ مَعِيَ فِي
الْجَنَّةِ" رواه الترمذي

*"Man ahya Sunnati faqad ahabanee, wa man ahabanee, kana
ma'iya fil jannah." (Tirmidhi)*

*"Who revives my Sunnah loves me, and who really loves me will
be with me in Paradise." (Prophet Muhammad ﷺ).*

# The *Sunnah* of Covering –
# Insulation of Energy

## Protection from Negative Energy
## Head, Hair, Turban, and Ring

وَمَنْ أَحْيَاءِ سُنَّتِيْ فَقَدْ أَحَبَنِيْ وَمَنْ أَحَبَنِيْ كَانَ مَعِيَ فِي الْجَنَّةِ" رواه الترمذي

*"Man ahya Sunnati faqad ahabanee, wa man ahabanee, kana ma'iya fil jannah." (Tirmidhi)*

*"Who revives my Sunnah loves me, and who really loves me will be with me in Paradise." (Prophet Muhammad ﷺ)*

*lhamdulillah,* for the great light of Allah ﷻ that shines upon Prophet ﷺ, that shines upon *Awliyaullah,* and shines upon our beloved guide, Mawlana Shaykh Hisham Kabbani, that is like a sun. As much as we stare into his reality, *alhamdulillah,* lights

313

are emitting and the blessings are shining. If we find anything good it is from his lights. Anything bad is from our own ignorance and we pray for Allah's ﷻ forgiveness.

## The *Sunnah* of Sayyidina Muhammad ﷺ is About Energy

From *Bismillahir Rahmanir Raheem, ati ullah ati ur Rasula wa Ulul amri minkum* (Holy Qur'an, 4:59) and from Mawlana Shaykh's teaching; that so many people are asking about energy and asking about difficulty. And asking, 'Shaykh how do we protect ourselves and take away negativity and increase our positivity?' *Alhamdulillah*, Allah ﷻ, through

His beloved Sayyidina Muhammad ﷺ, gave us everything. It is a matter of whether we want to keep it and what we want to incorporate in our lives; that is its secret.

The *Sunnah* of Sayyidina Muhammad ﷺ is about energy. It is a tremendous protection and a tremendous source of realities for us.

Prophet ﷺ brings it like every secret that, if you follow, you follow by love. Later pious people come into our lives and begin to teach its reality. That if you follow the way of Prophet ﷺ, it is completely about energy. It

is completely about how to bring that Divine Light and that Divine *Qudra* (power) upon the soul.

## Build and Keep Your Energy, Don't Let it Leak

At the same time the energy that you are building, Prophet ﷺ wants for us to keep it. It is one thing to build the energy and completely leak out everything; you always find yourself going two steps forward and three, four, five steps backward. Anybody who does construction or

home maintenance knows that a slow leak can destroy the whole house, the whole structure. If it is a big problem you can immediately see, 'Oh look there is a hole and I see the big problem.' It's the leak that destroys because you don't see it until it has damaged everything. It means the leaks in our life are our movement away from the *Sunnah* of Prophet ﷺ.

People think maybe it is a fashion statement, maybe I can do it, maybe I don't have to do it. It is not at all about that. We start from the beginning and the top (the head), that what the Prophet ﷺ wanted for us is that your head is the Crown of Creation. What Allah ﷻ is bestowing upon it of energies and realities, your *sura*, your face, is inheriting from the Divinely Face. It means in a battle there is no permission to touch the face because it is an inheritance from Allah ﷻ. It means the face, *wajh Allah*, the Divinely Face dresses the face.

## The Turban is the Crown on Your Head

It means the Crown of Creation is the head. If we understand the

grace and majesty that Allah ﷻ gave to the head, then you understand why Prophet ﷺ brought that and said, 'Put the crown upon your head.' The crown of the believer is the turban. And as soon as you wear the turban in *salah* (daily prayer); for anyone who wants to increase their blessings, to understand that as soon as you put the turban and you pray at home or anywhere you go, it is twenty-seven times more than if you prayed without it.

And the reward of every time you revive a *Sunnah* of Sayyidina Muhammad ﷺ, you get the *ajar*, the reward, of seventy martyrs!

$$\text{مَنْ أَحْيَاءِ سُنَّتِيْ عِنْدَ فَسَادِ أُمَّتِيْ فَلَهُ أَجْرَ شَهِيْدَ}$$

*"Man ahya Sunnati 'inda fasadi ummati flahu ajran Shaheed."*

*Narrated by al-Tabaraani in al-Awsat (2/31) Prophet Muhammad (pbuh) said: "Whoever revives my Sunnah when my ummah is corrupt, will have the reward of a hundred martyrs." (Bayhaqi)*

The turban of the Prophet Joseph

Even one martyr is enough for someone's soul. How Allah ﷻ loves Prophet ﷺ that don't let the *Sunnah* of Prophet ﷺ to vanish. So by reviving it in every generation, reviving it in our homes, reviving it in our lives, Allah ﷻ multiplies everything we do. So one building of energy, twenty-seven times your prayers (the rewards) by wearing your turban.

The turban signifies a state of death for the believer. This is like your tombstone, the cap that is going upon the turban. It is same for the *hijab*, it doesn't matter whether it is for the man or woman. Allah ﷻ wants us to guard our head. There is an opening upon the crown of your head, that you feel when the children are born, that softness (on their head). This is a tremendous opening for the soul.

As soon as you are building lights, what *Shaytan* wants is to take your head. He makes it to be unpopular so that you feel, 'Oh you know it is not going to be very stylish and I am not going to look so handsome if I walk around like that.' Or fear, which is the opposite of faith. 'Oh I fear they are going to beat me up if I wear my hat.' What fear? Everybody in the world is wearing a turban. You go to the airport and people are in a turban. The Minister of Defense (in Canada) is in a turban. Who is going to say anything? They have pride and are proud of the *Sunnah* that they carry. We should have even more pride for what Prophet ﷺ has given to us. *Shaytan* wants to make it from fear don't keep the *Sunnah*. But why he wants that; it's so you lose all your energy and that he can keep attacking the head.

It means the majesty is that when you cover your head, you wear a hat or wear your turban, that point of energy is covered. And increasing the humility of the believer, constantly feeling the hand of Allah ﷻ upon their head. They feel a state of humility that, *ya Rabbi*, with that hat on my head I am nothing.

## What Hair Represents to Male and Female

Then everything from the top of the head that Prophet ﷺ brought was of such an importance. When Prophet ﷺ ordered the shaving of the hair. As soon as you complete the *Hajj* (pilgrimage) you shave your head. The *Sahabah* (Companions) waited and they clipped their hair, and Prophet ﷺ was offended. When they went back home and they described that, '*Ya Sayyidi, Ya RasulAllah*, if you want them to shave their head, please shave your head.' And Prophet ﷺ came out and shaved his head and all the Companions immediately shaved their head.

317

## *Awliyullah* Shave Their Heads

They understood the *azemat*, the shaved head is stronger because the hair increases the feminine energy for men. For women it is the

opposite; the length of the hair for women is an honour for her. If two women die, the first one to be buried is going to be based on the length of her hair. (The one with longer hair would be buried first). That is not the truth for men, it is the opposite. The length of his hair increases his feminine energy. So what gives his *azemat*, and gives his

strength, is the shaving of his hair and to take away the animal kingdom's pride. We are the reverse of the animal kingdom. When you

look at the animal kingdom, the male in the animal kingdom have big hair, big feathers, to attract their mates. Prophet ﷺ doesn't want that for us. Your look is not for attracting anyone, unless you are not yet married and you have to get married, then you have to be

attractive. Once you're married and that is finished, it is no longer about being attractive. This is about *rijalAllah* and to have discipline against yourself and taking away of that negative energy.

So as soon as you begin to shave your head, realize that this bald head has to be covered. There is nothing on top of it, you put your cover, it is an energy source. As soon as you wrap your turban. You can't wear it to work but you go home, you put on your turban to make your *salah* (prayer). It is a reminder for you that this *taj* (cone-shaped hat) is my tombstone and this turban cloth is like my *kafan* (shroud).

*Ya Rabbi,* if I die at any moment – remember that before when the *Sahabi* and Companions and great followers were going through the desert, there was no ambulance to call upon. If someone died there was no mortuary to call. Your friends would make a *janaza* (funeral prayer) right there, take the turban off and wrap it as a *kafan* (shroud) and bury you. They would take your shoes and go because you don't bury the person with his shoes. It is a reminder always when you are walking and moving, that death is with you and the death is not far from you. *Ya Rabbi,* I am going to pass away one day and this is going to be my *kafan* (shroud).

## Cover Your Head in the Bathroom

That is why you don't take your turban into the bathroom. You don't take holy things into the toilet. That is why you take the turban off and put it aside and go in for *wudu* (ablution). When going in for *wudu* you have to go with your head covered. The whole concept of the head being covered and what we are talking about the *Sunnah* is a shield of armor for the believer. The headquarters for the *Shaytan* is the toilet. So

as soon as you are going in you are going into a battle zone with *Shaytan,* so it means you have to have your head covered and protect yourself within that environment.

## The Face and Beard

As soon as you go and shave your head and bring the energy, you realize that the energy of the face is going to be granted with the beard. So the beard is not something to scare people, because some people look very scary with their beards because they have an angry look. But there is a holiness in the hair. When it begins to grow it starts to protect these different *lataif* (energy points) of the throat and of the body. It means then that everything the Prophet ﷺ

brought for us was a protection. To build our energy and to protect our energy. So the biggest protection is the covering of the head.

*Alhamdulillah,* what we started with, the greatness of Mawlana Shaykh Hisham that, like a sun, when you look at the *kamil Shaykhs,* the perfected Shaykhs, because we are not *kamil* but we follow perfected Shaykhs, and we never saw them without a turban in an official capacity. It means they represent the office of Sayyidina Muhammad ﷺ

completely, because of the respect of the position, not for being proud and arrogant, but the position that it represents the majesty of Sayyidina Muhammad ﷺ. It means that at every official capacity wear the turban. It is a crown for the believer to hold the majesty of the *Sunnah* of Prophet ﷺ.

In our lives we never saw him (Mawlana Shaykh Hisham) without his head uncovered. If he didn't have his turban, he had his head always covered. We never saw him taking pictures on vacation without a head cover or having dark wavy hair and putting on sunglasses. These are from the bad characteristics and lack of perfection.

Why they are saying it is not to be judging people, but because people are looking at the *imams* and then copying. When they copy incorrect they have difficulties in life. When they see the *imam* has no head cover and he is going out amongst people. He is going out and dealing with people. Then (you think), 'Okay I don't have to wear a head cover either', and before you know it you are in difficulty.

## The Men Should Cover the Head and Hold the Flag of Islam

What we saw was from perfected Shaykhs, they never left their head uncovered. It wasn't that they put that responsibility on women that, no you have to have a head cover and I will go looking very sexy and handsome. No you keep the responsibility and you hold the flag of Islam in your family. You don't give it to your wife to hold it. It means you carry the responsibility, you carry the *Sunnah*. If she wants to, *alhamdulillah*, she can come along.

But now everybody wants to give the flag to their wives and they do as they like. If you go down Robson Street in Vancouver or any popular street and you see all these guys dressing however they want and they have a lady behind them in full *niqab* (face cover). And (the man) has no head cover and they are wearing shorts! They are wearing the latest sunglasses and a big bold watch. That is not the *Sunnah* of Prophet صلى الله عليه وسلم.

321

## *Sunnah* is an Insulation of Energy and Protection From Difficulty

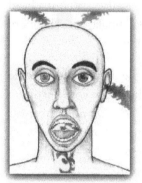 So when we copy that way and we get thousands of emails, 'I have a difficulty', or 'I have a sickness', and 'I have every type of difficulty and energy coming to me.' How is Allah ﷻ going to grant us *khayr* and goodness, if we are not upholding the way of Prophet ﷺ? And so we understood, we do it out of love to keep the respect of Prophet ﷺ. And later we found out that, Oh my God, this was a tremendous protection!

As soon as I shave my hair, I take that energy; as soon as I cover my head with my hat I have a protection upon my head. As soon as I come down (lower towards) my body and I wear clothes of modesty, I begin to understand that Prophet ﷺ was insulating us, like a wire; that this energy you are going to build within yourself and *shayateen* (devils) and *hasad* (jealousy) and bad eyes of people can take and pull the energy off of you.

Any energy you are trying to build within yourself, and as soon as you expose your body parts, people look and they pull the energy. It means somebody's *nazar* (gaze), when they see your flesh and they see your skin, they want to or don't want to, their eyes are pulling an energy and sending a negative energy to the body. So it means there was a secret in the dress of modesty, that it was an insulation; it was a protection for the body that whatever energy we are building it has to be protected within so that you have this energy to be using for your *salah*, using it for your worship.

## Prophet ﷺ Gave His *Sunnah* as a Gift to Other Prophets

As soon as you come to the hand you realize that all of these *Sunnahs* were granted from Prophet ﷺ to all the prophets because the one and true Messenger of Allah ﷻ is Sayyidina Muhammad ﷺ. So when Sayyidina Musa عليه السلام has an *asaa* (cane), it is a gift from Prophet ﷺ.

When Sayyidina Sulayman عليه السلام has the ring of power it is a gift from Sayyidina Muhammad ﷺ. So it means the real inheritance is always to Prophet ﷺ. Prophet ﷺ then gave that out. So what he gave to his Nation is that you can inherit. That is why the *ulama* are the inheritors of *Bani Israel.*

عُلَمَاءِ وَرِثَةُ الْأَنْبِيَاء

*"Ulama e warithatul anbiya."*

*"The scholars are the inheritors of the prophets."*

Prophet ﷺ was showing that you can inherit everything that I gave to those nations by keeping my *Sunnah.*

## The Secret of the Hand, Fingers, and Wearing the *Sunnah* Ring on the Right Hand

When you come to the ring and you come to the majesty of the hands, this ring is on the right hand, not the left hand. The left hand is for cleaning yourself. The ring is an allegiance to the Prophet ﷺ. When you wear your ring on your right finger, these hands represent your way and your allegiance to Allah ﷻ, that my *bayah* (covenant) with Allah ﷻ, my *bayah* to the Prophet ﷺ and to the *Ulul amr* (saints).

إِنَّ الَّذِينَ يُبَايِعُونَكَ إِنَّمَا يُبَايِعُونَ اللَّـهَ يَدُ اللَّـهِ فَوْقَ أَيْدِيهِمْ ۚ فَمَن نَّكَثَ فَإِنَّمَا يَنكُثُ عَلَىٰ نَفْسِهِ ۖ وَمَنْ أَوْفَىٰ بِمَا عَاهَدَ عَلَيْهُ اللَّـهَ فَسَيُؤْتِيهِ أَجْرًا عَظِيمًا (١٠)

*48:10 – "Inna al latheena yubayi oonaka innama yubayi AAoona Allaha yadu Allahi fawqa aydeehim faman nakatha fa-innama yan kuthu ala nafsihi waman awfa bima ahada alayhu Allaha fasayu/ teehi ajran AAatheema."*
*(Surat Al-Fath)*

*"Verily those who Swear Their allegiance to you do no less Swear Their Allegiance to Allah: the Hand of Allah is over their hands: then any one who violates his oath, does so to the harm of his own soul, and any one who fulfils what he has covenanted with Allah,- Allah will soon grant him a great Reward."*
*(Surat Al-Fath, 48:10)*

## Fingers Represent Prophet ﷺ and 4 *Khulafa Rashideen*

Your small finger has to do with the secret of Sayyidina Uthman ؓ. Your ring finger has to do with Sayyidina Umar Farooq ؓ. The tallest finger has to do with the secret of Sayyidina Abu Bakr as Siddiq ؓ. Your index finger, the *Shahadah* (testimony of faith) finger, has to do with the secret of

Sayyidina Ali ؏. And your thumb, which is like a finger but it is completely different, has to do with Sayyidina Muhammad ﷺ.

بَلَىٰ قَادِرِينَ عَلَىٰ أَن نُّسَوِّيَ بَنَانَهُ ﴿٤﴾

75:4 – *"Balaa qaadireena 'alaaa an nusawwiya banaanah."*
(*Surah Al-Qiyamah*)

*"Yea, verily. We are Able to restore his very fingers!" (The Resurrection, 75:4)*

Your identity and your secret when you understand your thumb that Allah ﷻ says, 'I have given everybody a unique print upon their thumb.' Your unique identity is upon your thumb. And it is like a finger but not like the other fingers. That Prophet ﷺ is a *bashar* and human but not like any other human.

That without that thumb, you are like a monkey. It is because this thumb and the honour that Allah ﷻ gave to us, this thumb makes us *insaan* (human being). This thumb gives us the ability to write and to grasp. It has a tremendous reality.

When the *Sunnah* ring is put on that finger (ring finger), it is from the characteristics of Sayyidina Umar Farooq ؏. *Qul ja al Haq wa dhaqal batil.*

وَ قُلْ جَآءَالْحَقُّ وَزَهَقَ الْبَطِلُ، إِنَّ الْبَطِلَ كَانَ زَهُوقًا ﴿٨١﴾

17:81 – *"Wa qul jaa alhaqqu zahaqal baatil, innal batila kana zahoqa."*
(*Surat Al-Isra*)

*"And say, "Truth has come, and falsehood has perished. Indeed falsehood, [by its nature], is ever perishing/ bound to perish." (The Night Journey, 17:81)*

That I stand for truth and I am completely against falsehood. And my whole life is to stand for truth and come against falsehood. It is an allegiance to Sayyidina Muhammad ﷺ. That is why the *Sunnah* of

Prophet ﷺ is on the right finger. Some people wear the ring on the left hand; that is incorrect. It is worn on the right hand. Mawlana Shaykh asks us to wear only one ring. If you wear too many rings, there is something wrong. It is the way of the *Sunnah* to keep that ring.

Mainly that ring is based of *aqeeq* (agate) or *firoz* (turquoise). Turquoise is given to students to defend themselves against *hasad* (jealousy) and bad energy. Anybody who is experiencing difficulty and bad energies, then they wear the *firoz* (turquoise) ring as protection for *nazar*. The *nazar* (evil eye) of people goes immediately to that blue ring, immediately catches that energy and it is able to take away the difficulty that would be coming upon the body.

Then when the student is progressing from *hasad* and wants to open their heart, then it becomes *aqeeq*. The *aqeeq* stone brings a warmth and an opening to the heart. From the *lataif* of the heart can begin to open and experiencing that energy, it begins to enter into the heart.

Again the shield of the clothes of modesty protects the body. The hat protects the body, the beard protects the body. Everything Prophet ﷺ gave was a shield for the believer and an energy. A lot of people think *Sunnah* is a fashion statement. No, you are doing it out of love, but more important it is a tremendous source of energy and protection of energy.

*Subhana rabbika rabbal 'izzati 'amma yasifoon, wa salaamun 'alal mursaleen, walhamdulillahi rabbil 'aalameen. Bi hurmati Muhammad al-Mustafa wa bi siri Surat al-Fatiha.*

# Protection Against Bad Energy
## *Siwak*, Ring, Cane, Body Energy, *Wudu*

*lhamdulillah*, in the teachings of the noble *Sunnah* of Sayyidina Muhammad ﷺ, that whatever Prophet ﷺ brought for us was for energy. That its real core and the reality is that we are an energy being. The soul is made from energy. It needs energy and it wants to be defended from negativity. There is positive flow of energy and the negative flow of energy. By understanding that reality, we reach a state of perfection, or move at least in that direction. It means everything that Prophet ﷺ brought for us out of the noble *Sunnah*, you follow it. Later they will begin to teach its reality and its importance.

## The Perfect Symmetry of Humans, the Codes on the Hands

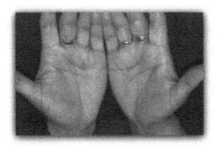

We left off last time at the importance of the hands, that the hands have tremendous secrets and encoding upon them, that your left hand has this upside down V, triangle shape and a line ٨١; the right hand has the line and the triangle ١٨. It means this is 18 on the right hand and 81 on the left hand, which means the perfect symmetry of who we are. One side is reflecting the other side. As a matter of fact, your brain, on the left side, controls your right side; your brain on the right side controls your left side. That's how nice Allah ﷻ designed the symmetry of *insaan* (human being).

### *Sunnah* of Prophet ﷺ is a Complete Solution to All Problems

By understanding when we are going for *wudu* (ablution). We talked last time about the importance of keeping the hair to be short, the importance of keeping your head to be covered. Because all of this is based on people asking, 'Shaykh I have negativity, Shaykh I have problems, I have difficulty.' Whether it is with sustenance, whether it's with energy, whether it's with sicknesses; all of these things that we incur upon this earth, Prophet ﷺ brought the complete solution, which was the *Sunnah*.

That *Sunnah* is a perfection of the energy. The practices built the energy; the *Sunnah* safeguards and protects that energy. It means that by keeping the hair, you take away that negative energy, by keeping the head to be covered, you sanctify the energy like a capstone on top of the pyramid. Its full power is when that cap is upon the head because everything else is just being released from the head.

The *shayateen* (devils) and the negative energies, they understand where the energy points of *insaan* (human being) are and they locate themselves upon those energy points and they basically withdraw everything. We talked before, that it's symbolic from the movie, 'The Matrix'. What Allah ﷻ wanted to show within that reality, when they showed that all the human beings, all they really were, was a battery; that they were in pods and all the *shayateen* were just pulling their energy. And that's how they view us on this earth. They don't have the heavenly energy. "*Wa laqad karamna Bani Adam*".

$$ وَلَقَدْ كَرَّمْنَا بَنِي آدَمَ ... (٧٠) $$

*17:70 – "Wa laqad karramna bani adama..." (Surat Al-Isra)*

"*And We have certainly honoured the children of Adam...*"
*(The Night Journey, 17:70)*

We are a paradise being walking upon the earth. And the *shayateen* (demons) are seeing, saying, 'Look at these energies.' They don't have access to that. So their whole interest is to ride upon *insaan* like a big battery. They lock themselves from the back and begin to take all the energy from that *insaan*, whether they're pulling it from the head, pulling it from the heart, pulling it from feet.

So the noble *Sunnah* comes to safeguard, that you are a paradise being and you are to be safeguarded while you are walking upon this earth. By following the way of Prophet ﷺ, then we are entitled to that protection and *malaika* (angels) are then protecting those who are following the way of the prophets, all the prophets brought that reality.

## Reality of the Fingers – The Holy Companions and Sayyidina Muhammad ﷺ

Then when we go to the secrets of the hands, we see that by washing the hands, we are releasing tremendous codes. And as soon as you are washing your hands and realize you have a ring on your right hand. We left off last time, that each finger is symbolic of a reality. That Sayyidina Uthman ؓ for *Jami al-Qur'an* and the reality of knowledge is your pinky; your ring finger is the finger of loyalty and struggle, which is to Sayyidina Umar al-Farooq ؓ, "*Qul jaa al haqq wa zahaqal baatil*".

وَ قُلْ جَاءَالْحَقُّ وَزَهَقَ الْبَطِلُ، إِنَّ الْبَطِلَ كَانَ زَهُوقًا (٨١)

*17:81 – "Wa qul jaa alhaqqu wa zahaqal baatil, innal batila kana zahooqa."*
*(Surat Al-Isra)*

*"And say, "Truth has come, and falsehood has perished. Indeed falsehood, [by its nature], is ever perishing/ bound to perish." (The Night Journey, 17:81)*

It means that you spend your life supporting truth and come against falsehood. Don't live a life in which you support falsehood, but support the truth of Allah ﷻ, and the truth of our reality and our soul.

Then to the longest finger (the middle finger), is for Sayyidina Abu Bakr as-Siddiq ؓ; where Prophet ﷺ described the greatness of Sayyidina Abu Bakr as-Siddiq ؓ, from what Allah ﷻ had poured into the heart of Sayyidina Abu Bakr as-Siddiq ؓ; *as-siddiq al-mutlaq.*

مَا صَبَّ اللهُ فِيْ صَدْرِيْ شَيْءَ إِلَا وَ صَبَبْتُهُ فِيْ صَدْرِي اَبِيْ بَكْرِ اَلصِّدِيقْ

*"Ma sabAllahu fi Sadri shay an illa wa sababtuhu fi sadri Abi Bakr as Siddiq."*

*Prophet ﷺ said: "Whatever I received, I poured in the heart of Abu Bakr as Siddiq."*

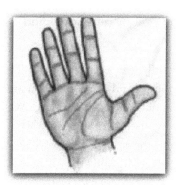

Then the index finger has to deal with the family of Prophet ﷺ and Imam Ali ؓ and that support. Then the noble finger upon these four fingers that are similar; the most different one is the thumb, which is the identity and this represents Prophet ﷺ. This gives *insaan* its majesty. Allah ﷻ says, 'We call you back all the way to your thumbprint.'

أَيَحْسَبُ الْإِنسَانُ أَلَّن نَّجْمَعَ عِظَامَهُ (٣) بَلَىٰ قَادِرِينَ عَلَىٰ أَن نُّسَوِّيَ بَنَانَهُ (٤)

*75:3-4 – "Ayahsabul insaanu al lan najm'a 'izaamah (3) Balaa qaadireena 'alaaa an nusawwiya banaanah. (4)" (Surat Al-Qiyamah)*

*"Does man think that We will not assemble his bones?(3) Yes. We have the power to restore (even) his very fingertips." (The Resurrection, 75:3-4)*

It means you have a unique identity that's uniquely for yourself.

Later when you begin to train with your energy, understand that as soon as you are touching your hands, you are activating codes. When you are beginning to understand the energy of your reality, that you have a unique energy for yourself. As soon as that energy begins to touch the hand, you are calling from your reality in *Bahr al-Qudra* (Ocean of Power), to become present with you, more than what you have now. From whatever energy you have now, as soon as you make *tafakkur* (contemplation) and begin to understand the importance of the hands, you are able to call and summon that reality, that uniquely identified on that thumb.

So that *shahadah* finger that brings the oceans of *Bahr al-Qudra*, why

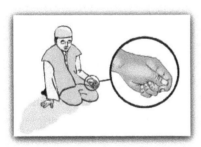

Allah ﷻ wants you to make your *shahadah* (testimony of faith)? It means that the power of the soul is moving through that finger. As soon as it scans your identity on the thumb, it calls for that energy to be present with the soul in excess of what's necessary for your day to day functioning. When Allah ﷻ wants to open that reality for the believer to bring their energy, to bring their *qudra* (power), so that they can achieve higher levels of understanding.

### *Sunnah* of the Ring on the Right Hand, Allegiance to Prophet ﷺ

So it means then the ring, and the *Sunnah* of the ring on the right hand, is the allegiance to the Prophet ﷺ. That ring is from *aqeeq* (Carnelian), so that it opens the power of the heart, brings a softness to the heart, or from *firoz* (turquoise). We said before that the turquoise is for taking away negative energy; taking away *hasad* (jealousy). For the ladies, same thing, that the ring is still there as a *Sunnah* and you can wear a necklace; you can wear different jewellery for women that have the turquoise. That turquoise is meant to deflect negative energy that people are looking through their eyes. When they look with their eyes, they are able to send a *hasad*, a jealousy to people. If that hits the turquoise, the turquoise takes it and, many times, may crack.

We are an energy being but people don't understand the extent of their energy. That's why Prophet ﷺ described that, 'Be humble and don't do things that gain people's *hasad*'. Don't go around with so much in front of people because their eyes are hungry. As soon as they look at what you have and they don't have, immediately an energy is produced and sent out; and if you are the recipient of that, then this leads to sickness and difficulties and lots of *mushkilat* (difficulties). So again, the *Sunnah* is a shield of protection. So as soon as that one has a turquoise ring, it's a deflection. If it's a female and they have the turquoise necklace or turquoise bracelets, it's a deflection from that energy.

Then you go to the body and the *Sunnah* clothes. The importance of the *Sunnah* clothes is that it is the dress of modesty (for men and women).

## Safeguard What You Eat, Negative Energy Contaminates the Food

Then we go to the *siwak* (teeth cleaning twig), where the importance of the *siwak* is that as soon as you use the *siwak*, it's a tremendous cleansing for the energy that's entering into the mouth. It means from everything that you are eating, drinking and breathing, it has an energy in it. The food doesn't have the energy, but the energy that's attaching to that food is what's important. If the person was not in a clean state, in *junub* or in a non-clean state and they are touching food, all of their badness is put upon that food. As soon as you eat it, you begin to take that energy within your being.

That's why Prophet ﷺ described that, 'Safeguard where you eat, how you eat, who you eat from'. If the person, when you are going out and going to restaurants and going to places, if the one serving you has no understanding of washing and they are in a completely dirty state, you don't know what they have been doing. They put all of that state that they are in into the food and serve you from that energy. As soon as you put it into your mouth, you have now gathered that energy. Many times, the *Ahl ul-Bayt*, (Family and descendants of Prophet Muhammad ﷺ), their teeth all cracked from *hasad*, from the bad energy of people. Because as this energy is going in it is affecting the teeth. The teeth that Allah ﷻ is putting is the first line of defense that protects that body.

## *Sunnah* of Using *Siwak* – To Clean Negative Energy of the Mouth

Exactly what goes in the mouth, has a direct correlation to the heart. So only now they found that plaque can cause heart disease; and this Prophet ﷺ was teaching 1,500 years ago! Why the *siwak/miswak*? A *siwak* was not meant to be only a toothbrush. When they say, 'No I have now big Crest; I can use Crest toothpaste.' No, no; the wood and the *siwak* and the reality of (the prayer said when you use the *siwak*) '*nifaaq min al qalbi wa shirk khafi*', was that, 'take away the hypocrisy in

333

my heart and the hidden *shirk* (polytheism)'. It had nothing to do with brightening your teeth, but it had to do with energy. As soon as you put the *siwak* into your mouth, you immediately grounded the mouth. Whatever energies are flowing into the mouth, as soon as you put the *siwak*, it is wood; that wood is pulling the negative energy out so that energy doesn't affect the heart.

Most important is to use it before you are going to do *amal* (good deed), you are going to recite Qur'an, you're going to pray. That is what Prophet ﷺ described Allah ﷻ is giving the *ajar* and the reward of 27 times your *salah* (daily prayer), if you use *siwak*. That is how Allah ﷻ wanted to stress that reality. Twenty-seven, 27, because it's the *baab* and the door to paradise; *Isra wal Mi'raj* is on the 27th; *Laylat ul-Qadr* is on the 27th. Allah ﷻ is then describing, this is the secret to that paradise.

If there's an *aalim* (scholar) or someone who professes to know something and you see them talk and you see them pray and they don't use *siwak*, immediately come to your understanding that are not conscious of energy; they are not conscious of the realities of the soul. So they are not reaching states of perfection because this is an important *Sunnah* that is the key to the heart. If the heart wants to open and they are not using *siwak*, how is it going to open?

It's impossible because everything they are eating and drinking is going in, and mainly from the *ghadab*, anger and bad energy. All of those energies go through the mouth and begin to affect the heart. So it means then the *siwak* and the importance of the *siwak;* we said it before, it's not a fashion statement. Prophet ﷺ gave everything as a perfection of energy.

### *Sunnah* of *Asaa* (Cane) – To Ground Your Energy

Go to the *asaa* (cane), they were all the inheritors of the prophets; the *asaa*, that when they carry the *asaa* and the reality of that *asaa*, is that it was the third prong. Women can also carry *asaa*; there are nice stores online, they have very elegant *asaas* that you order. That this cane is the third prong, which means a grounding. Prophet ﷺ was teaching 1,500 years ago electrical grounding, that your 2 feet are 2 currents that are touching this earth. When you begin to understand there is an electromagnetic field upon the earth, it moves on the earth; your 2 feet are plugged in. That ability (energy) is giving you the ability to stand straight.

Your feet are plugged into that energy, pulling that energy up.

If you begin to understand the flow of energy, that earth's energy is all negative and it's coming up, up, up (from your feet upward to the stomach). Prophet ﷺ describes that your biggest battle is going to be the equator of your reality. Your equator, like the earth, because we are a symbol of the earth, your equator is the belly button. So your body is like the earth. Prophet ﷺ described, the entire battle of your being is your stomach. It's going to be your equator.

It means all of your earth energy and negative energy, electromagnetic flow of energy is through the earth. All their desires, all their wants, all their bad character, are moving through the earth. They are moving up your body and clashing now into your belly. All your heavenly energy and heavenly dress upon the soul is your upper *lataif* (energy points). That's why the heart

*lataif* (chakra/energy points) and the heart is based on the upper portion of your body.

Allah ﷻ sends the *tanzil ar-Rahmah* (descending mercy) and sends the manifestations and the lights of paradise and the soul realities upon the soul. This is your yin and yang and this is the great conflict for *insaan* (mankind). That your energy, heavenly energy, is coming and dressing your soul through the upper portion of your reality, and all the material desires are upon the earth, clashing.

So every clash now is happening within the belly. The *asaa* was the grounding. As soon as your hold the *asaa*, it's a grounding for *insaan* to pull out the extra energy. Because as you are building your energy and you are building your positive charge and you are taking the negative charge of earth, it has to go somewhere. It's clashing, so these two energies are clashing from the top to the bottom. As soon as they hold the *asaa*, they are able to purge the negative charge out of the body.

It means then understanding that flow of energy, we begin to understand many things upon ourselves. When you go home and your feet smell, it's too much *dunya* (material world) energy upon you. That's why pious people, their feet don't smell. Their feet are from the feet of paradise. They are teaching that this *dunya* energy has a dirtiness and when you understand the flow of it coming up and trying to overtake you, every practice and everything that you are doing, from your *siwak* and controlling your head, covering the head, and washing with the understandings of *wudu*, is all a perfection of the energy.

## Importance of Washing Away Negative Energy

That's why people who have difficulties, these energies are coming up the leg; and from the leg it's moving towards the back. Then the clash is going to be into the spine and into the stomach. It means then the importance of understanding that energy, that whatever you are doing in life, you have to wash often. As soon as you shower and visualize that

water coming like a waterfall and your soul cleansing itself within the water, to relieve itself of these negative energies.

When the energy is too negative, then it's recommended to make a bath and put salt within that bath, the Himalayan salt or Epsom salt. Salt is a natural purifier which means salt takes away negativity. Even holding the salt stones takes away negativity. Even putting it in your meat and rolling it in salt and then rinsing it off takes away all the negativity. Allah ﷻ gave us that salt as a natural way of purification. So many *Awliyaullah* (saints), they sleep with salt right by their bed and they put that in their mouth as soon as they wake up to make sure that the negative energy is off of them, until they can reach to make *wudu* (ablution).

## *Sunnah* of *Wudu* (Ablution) – To Burn Away Fires of *Shayateen* (Devils)

It means then understanding the flow of energy; then you begin to understand how to wash, how to control that. Then the importance that Prophet ﷺ gave us *wudu* (ablution). That the water and the power of *wudu* burns away the fires of *shayateen* (devils).

### Pray *Salat al-Wudu*

So, as soon as you go to make your *wudu*, you wash and don't speak to anyone; come out and pray 2 *rakah* (2 cycle prayer). That 2 *rakah*, it becomes the seal of the *wudu* and the seal and the armor for the believer. It means as soon as they're washing, they're not speaking, they're entering into a purified state. As soon as they pray 2 *rakah*, Prophet ﷺ said to pray *salat al-wudu*, your *wudu* becomes like an armor, that it seals your body from satanic and *shaytanic* and evil attacks.

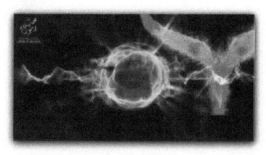

So the importance of *wudu*, it's not something that they say, 'Oh yeah, well they used to do that back home. We don't have to do that now. I took a shower in the morning'. But if you relieved yourself and lost your state of *wudu*, you are now best under the attack of *Shaytan* because the satanic attack is looking for deficiency in your energy field. So when you watch these sci-fi (science fiction) movies, they see the shield around and the *ifrit* and the *shayateen* are everywhere. They are waiting for an energy field to be void upon the believer and immediately enter into the attack.

So what Prophet ﷺ brought in the *wudu* (ablution) is that to wash the two dirtiest parts of your body. The way that you relieve yourself, from the front and from the back, are the big entry points for *shayateen* because those are the dirty entry points of the body. If those parts remain to be dirty and not to be purified and to be clean, again, all the negative charge immediately runs from below the earth and shoots up through the believer and enters into the body. And again, it becomes all the lower intestinal problems. So many people have a lot of difficulties in the lower body. And everything that Prophet ﷺ

brought was for perfection. It wasn't just something you did back home, you know, like old times.

Say, 'No!' This water and the use of water when you relieve yourself, from front or from back, was a way to sanctify and safeguard your body's entrance points, so that *shayateen* won't enter from those points. Then the reality of *wudu*, sealing the body with *salat ul-wudu*, and then all of the *Sunnah* that was given to us as a safeguard and a protection.

*Subhana rabbika rabbal 'izzati 'amma yasifoon, wa salaamun 'alal mursaleen, walhamdulillahi rabbil 'aalameen. Bi hurmati Muhammad al-Mustafa wa bi siri Surat al-Fatiha.*

# The *Sunnah* of Sleeping – Protection from Sleep Paralysis

## Defending Against *Jinns*, Demons, and Unknown Beings

وَمَنْ أَحْيَاءِ سُنَّتِيْ فَقَدْ أَحَبْنِيْ وَمَنْ أَحَبْنِيْ كَانَ مَعِيَ فِي الْجَنَّةِ" رواه الترمذي

*"Man ahya Sunnati faqad ahabanee, wa man ahabanee, kana ma'iya fil jannah."*

*"Who revives my sunnah loves me, and who really loves me will be with me in Paradise." Prophet Muhammad (pbuh)*

A sking always to be nothing and enter Allah's ﷻ oceans of *Rahmah* and Mercy and the Grace and blessings of Allah ﷻ to be upon us all, *InshaAllah.*

We are talking about the energy and the subjects of energy and the power of the holy *Sunnah* (the way of Prophet Muhammad ﷺ). One important thing that people ask is about night time, because of the effect of negative energy at night. It affects people's energy, it affects people's physicality and it affects people's dreams. Many people say they have attacks at night. They have night terrors; they have horrific dreams and all sorts of attacks. It means it is a time for us that we should understand when we are most vulnerable. When you are lying down and not defending yourself, we must know that there are many beings all around us.

341

This space we live in is not empty and anybody who wants proof of that, they should look into an electron microscope. They took a cup of water and looked inside the water with the electron microscope and they found so many levels of creation living in it. And when they looked at that creation again, they saw living things upon those living things. It means that there must be life everywhere. There must be positive energy and negative energy.

## Make *Wudu* (Ablution) Before You Go to Bed

*Alhamdulillah*, from Mawlana Shaykh Hisham's teaching for us which is all from *Bismillahir Rahmanir Raheem, ati ullah ati ar Rasola wa Ulul amri minkum.*

أَطِيعُوا اللّه وَأَطِيعُوا الرَّسُولَ وَأُوْلِي الْأَمْرِ مِنْكُمْ... (٥٩)

*4:59 – "...Atiullaha wa atiur Rasola wa Ulil amre minkum..."*
*(Surat An-Nisa)*

*"... Obey Allah, Obey the Messenger, and those in authority among you."*
*(The Women, 4:59)*

What Allah ﷻ gave to, and wanted Prophet ﷺ, to perfect Mankind

and that perfection is running within the hands of *Ulul amr* and the perfected guides. What they taught for us is that from the realities of sleeping, that when you are about to go to bed, that you go with *wudu* (ablution). That you wash before you go to sleep, make sure your private parts are washed and you complete your *wudu*. We talked before that you pray the prayer of *wudu*, the two cycles of *wudu* without speaking anything and you are sealing your energy. You finish all your washing, go and pray your two *rakats* (cycles) and seal yourself.

### *Du'a* – Supplication Before Sleep

At that time you can recite four *Surat Al-Falaq* (Chapter 113 of Holy Qur'an), three *Surat An-Naas* (Chapter 114 of Holy Qur'an) and two *Surat Al-Ikhlas* (Chapter 112 of Holy Qur'an) and blow it upon yourself.

*Qul a'udhu bi rabbil falaq* (Say; I seek refuge in the Lord of the Daybreak) [blow on your palms and around you], *Qul a'udhu bi rabbin naas* (Say; I seek refuge in the Lord of Mankind) and putting that light upon yourself [blow on your palms and lightly rub on your face and around you]. *Qul huwallahu ahad* (Say He is Allah, the One and Only) [blow on your palms and lightly rub on your face and around you], and asking Allah ﷻ to protect you while you sleep.

To read before sleep for protection:

4x *Surat Al-Falaq* (Chapter 113 of Holy Qur'an);

3x *Surat An-Naas* (Chapter 114 of Holy Qur'an)

2x *Surat Al-Ikhlas* (Chapter 112 of Holy Qur'an)

### The *Sunnah* is to Be Covered When You Sleep

When you are going into bed, it is the *Sunnah* to be covered. We talked before about the energy, that when you expose your body, you are exposing it to every type of energy. All these beings want to touch that human flesh; they want the access to that energy that they don't have access to. By keeping yourself covered with a long pajama for men and a T-shirt to cover the places of *hawa* and the places of the body that should not be exposed. And by having *ayat al Qur'an* (verses of Holy Qur'an) upon themselves and asking from *Bismillahir Rahmanir Raheem* and *Ayat al-Qursi* (Holy Qur'an, 2:255) and the names of pious people and having good things around their home. As soon as they go and lie down and are wanting to go to sleep, they are asking to be protected.

That to keep the head covered because this is the time when the most attacks come, when you sleep. Then your *Sunnah* is while you are awake as well as while you are sleeping. So it means you try to get a hat that you can pull over which does not keep slipping so that it does not keep popping off as you are sleeping. So a ski hat or toque or a knitted hat or whatever you can put over your head and it's secure on your head, which is the crown of Creation, and is guarded.

If you look back forty or fifty years ago at all the pictures of sleeping, everybody covered while sleeping. They have pictures of little children, even in cartoons, that they had long hats; they had sleep hats with a little tail. They had long underwear that were like long-johns which covered their entire body because they understood that reality. It is only a new concept where people sleep without any clothing and they go into the bed. Therefore they have many attacks, from the *jinn*, different nightmares and difficulty coming at night.

## Sleep on Your Back, Let the Force Field of the Heart Protect You

The defense that Prophet ﷺ brought for us was the perfection. That make your *wudu*, pray your *Salat al-Wudu*, recite Holy Qur'an upon yourself and blow that light upon yourself and as soon as you go to sleep you have something to cover your head.

Then, when you sleep get into the practice of sleeping on your backside because this is all about energy that Prophet ﷺ was bringing for us. That the *shayateen* (devils) are scared of approaching *insaan* (human being) from the front because of the energy to the heart.

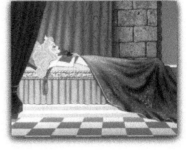

The heart is a tremendous protection for the human beings because this is where the light of the Divine is emanating. All the *zikr*, the prayer, every good action,

charity, everything is enforcing the light within the heart of the human being. So the heart is the force field. When you understand that, then as you sleep on your back, you realize there is a shield that your heart is emitting over you and defending you [Shaykh demonstrates a fan of light emitting from the heart].

As long as we keep that understanding, that the heart is there to defend. Then Prophet ﷺ described that when you are sleeping it is most preferable to sleep on your back. And if you have to move to your side, then again this is based on energy; as soon as you sleep you go to your right side. When sleeping on your right side you see again the heart is making a shield of protection because your heart is up. [Shaykh demonstrates a fan of light coming across from the left side to the right side of the body]. It's good for the heart, it is good for the conditioning of the heart, it is not putting stress upon the heart, and it is providing a shield of energy that encompasses all your body.

## Sleeping on the Left Side and on the Stomach Weakens Your Energy/Protection

The disliked position is if you go now and roll over to your left side. As soon as you move to the left what happens is that the heart is in duress because your weight from your body is being pushed upon the heart, the shield of protection is not there. There is nothing now defending you [Shaykh indicates overview of the body]; the heart's shield of protection is not there. Many people who are sensitive to energy become very uncomfortable when they sleep on their left.

The more you are aware of energy, the more you practice energy, the more you understand that this is all from the realities of the *malakoot* (heavenly realm). Prophet ﷺ came to perfect.

إِنَّمَا بُعِثْتُ لِأُ تَمِّمَ مَكَارِمَ الْأَخْلَاقِ

*"Innama bu'istu le Utammima makarimal Akhlaq."*

*"I was sent to perfect your manners."* Prophet Muhammad (pbuh)

Prophet ﷺ came to perfect but not necessarily the body. The body is going to be here for sixty or seventy years and go back into the grave. These teachings of the body were to perfect the soul, the inhabitant, the precious one from Paradise that is inside; it needs the body to understand these realities because it is the one suffering. What Prophet ﷺ brought were the rules to save the soul inside.

The one who is *jahl* (ignorant) and doesn't understand, as soon as they sleep like this (left side) their soul is going to be attacked. The heart is going to be attacked and that *insaan* (human) will be under attack because always visualize there are thousands of *ifrit*. There are very few people that have the ability, with their energy, with their *salah*, with their *namaz* (daily prayer), who will release tremendous energy that purifies that space. Most [people] don't have that energy and they can barely lift themselves in their *salah*, in their *amal* and actions.

## Close Your Windows/Blinds At Night

It means that negative energy is everywhere. It comes through the television, it comes through the music, it comes through the windows.

346

Even GrandShaykh said that at *Maghrib* (sunset) time close the windows, close the shades on your windows because of *Shaytan*. If you think you have a protection within your house because you put *Ayat al-Qursi*, you have Qur'an and *salawat* (praisings) playing in the house, you have made and fortified your house like a fortress, so the *Shaytan* won't be coming, but they become active at *Maghrib* time. The kids were watching a cartoon and the gargoyle came off the buildings. At five o'clock the gargoyles were coming alive and I was saying, 'Look, look, look, that's what *baba* (father) teaches.'

## You Give Permission to *Shayateen* (Devils) to Come to Your House

That at *Maghrib* time these *shayateen* become active. When they become active it means they are going into the house of believers. When you leave the window open, it is as if it's an opening for them that's inviting them. By closing the window it is a *hijab* (veil) that they don't have permission to break that *hijab*.

They teach you in movies all of the *Shaytanic* rules. So what are the most popular movies now? These vampires and young girls. As soon as the vampire wants to come into the house, they are teaching you even their *adab* (manners). That the vampire wants to come into the house and the girl says, 'Come on in,' and he says, 'No, you have to invite me in!' He is teaching what Prophet ﷺ brought almost 1,500 years ago; that we are under the power of '*Audhu billahi min ash Shaytani rajeem*' (I seek refuge in Allah, from Satan, the Rejected one.)

347

It means that *Shaytan* knows that no, no, you are protected. You have to break your *audhu* and invite me into your home. They are teaching that in the movies, that when you see the vampire you have to invite him in. And the greatness of what Prophet ﷺ, and what he brought for us, that to say '*Audhu billah*', live your life in '*Audhu billahi [min-ash Shaytani rajeem]*', seeking refuge from anything *Shaytanic* so that you will be under the *rahmah* (mercy) of *Bismillah ar-Rahmaan ar-Raheem*.

*A'udhu Billahi Minash Shaytanir Rajeem*
*Bismillahir Rahmanir Raheem*

*I seek refuge in Allah from Satan, the rejected one,*
*In the Name of Allah, the Most Beneficent, the Most Merciful*

## The Devils Can Send Difficulties From Far

So even the windows to be closed at night so that evilness doesn't come in. Even if you have all your protection, as soon as you open your windows, from a distance, they have no permission to come in, but their *nazar* (gaze) from a distance can strike through the window. So they are like shooting arrows. They don't have permission to come in but from a distance they can look through the window and begin to shoot all sorts of difficulty. You feel that difficulty and then you feel the arguments begin in the home. Every type of *fitna* and anger and

aggression begins to start around *Maghrib* time.

It means all of what Prophet ﷺ brought and what the real *Ulul amr* (saints) who not only translate the *Hadith* but they understood the reality of the *Hadith* and they are able to talk to you in very basic simple English. That is the miraculous nature of the *turooq* (Islamic spiritual paths); They can take very complicated realities and talk in a way that five or six-year-old kids can understand!

It means to protect the home from negative energy. Then when you are sleeping and you realize that if you sleep on your left, you will put duress upon the heart. It's not going to have a shield of protection. The worst position is if you sleep on your stomach. That is a complete inviting of negative energy. As soon as you sleep on your stomach, the most vulnerable part of your body is exposed to the air. And every type of negativity is entering in now through the rear end. As they enter in, they increase the negativity, increase the anger, increase every horrific characteristic into *insaan* which is coming through the nighttime visitations.

Again the greatness of Prophet ﷺ was to teach about these energies and teach the realities about the *jinn*. So when you are watching YouTube and all the television shows that the children are watching alien abductions. What alien abductions? These are the *jinn*! They are not coming with a UFO ship from somewhere else, they are right there in your room. That is why they are molesting you, abusing you and beating you. Everything that the Prophet ﷺ brought was this. There are no aliens coming on a ship from a distant planet, they are right there in the room. Protect yourself against the unseen creations of Allah ﷻ. That protection is to wash, to keep the *wudu*, to keep yourself clothed when you are sleeping, sleep on your back and sleep on your right.

## Constantly Make *Salawat* (Praise Upon Prophet ﷺ) to Protect Yourself

And constantly be in the practice of making *salawat* on Prophet ﷺ. So when you feel an attack coming, something that has grabbed you or something trying to grab you, it is second nature to call upon Prophet

ﷺ by saying, *allahumma salle ala Sayyidina Muhammad wa ala aali Sayyidina Muhammad.*

اللَّهُمَّ صَلِّ عَلَى سَيِّدِنَا مُحَمَّدٍ، وَعَلَى آلِ سَيِّدِنَا مُحَمَّدٍ وَ سَلِّمْ

*"Allahumma salli 'ala Sayyidina Muhammadin wa 'ala aali Sayyidina Muhammadin wa Sallim."*

*"O Allah! Send Peace and blessings upon Muhammad and upon the Family of Muhammad (Peace be Upon him)"*

It has in it the *zikr* of Allah ﷻ and the praising upon Prophet ﷺ. So you have double protection. You have Allah's ﷻ attention with His most beloved. You get the *nazar* (gaze) of Prophet ﷺ upon you and Prophet ﷺ comes to give back your greeting and salutation; that is when the *haqq* (truth comes and every falsehood has to leave that environment and in that room).

وَ قُلْ جَاءَالْحَقُّ وَزَهَقَ الْبَطِلُ، إِنَّ الْبَطِلَ كَانَ زَهُوقًا

*17:81 – "Wa qul jaa alhaqqu zahaqal baatil, innal batila kana zahooqa." (Surat Al-Isra)*

*"And say, "Truth has come, and falsehood has perished. Indeed falsehood, [by its nature], is ever perishing/ bound to perish." (The Night Journey, 17:81)*

But it has to be second nature. Otherwise people say they have an attack all night long and it's not coming to them what to say. That is why *Awliya* (saints) are coming into our life to remind that to be in the practice of constant *darood shareef* because that is praising upon Allah ﷻ and mentioning His most beloved Creation whom Allah ﷻ loves dearly, Sayyidina Muhammad ﷺ. By making it second nature then you are constantly in *darood shareef.* Then keeping the head covered, sleeping on the back and not sleeping on the stomach where every negativity enters the body.

We pray that Allah ﷻ gives us more understanding from the *malakoot* and what they call these energies and these realities. Especially with the world of the unseen that people are calling the alien and alien abduction. No, no, this is the world of the *jinn*, they are all around us. And to become familiar and to understand that Creation is part of the faith. To believe in the Unseen, to believe in angels, to believe in these things from *malakoot* (heavenly realm) and from a dimension that we don't see.

*Subhana rabbika rabbal 'izzati 'amma yasifoon, wa salaamun 'alal mursaleen, walhamdulillahi rabbil 'aalameen. Bi hurmati Muhammad al-Mustafa wa bi siri Surat al-Fatiha.*

# Pyramids and
# The Perfection of Our Energy

سَنُرِيهِمْ آيَاتِنَا فِي الْآفَاقِ وَفِي أَنفُسِهِمْ حَتَّىٰ يَتَبَيَّنَ لَهُمْ أَنَّهُ الْحَقُّ... (٥٣)

*41:53 – "Sanureehim ayatina fil afaqi wa fee anfusihim hatta yatabayyana lahum annahu alhaqqu ..." (Surat Al-Isra)*

*"We will show them Our signs in the horizons and within themselves until it becomes clear to them that it is the truth..." (The Night Journey, 41:53)*

Allah ﷻ describes in Holy Qur'an that, 'We show you Our signs upon the horizon and within yourself.' We live in a society, universal society, not that we're talking about only the location that we're living; we live in a time, in a world now, where the philosophy they have is, we come from a state of ignorance and gradually we are increasing in our competence and our level of intelligence. And we are supposedly at the height of our civilization.

## We Were Intelligent and Now We Are in Worst of Conditions

Where Allah ﷻ tells us in Holy Qur'an that, "No, I taught the holy prophet Adam ﷺ, peace and blessings be upon him, I taught him all the names.

وَعَلَّمَ آدَمَ الْأَسْمَاءَ كُلَّهَا... (٣١)

قَالَ يَا آدَمُ أَنبِئْهُم بِأَسْمَائِهِمْ... (٣٣)

وَإِذْ قُلْنَا لِلْمَلَائِكَةِ اسْجُدُوا لِآدَمَ فَسَجَدُوا إِلَّا إِبْلِيسَ... (٣٤)

*2:31 – "Wa 'allama Adamal Asma a kullaha,…"*

*2:33 – "Qala ya Adamu anbi hum bi asmayihim…"*

*2:34 – "Wa idh qulna lil malayikati osjudo li Adama fasajado illa ibleesa…"*
*(Surat Al-Baqarah)*

*"And He taught Adam the names – all of them…" (2:31)*

*"He said: O Adam! Tell them their names …" (2:33)*

*"And [mention] when We said to the angels, "Bow Down to Adam"; so they prostrated, except for Iblis…" (2:34) (The Cow)*

'I told him all realities.' And the angels were astonished and bowed down in prostration. And that was the prostration of respect, of that Divinely Knowledge, that the Prophet Adam ﷺ came and delivered to this holy earth.

We are then of an understanding that we were very intelligent before and we are in the worst of conditions now. We are closer to the 'Planet of the Apes' movie where pious people consider us talking animals. We have very little of our humanity left, very little of our resemblance of our paradise dress. And we are very close to the understanding where Allah ﷻ shows us in the movie 'Planet of the Apes', you are just a gorilla that talks a lot, with all sorts of different characteristics.

But at one time there was knowledge and realities upon this earth. One of them because you see the outward sign and then they begin to teach the inward reality within ourselves. The spiritual world, they teach these realities for the soul and they don't have permission to bring that reality for the material world. And the bad ego and bad characteristic takes that reality and wants to use it for the material world, hence we see the sign outside as a way of reflecting, because there's more negativity than positivity. There's more of a negative ego trying to inspire and bring out all these realities for material benefit versus spiritual benefit. So spiritual pursuit is smaller; material pursuit is always greater.

Then Allah ﷻ is saying, 'I'll show you the sign on the horizon,' because there will be many, because people's material desires, they use realities for material desire, profit and benefit.

$$ \text{سَنُرِيهِمْ آيَاتِنَا فِي الْآفَاقِ وَفِي أَنفُسِهِمْ حَتَّىٰ يَتَبَيَّنَ لَهُمْ أَنَّهُ الْحَقُّ...(٥٤)} $$

*41:53 – "Sanureehim ayatina fil afaqi wa fee anfusihim hatta yatabayyana lahum annahu alhaqqu …" (Surat Al-Isra)*

*"We will show them Our signs in the horizons and within themselves until it becomes clear to them that it is the truth…" (The Night Journey, 41:53)*

Spiritual realities, there is no profit. They follow the real Prophets ﷺ but not the profit, getting some benefit.

## Pyramids Were Not Tombs But Source of Energy

They begin to teach us that when you look just at the symbols of the earth, the pyramid, it was not a tomb, it had nothing to do with being a tomb. It had to do with a source of energy and a symbol of power.

And they begin to teach, because of the benefit of the Internet, which some people can use for negativity and some people can use for positivity; is that when they have only one way of teaching, that no, 'We are monkeys and we are coming towards our height of civilization,' then you have no access to knowledge. As a result, with the opening of the Internet, no, you can pretty much Google everything and find what needs to be found and realities to be taught.

That, based on that philosophy, they will never show anything of intelligence. All of the science and physics and history will be based on the foundation that, 'We were a gorilla and now we're at the height of our civilization', not that, 'No, we were at the height of our civilization; we had technologies ahd realities and we are gorillas now'. We've devolved, not evolved, you go down.

## Pyramids Were Power Sources Using Water and Sun

When you Google and they say, 'These pyramids, these were power sources. These were tremendous realities.' And they say that it was built in such a way as a perfection of insulation, certain stones on the inside, another layer of stones on the outer and a completely different type of stone on the outermost. And it was like a wire. They are showing us now in today's technology the layers of wiring, because you have the copper on the inside which conveys the energy and the energy moves on that. And the shield that holds it and protects it so not to lose the energy.

Its source they say came from water and there were water tables and water pools all around. And they merely had the sun to reflect on these water pools, move them in different directions and this water would hit these granite stones, marble stones and all the different structure they put together and begin to release and they would capture its energy.

Based on its insulation then, they would perfect that energy because once that energy is well-insulated it begins to reflect to each other. That is clean energy. It's not made from exploding anything. It's not made from making anything to be dirty, but as a healing energy. And that energy multiplied, multiplied, multiplied, and became a tremendous source of power.

Then somebody asked, 'Well, where is that today?' Well because holy people are not permitted and not allowed to bring for the material world. Because any of these realities that you introduce into the material world, somebody wants to profit from it. Somebody wants to sell it. Somebody wants to make an exchange from it. You cannot buy and sell and trade Allah's ﷻ realities. Then the Divine says it's hidden. But *Shaytan* and bad character gets an inkling, a whiff, of that reality and they bring it and manipulate it.

## The Perfection of Our Being and the Sun in Our Heart

For us, the teaching of that reality is in our being. Our being is more perfect than that pyramid. It means what Prophet ﷺ brought of the *Sunnat an-Nabi* ﷺ, the *shari'ah* and the law of Sayyidina Muhammad ﷺ and the power of Holy Qur'an; these are the insulations.

It means Prophet ﷺ is teaching, and all the prophets, they are brothers, teaching, if you follow the Divine understandings of good and bad, right and wrong for your being, you'll perfect your inside, because you need a water source shined with sun. That sun is an imitated energy source. So all the prophets came to teach, because they take a very difficult religious jurisprudence or religious understanding and simplify it for everybody to take; very basic, like children you can eat it, you can understand it.

The rules of the do's and don'ts of reality, of the *deen*, of the way of Allah ﷻ was to perfect the heart. If you listen to the do's and don'ts and correct the character, the heart will become perfected. If the heart becomes perfected, it becomes a sun within the being. An eternal flame will be lit within the heart because God occupies the heart, *"Qalb al-mu'min baytullah."*

قَلْبَ الْمُؤْمِنْ بَيْتُ الرَّبّ

*"Qalb al mu'min baytur rabb."*

*"The heart of the believer is the House of the Lord." (Hadith Qudsi)*

It means that when the Divine is happy that the servant is keeping the boundary and the limits of the Divine, keeping the character of what the Divine wanted for himself, for his family and for his community, He begins to occupy that heart. If Allah ﷻ occupies, when we say occupy, not that God comes into the heart, nothing can contain Allah ﷻ, but merely Allah's ﷻ *Rida* and Satisfaction, God's Happiness and Joy begins to gaze upon that heart and it becomes illuminated and eternal.

And the eternal flame within the heart, it is the seed of the soul. It is the power source of the entire universe of our being. If that is lit and that heart is a sun, it merely begins to shine on the water of our body which is the blood.

And Divine is teaching that everything you see outside, when you're amazed by it and understand its science, it was already given to us as a reality. But we lost the internal reality and people are mesmerized by the external, what they're seeing. Every technology is based on a deep spiritual reality. They say they were producing power with sun, water and specific stones that emit the energy, and the molecules, the atomic reality of the water.

## *Sunnah* of Prophet ﷺ is Insulation For Our Body

The Divine is teaching keep the *Sunnah* of Sayyidina Muhammad ﷺ. Keep the do's and don'ts of what Prophet ﷺ wants; you will be insulated. Dress in modesty so that your energy stays with you and is not dissipated.

This pyramid is very interesting because you watch these shows, which say that if the cap stone is taken off, it didn't function. So they made a big structure, went to so much difficulty that every stone is precise, that you couldn't put a razor blade inside the stone. Anything off, it doesn't function; the energy comes and goes, not to the perfection of what they wanted. If for a pyramid of stones that preciseness has to be there, what about for ourselves, to support the reality of the soul?

## Keep Your Head Covered to Insulate Your Energies

So why then every prophet came with these realities? If the pyramid needs a cap, they say, 'Where's the cap for the pyramid, they took it off.' If it didn't have the cap, the function of its energy was not coming out and was not directing its source. The Divine is saying that, 'Where's your cap? You are more powerful than that pyramid. Keep your head to be covered.'

There's a reality. There's a reality in which you are emitting energy. And not only you're emitting and losing all your energy, because as soon as we do a little bit of good, we don't feel it; we don't feel ourselves to be a reservoir of power. We feel ourselves good and energized and they begin to teach that Allah ﷻ says, 'I'll show you the signs on the outside so that you can understand the greater reality within.'

Why you are worried about the stone structure? See how it's all insulated? Look at a wire, it has all these layers of protection just to carry the electricity on the copper. What about the electricity that's moving within your body? Then keep yourself to be protected. Insulate yourself so that your energy doesn't leave. Insulate yourself so that people's negative eyes and negative energy, that they merely

gaze upon you and they send you difficulty and they pull from you light, what we call the eye of envy, not that they're bad and not that they know it.

## Protect Your Energy – Positive Energy Leads to Positive Choices

We're energy beings. You don't understand the extent of our power, that when you look, and somebody looks at you, they have thrown all their burdens upon you. And if you are not shielded and protected, whatever you had of energy was now taken and you feel your battery to be empty. And when your battery is empty, it leaves you to make bad choices, negative choices.

The abundance of positive energy within us leads us to make positive choices, a very simple formula, nothing complicated, that when you do good, you are good, you do good. We build the goodness within ourselves, build the positive energy within ourselves, build that energy, build that energy; you find yourself doing good, good, good, good, good, because you must have an energy inside to protect you outside. How can we have good choices when there's nothing inside?

Then the prophets came and taught all this simplified reality that wear like this, dress like this, put your hat onto yourself, not teaching advanced electronics at that time, it was too difficult. But there's a time in which people would understand energy and understand positive energy, and understand how negative energy is attracted to positive energy, and it merely just moves towards it and grabs, and takes that positive energy.

And then Prophet ﷺ is giving all that information that what an important *lataif* (energy point) your head has. It is like the cap of that pyramid, that everything within the being to be perfected and to be shielded. Then teaching that use water to wash, purify your energy source, purify your being, purify your reality and you begin to be more powerful than that pyramid. No doubt, Allah ﷻ, *"Wa laqad karamna Bani Adam."*

وَلَقَدْ كَرَّمْنَا بَنِي آدَمَ وَحَمَلْنَاهُمْ فِي الْبَرِّ وَالْبَحْرِ وَرَزَقْنَاهُم مِّنَ الطَّيِّبَاتِ وَفَضَّلْنَاهُمْ عَلَىٰ كَثِيرٍ مِّمَّنْ خَلَقْنَا تَفْضِيلًا (٧٠)

*17:70 – "Wa laqad karramna banee adama, wa hamalna hum filbarri wal bahri wa razaqnahum minat tayyibati wa faddalnahum 'ala katheerin mimman khalaqna tafdeela." (Surat Al-Isra)*

*"And We have certainly honoured the children of Adam and carried them on the land and sea and provided good and pure sustenance and bestow upon them favours, and preferred them over much of what We have created, with [definite] preference." (The Night Journey, 17:70)*

The Divine is saying, 'I have honoured your creation. Those they made with their hands; you, I made with My Hands and I breathe onto you from My Spirit.' It means the Magnificence and Munificence of the Divinely Presence and teaching what our reality, its potential, is.

## Shield Yourself With *Sunnah* of Prophet ﷺ

Then you begin to think and understand yourself, that when I shield myself and follow what Prophet ﷺ was bringing, it's a shield of protection. Then I follow the laws and the discipline of what the Prophet ﷺ was bringing and I begin to understand that my blood and my heart should be perfected.

If I want God to occupy my heart, if I want Allah ﷻ to occupy my heart, He wants it to be clean because there are no two kings that can occupy one throne.

It means that, 'Throw that one off your throne and I will occupy,' which means, 'My Authority will come and sit upon your heart.' So then we begin to understand that I have to purify my heart. I have to purify my way and I have to purify that example.

## Purify Your Heart by Purifying Your Blood

And then Prophet ﷺ is teaching that all of that purification will begin to purify the blood. And then the importance of every breath that comes in, because if you are now purifying that blood, what Prophet ﷺ said about the blood, that *Shaytan* (Satan) moves through that blood.

It means for us to understand when we're sick and have difficulties and affected by negative energies, they are teaching us that build your energy, build your reality. Shield so that you don't lose what you're building first because if you don't take all the plugs and all the holes and plug all the holes, whatever you pour into it is already lost. So shield yourself, protect yourself.

Once you have that shield then go in now and reflect upon the self and the reality that my heart needs to be purified. Eat what is *halal* (permissible), dress what is *halal* and understand the reality of the heart.

## Guard and Purify Your Breath

Then the blood has to be purified. If it's the blood that I want to be purified, then they say, 'Where is that blood coming from?' Oh, it's your breath.'

My breath has to be purified. Where is this breath going and what is it breathing? How can you put something into your breath and kill your lungs and kill your heart and kill your being?

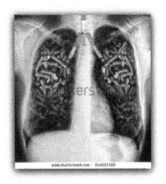

They begin to teach that my breath is the Holy Breath of the Divine. It means every energy of Allah ﷻ is all around us: *Qul Hu.*

The essence of every atom is a Divine reality of power making it exist. The breath brings that reality into the lungs. The lungs take that energy and dress the blood. That blood moves into the heart.

It means now we're understanding the power of the blood and the energy, that the quality of my blood is going to be based on the quality of my breath. How can you say you have clean blood if the breath is contaminated?

It means then where I go and what I do and what's happening in that air is important. You hang out with a lot of people who are hurting their breath and you're breathing it in. They say that who breathes on the second-hand is in more danger than the one who did on the first-hand.

Now they want to legalize everything for everyone, why? To destroy the breath, because they understand that once you destroy the breath, you destroy the blood; if you destroy the blood, you've already killed the heart. If you kill the heart, there's another one lost, no heart, no soul, it's very scary. We might as well be living in 'The Walking Dead', where people, where Allah ﷻ says that, 'Their food becomes the flesh and bone of men.'

It means all these realities Prophet ﷺ is bringing. As soon as you purify the heart, purify the blood, bring that energy in and begin to bring that breath in, the importance of that breath that's coming in, the purity of that breath.

Then they teach you make a *zikr* (recitation) on your breath, breathing in '*Allah*', breathing in '*Hu*'. Conscious of that breath, conscious of what's coming, conscious of that energy, asking, '*Ya Rabbi*, from Your *Rahmah*,' that, 'Your Mercy that is all-encompassing and everywhere, dress me from that *rahmah*.'

To be conscious of God's mercy is to be dressed from that reality, because God is saying, 'Now that you're conscious of it, I send you even more. Before you were benefiting from it but not caring.' As soon as you become conscious of something, you're asking for more of it, and Divine wants us to be conscious, wants us to be awake. As soon as you breathe in that mercy, that energy, that light begins to power every cell in the lungs, and dress the blood. And then that blood now moves directly into the heart, it's the physiology of our body, moves into our heart. What is that blood now going to face the heart?

## Dirty Heart Contaminates the Blood

Is the heart clean and free from bad character or is the heart contaminated? So again, visualize if a heart is contaminated, filled with black sludge, whatever the blood goes in is going to be dressed by that. It will take all the energy of what's in the heart and begin to move through the eleven essential openings of the body.

They are teaching, purify your breath. At the same time, it's not either or, as you're purifying your breath, purifying your meditation, purifying your understanding, have a shield of energy always with you, understand where you go and where you come and perfecting yourself and your energy.

### *Zikrullah* – Remembrance of Allah ﷻ Purifies Your Heart

Then as soon as you're looking to your heart, that the heart has to be clean, the heart has to be purified, "*zikrullahi tatma'inul Qulob*".

الَّذِينَ آمَنُوا وَتَطْمَئِنُّ قُلُوبُهُم بِذِكْرِ اللَّـهِ ۗ أَلَا بِذِكْرِ اللَّـهِ تَطْمَئِنُّ الْقُلُوبُ (٢٨)

13:28 – "*Alladheena amano wa tatma'innu Qulobu hum bidhikrillahi, ala bi dhikrillahi tatma'innul Qulob.*" (Surat Ar-Ra'd)

"*Those who believe, and whose hearts find satisfaction in the remembrance of Allah. For without doubt in the remembrance of Allah do hearts find satisfaction.*" (The Thunder, 13:28)

That the mentioning of God's name, the chanting and the praising upon the Divinely Presence, it begins to purify the heart. The remembrance of God and Allah ﷻ saying, 'Remember Me and I will remember you.'

فَاذْكُرُونِي أَذْكُرْكُمْ وَاشْكُرُوا لِي وَلَا تَكْفُرُونِ (١٥٢)

2:152 – "*Fadhkuronee adhkurkum washkuroli wa la takfuroon.*" (Surat Al-Baqarah)

"*So remember Me; I will remember you. And be grateful to Me and do not reject faith.*" (The Cow, 2:152)

When Allah ﷻ remembers us, it's not at our level. As soon as you are remembering say, "*Allah, Subhanallah, Alhamdulillah, La ilaha illallah, Allahu Akbar*", Allah ﷻ is remembering us at a higher association.

Then Allah ﷻ says, 'Be *shukur*, be thankful to me.' Why? Because we are thankful for the breath, not thankful for the money, the cash and all the things we wanted from God; those are all very secondary. But be thankful for the greatest gift you have, this is the gift of life. The gift of your life is a breath. 'If I take that breath away, all the other things you want from Me will be nothing.'

Then Allah ﷻ is saying, 'Remember Me and I will remember you.' Remember means you're breathing with remembrance, and being *shukr*, being thankful. And don't be "*takfuroon, thuma amano, thuma kafaro.*"

إِنَّ الَّذِينَ آمَنُوا ثُمَّ كَفَرُوا ثُمَّ آمَنُوا ثُمَّ كَفَرُوا ثُمَّ ازْدَادُوا كُفْرًا لَّمْ يَكُنِ اللَّـهُ لِيَغْفِرَ لَهُمْ وَلَا لِيَهْدِيَهُمْ سَبِيلًا (١٣٧)

*4:137 – "Innal ladheena amano thumma kafaro thumma amano thumma kafaroo thumma izdado kufran lam yakuni Allahu liyaghfira lahum wa la liyahdiyahum sabeela." (Surat An-Nisa)*

*"Indeed, those who have believed then disbelieved, then believed, then disbelieved, and then increased in disbelief – Allah won't forgive them, nor will He guide them on a path/way." (The Women, 4:137)*

Don't become in disbelief, saying, 'No, God doesn't exist,' and then every five minutes, 'I believe, I don't believe; I believe, I don't believe.'

## Purify Your Heart For Divine's Love

You're trying to activate the reality. Be firm on that belief; you begin to purify the heart. You begin to cleanse the heart; you begin to ask every day, 'Thy kingdom will come, Thy Will be done on earth as it is in heaven.' All holy books are the same, that 'we want Allah's ﷻ kingdom, we want God's kingdom upon the throne of my heart'.

The first thing He tells is then, 'Remove the evil one. Remove the false one sitting upon your heart telling you what to do.' Then everything is about my internal struggle now, what I want and what I know the Divine wants for me, what I want and what the Divine wants for me, what I want and what the Divine wants for me; one of us submits. Allah's ﷻ not going to submit to me so I'm going to submit to Allah ﷻ. I'm going to submit to the Divinely Presence.

## Keep the Company of the Guides

They begin to teach that is the perfection of your energy. As soon as we begin to understand that and build that energy, build that reality, purify that heart, purify the breath, bring that energy in, then they begin to teach us where there's a secret happening inside that pyramid. There's an energy that is moving back and forth at a very high rate of speed [inside that pyramid] and that becomes the concept of guidance, that, *"Wa kunu ma'al Saadiqeen."*

يَا أَيُّهَا الَّذِينَ آمَنُوا اتَّقُوا اللَّـهَ وَكُونُوا مَعَ الصَّادِقِينَ (١١٩)

*9:119 – "Ya ayyuhal ladheena amanoo ittaqollaha wa kono ma'as sadiqeen." (Surat At-Tawba)*

*"O you who have believed, fear Allah and be with those who are true (in words and deed)." (The Repentance, 9:119)*

Keep the company of the guides, because once you keep the company of the guides, now you're opening the reality of the laser. We said before the laser and the power of light because these are all now light realities. Why is it that if you flash a flashlight it just falls and drops? The energy of the flashlight is not reaching you, you are not feeling that energy; it's not cutting anything.

## Guides Mirror Divinely Light and Magnify Your Light

How is that light working? It's that, oh, they magnify the light to reflect off itself; it means they use mirrors. The light comes to a reflector, and reflects they say a million times in a fraction of a second and they add a resonance to the light. They add a frequency to the light. Resonance for us is *zikr*. They add a *zikr* to the light in its mirroring in its reality.

367

It means then the concept of the Shaykhs are teaching they are that mirror. That as soon as you're in their company and you're learning how to meditate, you're sending your light, they're sending their light, they're magnifying that light; you're taking that light, they magnify that light. That is the reality of that Divine love.

The light moves to them; they take that light, pray for that light, they add a resonance and they add a *zikr* to that light and send it back. And

 you take it and send it back in appreciation. That becomes the reality of love. That energy goes to them, they take it and bless it, send it back; we take that energy, thank them, send it back, and back and forth, back and forth. In a fraction of a second, your

light becomes more and more powerful, like a laser. And if well-insulated, your energy begins to stay. It's not lost every five minutes. That they're teaching you, like a laser, open the reality of these lasers. *Shaytan* is using it for *dunya*; you use it for *Rahman*.

It means go into the company of these mirrors. They merely send their *nazar*, (when we say 'Send your *nazar* upon us, *ya Sayyidi*, send your *nazar*'). When Allah عزّوجلّ is saying and describing to Prophet صلّى الله عليه وسلّم, 'Don't tell Prophet صلّى الله عليه وسلّم to listen to you, but to look and to gaze at you.'

يَا أَيُّهَا الَّذِينَ آمَنُوا لَا تَقُولُوا رَاعِنَا وَقُولُوا انظُرْنَا وَاسْمَعُوا...(١٠٤)

*2:104 — "Yaa ayyuhal ladheena aamano, laa taqolo ra'yina wa qolu unzurna wasma'o; ... " (Surat Al-Baqarah)*

*"O you who believe! Do not say (to Prophet Muhammad (pbuh)) Raina, listen to us, and say Unzurna (gaze upon us) and you listen (to him (saws), ... "*
*(The Cow, 2:104)*

*"Ishfa lana"* (intercede for us), means we want the gaze of Prophet صلّى الله عليه وسلّم, not he listening to us, his listening to us is in perfection for the

Divine Presence. What we want is his gaze because from his holy face is light. That we are sending our light as a gift. He takes that light, intercedes for us, increases the frequency of that light, the blessing of that light and sends it back. Again now we are higher. We take that light, we pray on that light, we send it back as a gift; Prophet ﷺ takes that light, sends it back, sending, sending, sending. And the reality of fusion, the power of that light is opening, multiplying.

That's why Mawlana Shaykh says that then their hearts are like lasers. It means they merely reflect on something and like a laser beam their heart can come out, the light of their hearts come out and they touch the heart and souls of people.

We pray that all these realities and every technology has a deep spiritual reality. We pray that Mawlana Shaykh open for us more and more understanding of our self and the extent of the treasure that's available to us but nobody coming to take it.

*Subhana rabbika rabbal 'izzati 'amma yasifoon, wa salaamun 'alal mursaleen, walhamdulillahi rabbil 'aalameen. Bi hurmati Muhammad al-Mustafa wa bi siri Surat al-Fatiha.*

# Chapter Eight

## Meditation and *Muraqabah* (Spiritual Connection)

الَّذِينَ يَذْكُرُونَ اللَّهَ قِيَامًا وَقُعُودًا وَعَلَى جُنُوبِهِمْ وَيَتَفَكَّرُونَ فِي خَلْقِ السَّمَاوَاتِ وَالْأَرْضِ رَبَّنَا مَا خَلَقْتَ هَذَا بَاطِلًا سُبْحَانَكَ فَقِنَا عَذَابَ النَّارِ (١٩١)

*3:191 – "Alladheena yadhkurona Allaha qiyaman wa qu'odan wa 'ala junobihim, wa yatafakkarona fee khalqis Samawati wal ardi, Rabbana ma khalaqta hadha batilan subhanaka faqina 'adhaban nar." (Surat Al-Imran)*

*"Who remember Allah while standing or sitting or [lying] on their sides and Contemplate the creation in the heavens and the earth, [saying], "Our Lord, You did not create this aimlessly; exalted are You [above such a thing]; then protect us from the punishment of the Fire." (Family of Imran, 3:191)*

الَّذِي خَلَقَ الْمَوْتَ وَالْحَيَاةَ لِيَبْلُوَكُمْ أَيُّكُمْ أَحْسَنُ عَمَلًا ۚ وَهُوَ الْعَزِيزُ الْغَفُورُ (٢)

67:2 – *"Alladhee khalaqal Mawta wal Hayata liyabluwakum ayyukum ahsanu 'amalan, wa huwal 'Azizu ul Ghafoor."*
*(Surat Al-Mulk)*

*"He Who created Death and Life, to test you [as to] which of you is best in deed - and He is the Exalted in Might, the Forgiving." (The Sovereignty, 67:2)*

# Muraqabah
# (Spiritual Connection)

*Alhamdulillah*, there are many different realities in *tariqa* (spiritual path) and these are gifts from Allah's ﷻ Divinely Presence to the presence of Sayyidina Muhammad ﷺ and from Sayyidina Muhammad ﷺ to *Awliyaullah* (saints). From the teachings of the saints and guides and perfected ones, it is a reminder that out of the many oceans of realities that we have talked about is the meditation and *muraqabah*.

It means all of it is based on how to open the heart. The heart has its subtle openings, what they call *lataif*, like satellite dishes of energy that open the layers of the holy heart to the holy presence and the Divinely lights of the Heavenly Kingdom to come. It means we are asking from

Allah's ﷻ Heavenly Kingdom to come onto Earth and come into our hearts and to make our heart be a Heavenly Kingdom.

## The Head Must Submit First, Then the Heart Opens

### Submit the 7 Holy Openings of the Head

For the heart to open, the holy head has to be in submission. It means that when the ears are in submission, the eyes are in submission, and the breath is in submission. Then the last and most difficult is the holy tongue; that all of it must be in submission. So all of the *tariqa* training comes to teach us that when we accompany the Shaykhs,

accompany our perfected masters, they teach us how to perfect our *samina wa atana*, "we hear and we obey."

## The Ears Have Direct Connection to the Feet – Keep You Balanced

سَمِعْنَا وَأَطَعْنَا غُفْرَانَكَ رَبَّنَا وَاِلَيْكَ الْمَصِيْرُ (٢٨٥)

*2:285 – "...Sam'ina wa ata'na, ghufranaka Rabbana wa ilaykal masir."*
*(Surah Al-Baqarah)*

*"...We hear, and we obey: (We seek) Thy forgiveness, our Lord, and to Thee is the end of all journeys." (The Cow, 2:285)*

So Allah ﷻ is teaching directly, your ears are locked to your feet. So if you have vertigo you can't walk. There are two levels of ears. We have an outer ear and an inner spiritual ear. Allah ﷻ describes they have ears but they don't use it, they use it like the animal kingdom but we don't really hear into the heart.

### Keep Your Vision Upon Your Feet – *Nazar Bar Qadam*

Keep your vision upon your feet, *nazar bar qadam*, why? Because your *nazar* has your *hawa*, your desires. You don't see blind people have *dunya* (material world) desires. There is no blind person out there trying to conquer the Earth and buy a Ferrari, he can't see, he can't use it. There are no blind people with material desires.

Then seeing is directly connected to your desires. Keep your desire closed and keep your vision on your feet. It means watch where your feet are taking you in life. If these feet go dancing we have got trouble. If these feet go to *masjid* to worship and do prayers, *alhamdulillah*, we are on the footsteps of piety and on the footsteps of Sayyidina Muhammad ﷺ *qadam al Haqq, wa qadam as Siddiq* (The Footstep of the Truthful). And those who are inheriting from holy Companions and *Ahl al-Bayt an-Nabi* ﷺ, inherit the footsteps of Prophet ﷺ.

## *Tafakkur* (Contemplation/Meditation)

### In *Tafakkur* (Meditation) See Your *Imam* In Front

From the previous teachings, if all of the head openings are understood and are submitting from its animal nature, and coming down towards its heavenly reality, immediately at that time they begin to teach us in the meditation and in the *tafakkur* (contemplation). That when you are making *tafakkur* and contemplation, you have to always be with the people of light. You always have to be with your *imam*. It means there is never a time that we accompany physically the Shaykh and that spiritually we are not with him.

It means every concept of our life is of that nature, that, *ya Rabbi*, the biggest *imam* (spiritual leader), the greatest *imam* is Sayyidina Muhammad ﷺ. When we teach ourselves – or Sayyidina Isa عليه السلام or Nabi Musa عليه السلام or whatever nation they are from, and whichever prophet they are following – our life is based on, 'The Prophet is always in front of me.' That my life is always behind them, I pray that God accepts me to be dust under their feet.

But because we are not at that time then Allah 🕮 gives to us guides. So our holy Shaykh is always my *imam*, whether I am accompanying him

and praying behind him, and memorizing in the vision of my eye in my heart. It means I try never to leave that presence. It means that you are keeping the love of the Shaykh. And that love of the Shaykh, because we accompany based on love,

not by force. Nobody can force us to sit here at spiritual associations; nothing will open by force.

## Love Opens The *Hudur* (Presence) of the Shaykh

We accompany by love and they begin to teach with that love you begin to have a *hudur*, you feel a presence. That presence means you merely look at them and when you close your eyes you can see them with the eye of the soul, with the eye of the heart. That you see them and you build the relationship physically with them, and spiritually with them. That to always be in their company, that *muhabbat* and love for that reality, begins to develop the *hudur* and

the presence of the Shaykh. It means the physical presence of accompanying these masters and their spiritual presence, because Allah 🕮 says; go through every house through the correct door.

وَلَيْسَ الْبِرُّ بِأَن تَأْتُوا الْبُيُوتَ مِن ظُهُورِهَا وَلَٰكِنَّ الْبِرَّ مَنِ اتَّقَىٰ ۗ وَأْتُوا الْبُيُوتَ مِنْ أَبْوَابِهَا ۚ وَاتَّقُوا اللَّهَ لَعَلَّكُمْ تُفْلِحُونَ

2:189 – *"... wa laysal birru bi-an tatol buyoota min zuhooriha wa lakinnal birra manit taqa, wa' tol buyoota min abwabiha, wat taqollaha la'allakum tuflihoon." (Surah Al-Baqarah)*

*"... And it is not righteousness to enter houses from the back, but righteousness is [in] one who fears Allah. And enter houses from their doors. And be Conscious of Allah that you may succeed." (The Cow, 2:189)*

# *Muraqabah* (Spiritual Connection)

### Connect With the Shaykh at the Level of Soul

The house of Allah ﷻ is *qalbun mu'min baytullah* which means come through the heart not through the head. It means open the soul and make a connection with them through the level of the soul.

قَلْبَ الْمُؤْمِنْ بَيْتُ الرَّبْ

*"Qalb al mu'min baytur rabb."*

*"The heart of the believer is the House of the Lord." (Hadith Qudsi)*

There are people who accompany the Shaykh fifty years, forty years, ten years physically but they never attempted to connect spiritually. And that is the great error that is the great difficulty because all you are taking is from his physicality and it is such a small reality compared to the spirituality of the Shaykh. That is the light and the eternal presence of the Shaykh, he is the reflection of Sayyidina Muhammad ﷺ and Sayyidina Muhammad ﷺ is the Divinely reflection upon Earth.

The perfection of what Allah ﷻ wants is known through all the prophets. All the attributes of the Divine reflect through the prophetic reality and from the prophetic reality to the pious servants. *Atiullah wa ati ar rasula wa Ulul amri minkum.*

يَاأَيُّهَا الَّذِينَ آمَنُوا أَطِيعُوا اللَّه وَأَطِيعُوا الرَّسُولَ وَأُولِي الْأَمْرِ مِنْكُمْ (٥٩)

*4:59 – "Ya ayyu hal ladheena amanoo Atiullaha, wa atiur Rasola, wa Ulil amre minkum..." (Surah An-Nisa)*

*"O You who have believed, Obey Allah, Obey the Messenger, and those in authority among you..." (The Women, 4:59)*

The *Ulul amr* (those with heavenly authority) inherit that reflection. So they begin to teach by keeping their presence, by meditating and contemplating that my Lord I never want to be without them, that I am always with them.

## Realm of the Heart is Spiritual and Requires Spiritual Connection

As soon as you begin to learn to make *tafakkur* (contemplation), we are now leaving the level of the mind and the level of the physicality. Through the head at the initial stage, it was to discipline the physicality.

Now when we enter into the realm of the heart it is the realm of faith. This is no longer of a physical nature, this is of a spiritual nature, and we have to make a spiritual connection with our guide. Sultanul Awliya Mawlana Shaykh Nazim ق, is the ultimate in that connection but, *alhamdulillah*, Allah ﷻ gave for us a perfect example of that reflection and making connection with that and asking always to be in the presence of Mawlana Shaykh Hisham Kabbani. For us in this region we seek his example, we seek his travelling, we hear his *suhbahs*, we hear all the teachings.

## At First Stage We Try to Connect With the Shaykh

By that example we are asking, *ya Rabbi*, let me to serve the one who is serving the *sultan* who is serving Prophet ﷺ. Let me have access to that one and be able to travel to see him, to take *bayah* (allegiance) with him, to accompany them, to serve them. That begins to open the concept that as soon as we are meditating and contemplating, *ya Rabbi*, let me always be with him, from Your Holy Qur'an, *ittaqullah wa konu ma as-sadiqeen*.

$$...اتَّقُوا اللّٰهَ وَكُونُوا مَعَ الصَّادِقِينَ (١١٩)$$

*9:119 – "...ittaqollaha wa kono ma'as sadiqeen." (Surah At-Tawba)*

*"···have conscious of Allah and be with those who are truthful/pious/sincere (in words and deed)." (The Repentance, 9:119)*

I am asking to always accompany Your pious servants. As soon as I am meditating and contemplating, asking, *ya Rabbi*, I want to be with the soul and its reality, and you begin to visualize as if you are there physically with them. Their soul is right there in the presence, their soul is right in front of us and asking, *ya Rabbi*, let me open my heart and build my connection from soul to soul with my guide.

At the first stages it is me trying to connect. There is no way to hear him until he has given permission that the connection is correct. I merely send out the line, send out the request, it is for them to find acceptance. If they accept, they feel it to be sincere, they deem it to be correct, then they begin to send their *nazar*. *Nazar* means their spiritual attention upon the soul.

As soon as they send their spiritual attention it means all of this knowledge is based on the heart, based on the spiritual connection. We begin to learn the physical is what we are hearing through our ears, but it is opening a spiritual connection of the Shaykhs.

# *Ka'bah* and the Heart

### Four Corners of *Ka'bah* Represent Four Categories
### *Nabiyeen, Siddiqeen, Shuhada* and *Saliheen*

They are teaching us, for that (spiritual connection) reality to open up Allah ﷻ says, if you want to be with Me, you have to be with four categories; the *Nabiyeen, Siddiqeen, Shuhada* and *Saliheen* (Prophets, Truthful, Witness/Martyrs, and Righteous).

وَمَن يُطِعِ اللَّهَ وَالرَّسُولَ فَأُوْلَئِكَ مَعَ الَّذِينَ أَنْعَمَ اللَّهُ عَلَيْهِم مِّنَ النَّبِيِّينَ وَالصِّدِّيقِينَ وَالشُّهَدَاء وَالصَّالِحِينَ وَحَسُنَ أُولَئِكَ رَفِيقًا (٦٩)

*4:69 – "Wa man yuti' Allaha war Rasola faolayeka ma'al ladheena an'ama Allahu 'alayhim minan Nabiyeena, was Siddiqeena, wash Shuhadai, was Saliheena wa hasuna olayeka rafeeqan." (Surah An-Nisa)*

*"And whoever obeys Allah and the messenger, then those are with the ones on whom Allah bestowed his softness amongst the prophets, the highly Righteous [Truthful], the Witnesses to the truth, and the Righteous. And excellent are those as companions." (The Women, 4:69)*

That is why the *Ka'bah* is a symbol from them. If you want to be with Allah ﷻ, you have to be with the *Nabiyeen* (Prophets) which is the *Hajar al-Aswad* (Black stone in *Ka'bah*), with the *Siddiqeen*

(Truthful), the corner that is closest to Prophet ﷺ. The *Shuhada* (Martyrs) because they see and those *Shuhada* produce the *Saliheen* (Pious People).

380

**1. *Nabiyeen* (Prophets)** – Corner of *Hajar al Aswad*. (*Nabiyeen* are all the 124,000 prophets).

**2. *Siddiqeen* (Truthful Ones)** – Corner close to Prophet ﷺ. *Siddiqs* are the big Companions of Prophet ﷺ.

**3. *Shuhada* (Those Who Witness)** – The martyrs. Not only the people who died in battle, but those who die in their physical world. It means the big *alims* (scholars) of reality, who were able to destroy their characteristic. They are deemed not to be very much alive in this *dunya* because they are alive in the Divinely Presence.

The *Shuhada* are witnessing. If not a *Shuhada* and not from one who sees in their association, they are never going to reach to be the *Saliheen*. It is just the formula which Allah ﷻ is creating that reality.

**4. *Saliheen* (Righteous Ones)** – So by entering in and finding the groups of *Saliheen*, they must have from amongst them *Ahlul Basirah* (People of Spiritual Vision), whom they have trained and their desires have dropped. As a result of the desires dropping Allah ﷻ describes, We took the lock of their ears, We took the lock of their eyes which is the *ayn* (vision) of the heart, and We removed the *Kiswah*, the veils that are blocking them.

It means by keeping their company their whole purpose is not the physical association but by means of the physical they are able to pull the souls of people. So from '*Malakut kulli shay*' it means we come into a physical association and we seek out a physical association but these *Ahlul Basirah* are from the people of light. That immediately their soul in the room is able to grab all the souls of everyone present, and takes them to what Allah ﷻ wants from the fulfilling of the Contract.

فَسُبْحَانَ الَّذِي بِيَدِهِ مَلَكُوتُ كُلِّ شَيْءٍ وَإِلَيْهِ تُرْجَعُونَ (٨٣)

*36:83 – "Fasubhanal ladhee biyadihi Malakutu kulli shay in wa ilayhi turja'oon." (Surah Yaseen)*

*"Therefore Glory be to Him in Whose hand is the [heavenly] dominion/ kingdom of all things, and to Him you will be returned." (Yaseen, 36:83)*

It is the same from Holy Qur'an and Allah ﷻ is saying, if you want to be with Me you must be with *Nabiyeen* (Prophets), *Siddiqeen* (Truthful Ones), *Shuhada* (Martyrs/Those Who Witness), *wa Saliheen* (Righteous).

So *Shuhada* are witnessing. One way of becoming a witness is you die and now you witness the light Allah ﷻ wanted to show. Or your desires drop and your heart begins to open; your soul begins to see what Allah ﷻ wants it to see, and now you are from the *Shuhada* and *Ahlul Basirah* (People of Spiritual Vision), those whose hearts are open.

Allah ﷻ says you have to be from these four realities, from the *Saliheen*, from the *Shuhada*, the *Siddiqeen* and they are all connected to Sayyidina Muhammad ﷺ, *Nabiyeen*.

## Holy *Ka'bah* and the Four Inner and Outer Points of *Lataif al Qalb*

It means then there are the levels of the heart. Before we go into the understanding of the *Lataif al Qalb*, you will see that around the heart encompassing the circle of reality is a square which each points to, the outermost point of each *lataif*, makes four.

382

That four is the *Ka'bah, qalbun mu'min baytullah.*

قَلْبَ الْمُؤْمِنْ بَيْتُ الرَّبْ

*"Qalb al mu'min baytur rabb."*

*"The heart of the believer is the House of the Lord." (Hadith Qudsi)*

There is an outer four and an inner four. The outer four is the *Ka'bah* of the physicality. The inner four is the innermost reality, the *Baytul Mamur*, the Divinely House in the oceans of light.

They teach us to accompany the guides, to learn and understand from them, to open our souls into their presence. Then Allah ﷻ begins to open the reality of the soul, and the true connection of the soul. And only at that time can this conveyance begin to open.

*Subhana rabbika rabbal 'izzati 'amma yasifoon, wa salaamun 'alal mursaleen, walhamdulillahi rabbil 'aalameen. Bi hurmati Muhammad al-Mustafa wa bi siri Surat al-Fatiha.*

# Introduction to Healing:
# Don't Compete with Allah 𐎟
## Don't Pray for Difficulties to be Taken Away

They are the perfected Shaykhs, who are of a tremendous nature of perfection and that we are students of their way. They teach from the perfected way of realities, so that to reach Allah's 𐎟 satisfaction, Prophet's ﷺ satisfaction and happiness for us, and that the *Ulul amr* (saints) to be happy with us and their *nazar* (gaze) always upon us.

We may meet many people from many different backgrounds but it doesn't mean that everything that they're learning or they've been taught is from the *kamil* and the most perfected way of reaching Allah's 𐎟 *Rida* and Satisfaction. One, because the *tariqa* (spiritual path) and the days that we live in now is based on healing. That's very important because so many people want to claim that they can heal when yet they don't heal themselves, and they themselves, may be very sick.

It means that from our understanding and from the way and through this clinic and through this location and wherever this voice is broadcasting and being heard, it has an *ijazah,* and a permission, from Allah 𐎟, from Prophet ﷺ, from *Ulul amr:* Sultan al-Awliya and Mawlana Shaykh. It means that if you are hearing that voice, it's from their teachings, that reality.

## Allah's ﷻ Hand is Upon Everything – Never To Compete With Allah ﷻ

In the world of healing is that we believe in everything to be in submission and that Allah's ﷻ Divinely Hand is upon everything. And nothing can escape the Hand of Allah ﷻ ,

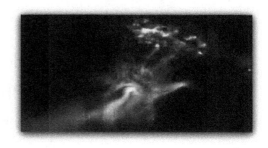

whether it's under the *tajallis* of *Rahman* or been under the influence of *Shaytan* (Satan). So when Allah ﷻ inspires somebody to come towards these clinics and these realities, these centres of Naqshbandiyatul Aliya, and I can't speak for other Shaykhs and other *tariqas*, but through what we have been trained, is then never to compete with Allah ﷻ.

So it means there has to be always a foundation for everything. The foundation is that Allah's ﷻ Hand is on everything and there must be a wisdom in everything that Allah ﷻ bestows upon the servant, from good and from bad.

When we understand that the *kamil* and the perfected Shaykhs, they don't want to be in a situation in which they are coming against Allah's ﷻ Will, God's Will. 'God's Will shall be done, on earth as it is in heaven' means every book describes the same reality. We live by that reality; we breathe and eat by that reality.

## Allah ﷻ Doesn't Send People for You to Take Away Their Issues

It means who Allah ﷻ sends to the clinic or sends within our vicinity or sends to our eyes and our ears, Allah ﷻ doesn't send them for you to change them. What, He doesn't know what He gave the servant? He doesn't know that He gave them a sickness or a difficulty, an imperfection within their character, within their eyes, their hands, their feet, their anger, their *akhlaaq* (character)? Whatever it is, Allah ﷻ gave it!

When you're not *kaamilan* and not understanding the way of perfection, you feel it's necessary to change everything. That something comes crooked to you, 'Oh, this means I have to  straighten it'; that somebody comes sick to you, you have to heal it; somebody comes with whatever difficulty they have, that you have to resolve it at that issue and at that time.

They come and they teach and they inspire. They inspire within the self that you're not there to compete with God. Whom Allah ﷻ gave, He knows what He gave. He knows why He gave them their sicknesses, their difficulties; whatever it is that's making the person to come here. Allah ﷻ knows what He gave to them and He doesn't need you to take it away because now you are in a competition with the Divine.

For example somebody comes with lots of pains and lots of sicknesses and lots of difficulties, Allah's ﷻ not in need of the servant and that's when those *ayahs* (verses) of Qur'an describe that they take for themselves *awliya* instead of Allah ﷻ. Allah ﷻ is the only One who can protect.

أَمِ اتَّخَذُوا مِن دُونِهِ أَوْلِيَاءَ ۖ فَاللَّـهُ هُوَ الْوَلِيُّ وَهُوَ يُحْيِي الْمَوْتَىٰ وَهُوَ عَلَىٰ كُلِّ شَيْءٍ قَدِيرٌ (٩)

*42:9 – "Amit takhadhoo min doonihi Awliya a, fallahu huwa alwaliyu wa huwa yuhyee almawta wa huwa 'ala kulli shay in qadeer." (Surah Ash-Shura)*

*"Or have they taken protectors/ helpers besides Him? But Allah – He is the Protector, and He gives life to the dead, and He has Power over all things."*
*(The Counsel, 42:9)*

It means they go to something of an incorrect nature; an incorrect nature not understanding Divine Will, that if you have been granted something of a blessing, of a *barakah*, of a reality, then who are you to compete with God?

## *Awliya* Guide People to Know Themselves

When God gives something, what He wants from pious people is, 'Don't change what I have put upon that person because they have not changed what's within themself. I don't change a condition of a people until they change what's within themselves.'

$$ ...إِنَّ اللَّـهَ لَا يُغَيِّرُ مَا بِقَوْمٍ حَتَّىٰ يُغَيِّرُوا مَا بِأَنفُسِهِمْ ۗ وَإِذَا أَرَادَ اللَّـهُ بِقَوْمٍ سُوءًا فَلَا مَرَدَّ لَهُ ۚ وَمَا لَهُم مِّن دُونِهِ مِن وَالٍ (١١) $$

*13:11 – "...InnAllaha la yughayyiru ma biqawmin hatta yughayyiro ma bi anfusihim, wa idha arada Allahu biqawmin soo an fala maradda lahu wa ma lahum min doonihi min wal...." (Surat Ar-Ra'd)*

*"Indeed Allah will not change the condition of a people until they change what is in themselves. And when Allah intends for a people ill, there is no repelling it. And there is not for them besides Him anyone to protect/patron."*
*(The Thunder, 13:11)*

It means then, take them to find themselves. That's what Allah ﷻ wants from the Shaykhs and pious people, is that they guide them. Guide them to themselves. Teach them about themselves. Teach them how to fish versus giving them a fish.

## Healing is Not a "Drive Thru"
## Difficulty Will Be Intensified If Lessons Are Not Learned

In this day and age, the sickness that we have is that this is the

McDonald's era; where everybody drives thru, pays three bucks and gets their cure. And everybody is willing to do that but it's only going to be much more significant the next time it comes because not yet the change has occurred within that person.

One, for the Shaykh who practices like that or the guru or whoever the person is; when they constantly changing what Divine Will, they will be accountable for what they are doing. And that difficulty will come upon them in their life and in their grave.

And for the one that you keep taking away what Allah ﷻ is sending upon that person; it means they have not learned a lesson that Allah ﷻ wanted them to learn. So you've actually made it more difficult for that person. What they could have learned with a cut on their hand or a broken arm, they didn't learn it. And by whatever *barakah* (blessing) comes your way and whatever Allah ﷻ bestows upon you of accepting your prayers, whom Allah's ﷻ *Rida* and satisfied with, you took something away but yet that servant didn't learn the lesson that Allah ﷻ wants. It means something far more powerful may be coming that way to get the effect that Allah ﷻ wanted, which could have been learned by the first.

## Every Illness Has a Remedy

We know it as common sense that if somebody has a pain and they have chronic pain, you find them sitting here on the carpet, because they know that by means of that difficulty they seek a remedy from the Divinely Presence.

Nabi Musa ﷺ was cold and he saw God as a fire. Allah ﷻ is not a fire but the condition which Allah ﷻ puts you in is perfect for you to seek out its remedy; and for every sickness, Allah ﷻ has provided a remedy.

*"Every illness has a cure, and when the proper cure is applied to the disease, it ends it, Allah willing." Prophet Muhammad (pbuh) (From Sahih Muslim)*

It means then from the perfected way is not to constantly be changing what Allah ﷻ wants. 'No we came and we want this to be taken away, we want this difficulty be taken away. The cure is like that. Oh how come we're not being cured, this person can cure.' No, no, it's wrong! The understanding is wrong.

## Real Guides Are Not in Competition with Allah ﷻ

What Allah ﷻ has given to them may be astonishing for people. But in the *kaamilan* way, and the perfected way, they are not in competition with Allah ﷻ. They are merely a servant and trying to reach servanthood for Allah ﷻ. That's the difference, in *ayahs* of Qur'an when you hear the *ayahs* of Qur'an, where Allah ﷻ says, 'They've taken these people as saints or *walis*' that can change things and compete with Allah ﷻ but that's not the way.

That is not the way that Naqshbandiya is teaching, no, no! These *Awliyaullah* are the servants of Allah ﷻ *(Ibadullah)*. They are not in competition with the Divinely Presence. They're not here to change anything in which Allah ﷻ is bestowing upon humanity but merely to guide humanity to Allah's ﷻ Satisfaction.

## Saints Guide Humanity to Struggle for Allah's ﷻ Satisfaction

The first *zikr* of Naqshbandi way is:

$$\text{اِلَهِى اَنْتَ مَقْصُوْدِيْ وَرِضَاكَ مَطْلُوْبِيْ}$$

*"Ilahi anta maqsudi wa radhaaka matloob."*

*"My God, You are my aim, and Your Satisfaction is what I seek."*

I am begging Your Forgiveness and seeking Your Satisfaction. It's the Shaykh's job to instill that upon the soul and in the heart of the person that, seek God's Forgiveness and seek a way towards His Satisfaction.

We're not here to take anything away and compete with the Divine but merely to teach you how to reach towards His Satisfaction. That if you sit on the carpet and begin to do your *zikr* (remembrance), to do your practices, to do your *wudu* (ablution), to do your *salah* (daily prayer) and struggle against yourself, to come, to come, to come. As soon as you begin to come and struggle against yourself you feel the emanations of light and blessings begin to dress the soul.

If those lights and blessings dress the soul, by means of that blessing, Allah ﷻ takes everything away. Now if Allah ﷻ didn't take something away, by means of those lights and those blessings, you will be still content with Allah's ﷻ Will. It means you will begin to learn *tasleem* and submit. 'Ya Rabbi, whatever you are bestowing upon me, *inshaAllah*, You'll find me to be patient'.

If it's a difficulty that I must endure, a difficulty I must carry, *inshaAllah* with the *zikr*, with the practices, with my *salah*, with my fasting, with my reading of Holy Qur'an, and following the holy way of Sayyidina Muhammad ﷺ, you find within your soul a strength to be patient in Allah's ﷻ Will.

## When in Difficulty, Contemplate on What Allah ﷻ Wants From You

It means our way is not based on taking away what Allah ﷻ sends. Not to get it and to try throw it and then run all over town trying to find somebody to try get rid of it. The way is the way of wisdom and *hikmah* (wisdom) and '*Ya Rabbi*, what's the *hikmah* of this difficulty in life and what is it you want from me?' And that is the perfected character of not only the Shaykh but the student.

When the student reaches perfection, they submit to God's Will. Through prayer and contemplation, through all their practices that Prophet ﷺ brought for them, they find within their heart a contentment. *Zikrullahi tatma'inna qulub.*

الَّذِينَ آمَنُوا وَتَطْمَئِنُّ قُلُوبُهُم بِذِكْرِ اللَّهِ ۗ أَلَا بِذِكْرِ اللَّهِ تَطْمَئِنُّ الْقُلُوبُ (٢٨)

*13:28 – "Alladheena amano wa tatma'innu Qulobu hum bidhikrillahi, ala bi dhikrillahi tatma'innul Qulob." (Surat Ar-Ra'd)*

*"Those who believe, and whose hearts find satisfaction in the remembrance of Allah. For without doubt in the remembrance of Allah do hearts find satisfaction."* (The Thunder, 13:28)

That through their *zikr*, through their chanting, through their practices they find within their heart, they find a sense of communication. That through that communication, they begin to find tranquility that, '*Ya Rabbi*, You want something from me'.

And it's going to take time, and you find always in life, those that their difficulty went quickly away, so did their presence from the *zikr*. They ran; they got some sort of a cure and they ran away and that's not what

Allah ﷻ wanted. Whether the difficulty is that you got freed from being alone, you got freed from sickness, you got freed from jail; whatever it is that you thought as a burden that was placed upon us. If it be taken away quickly, we find ourselves running because the reality had not yet really set within the heart.

## Difficulty Brings You Closer to the Divine Presence

That through that means of difficulty is a tremendous opening to the Divinely Presence. We've said many times throughout our life and

*tariqa,* as soon as difficulty visits you, your prayers become very sweet. Your meditation and contemplation, your *tafakkur* becomes very sweet; sweet in the sense that you are crying to God, that you feel an intimacy with the Divinely

Presence. And that's what Allah ﷻ loves. That, 'Look, My servant through this difficulty, you have such an intimate dialogue with Me. And constantly asking for My Help and My relief.' And the intimate relationship is what Allah ﷻ wants.

What made pious people to be pious is that they kept that intimacy whether good or bad times were delivered to them. Because if they can be intimate with the Divine and intimate in their love and in the purity of their request, as if the whole world was collapsing upon your head; how would you make your *sajdah* (prostration), which is begging Allah ﷻ for relief, begging for the *nazar* (gaze) of Sayyidina Muhammad ﷺ and *Awliyaullah* that their gaze to be upon us.

## Remember Allah ﷻ in Best of Times

It means then they say, then never leave that sincerity, whether your times are bad or whether Allah ﷻ turns those times to good, that even in the best of times, be sincere. In the best of times, seek the satisfaction of the Divine with *zikr*, with chanting, with practices. And you see then many people, their characters begin to grow. That everything is great for them and they still coming for *zikr*, everything great for them and they're deep in the love and in the remembrance of Allah ﷻ and Sayyidina Muhammad ﷺ.

## There is a *Hikmah* (Wisdom) in What Allah ﷻ Wants From Us

And this is what Allah ﷻ wants us to inherit, this great characteristic

of Sayyidina Muhammad ﷺ. That not to run from the Divine but run towards the Divinely Presence, and to be satisfied with whatever Allah ﷻ bestows upon us. And that Allah ﷻ knows the best, the best for us that is unimaginable. Whether it was  our experiences in our early beginning, with our experiences with our parents, with everything around us, there must be a tremendous *hikmah* (wisdom), a tremendous *hikmah*.

That, '*Ya Rabbi*, all my relationships prepared me for this day today, and my seeking of Your Realities.' So many times, my relationship with my father and the struggles I had were very similar to my relationship with my beloved Shaykhs. The character and the whole atmosphere of that life prepared me for meeting with them and to take a life in that path.

We pray that Allah ﷻ always inspire within us the higher reality. That in this day of McDonald's and fast food, that there is no quick solution. Anything that we think that we are taking away quickly, something much more difficult will be taken (its place). And there is a wisdom in why Allah ﷻ wants something for us. And that the *kaamilan*, the *kamil* and the perfected way, is to seek out that wisdom.

We pray that Allah ﷻ grant us these wisdoms, and patience through difficulty, *inshaAllah*.

*Subhana rabbika rabbal 'izzati 'amma yasifoon, wa salaamun 'alal mursaleen, walhamdulillahi rabbil 'aalameen. Bi hurmati Muhammad al-Mustafa wa bi siri Surat al-Fatiha.*

Printed in September 2023
by Rotomail Italia S.p.A., Vignate (MI) - Italy